Queer People of Color in Higher Education

A Volume in
Contemporary Perspectives on LGBTQ Advocacy in Societies

Series Editors

Joshua Moon Johnson
University of Wisconsin-Madison

Lemuel W. Watson
University of South Carolina

Queer People of Color in Higher Education

edited by

Joshua Moon Johnson
American University of Malta

and

Gabriel Javier
Multicultural Student Center

INFORMATION AGE PUBLISHING, INC.
Charlotte, NC • www.infoagepub.com

Library of Congress Cataloging-in-Publication Data

CIP record for this book is available from the Library of Congress
http://www.loc.gov

ISBNs: 978-1-68123-881-4 (Paperback)

 978-1-68123-882-1 (Hardcover)

 978-1-68123-883-8 (ebook)

Printed in the United States of America

DEDICATION

This book is dedicated to the fierce activists, leaders, and scholars who sacrificed to make a book like this possible.

I dedicate this book to my loving parents who made me proud to be unique, critical, and authentic. My motivation and inspiration in my recent adult life has come from my supportive partner, love, and husband, Aaron Faucher.
~Joshua Moon Johnson

Dedicated to my family: my parents Roberto and Carolina, my brother, Rob, and Sarah, Brennan, and Lilly. Thank you for keeping me rooted.
~Gabe Javier

CONTENTS

PREFACE

This book emerged out of a desire to have more information, knowledge, and resources to best serve the students on our campus. Both Gabe and I (Joshua) have served as directors of LGBT centers and at multicultural centers at large, public, and often well-resourced institutions, yet we were always left having to figure out how to best serve those students with lives intersecting and trying to navigate how to live in communities that fully accepted their racial, sexual, and gender identities. We both live at this intersection as queer men of color, and we have existed on college campuses for much of our lives. Our colleagues and even friend circles rely on us to educate and speak for those not present, those excluded, and those oppressed in a society that does not value them. Out of this professional experience and out of our lived experiences, this book emerged.

Over the decades, our universities began to recognize that not all students were white, so they offered a few services and built a center or building. A few decades later, they realized that not everyone was heterosexual, so they added a few others services and a building (or a closet). A decade or so later, some are now realizing that everyone is not cisgender or gender-conforming, but little has yet to be done about this fact still. As our institutional structures created "special services," they were created in simplistic ways, but our students are not created in simplistic ways. In my work in LGBT and multicultural student affairs, I have always struggled to be inclusive of other marginalized groups; it is not what our stakeholders want, our missions want, or what our assessment or data can handle or care about. As far as we have come, we continue to exclude, and this book aims to draw attention to one population that continues to be pushed aside: the queer people of color (QPOC) in higher education.

As we solicited contributors to this book, we were blown away by the brilliance, passion, and insight that came forth. Many of the authors are QPOC and have lived this experience as undergraduate students, student leaders, student activists, graduate students, staff members, and faculty members. The research and direction provided in this book are like no others that I have found in the literature. As I began my career as a social justice educator in higher education, I wish I had had this book as a guide to better serve students as well as an affirmation of my experience and struggles trying to exist and lead as a queer person of color.

The structures that make life difficult for queer students of color do not disappear once they graduate; our staff members have to survive in the same racist, homophobic, and transphobic worlds our students do while trying to be a mentor, counselor, and guide to wounded students. The experience of trying to heal the wounded when you too are wounded leads to retention, recruitment, burnout, and mental health crises. The authors of this book speak to the experiences beyond just students, and all recall their own personal experiences. Moreover, one chapter focuses entirely on faculty and staff who are QPOC. I have been in far too many meetings where we try to figure out how to get or keep faculty and staff of color, and yet we never look at the bigger picture—the climate, systems, and culture that make this task impossible. If those QPOC faculty and staff are not leaving to go to a campus they hope is better, then they are often too worn down to function.

This book comes from a place of pain: the pain of seeing students giving up on college, being disowned by their families, experiencing hate crimes because of their identity, or being institutionalized because their mental health was taking a beating. This book also comes from a place of hope: hope that we can do better; that we can adjust our services; that we can recognize the complexity of racism, sexism, homophobia, and transphobia; and that we can listen, comfort, and support those in our lives and on our campuses who need us to drastically shift how we serve students. As you read each chapter, we hope you ponder the impact it has on you as a person, your role in your career, and your ability to effect change on your campus. We are honored you have cared enough to read this far, and we are encouraged that this book has come to life and made it to press. Be patient with yourself, with each other, and find hope.

CHAPTER 1

AN INTRODUCTION AND OVERVIEW TO QPOC IN HIGHER EDUCATION

Joshua Moon Johnson and Gabriel Javier

College campuses are enriched, enlivened, and strengthened by the celebration of diversity on campus. Diversity, in its widest and most general sense, continues to be a key element of the educational experience in higher education. The conversation about the changing complex nature of diversity, however, remains nascent on many campuses (Smith, 2015). As such, most educators on college campuses are concerned with aspects of diversity, but many do not actually have an understanding of the complexity of marginalized populations' identity (Ahmed, 2012). Institutions of higher education segment into functional areas, such as academic affairs, research, student affairs, and external relations; these institutions also attempt to segment students' lives into convenient boxes that are addressed without relation to each other. The challenges that campuses face are not new, nor are they close to being fully addressed all institutions of higher education face obstacles attempting to create inclusive environments where all people can feel valued, feel safe, and succeed inside and outside of the classroom. Across these functional areas, there should be a commitment to serving students at the intersection of their multiple and complex identities. Campus

Queer People of Color in Higher Education, pp. 1–7
Copyright © 2017 by Information Age Publishing
All rights of reproduction in any form reserved.

academic advisors, housing staff members, health center staff members, and even financial aid staff members must all foster a sense of students' concerns related to their social identities to capture the full context of their lives and, therefore, college experience. As we examined research, institutional services, and community resources, it became obvious that gaps exist related to serving students of color who are lesbian, gay, bisexual, transgender, and queer (LGBTQ)—from here on, "queer" will be used to represent the LGBTQ population. Although campuses have made strides toward providing services for students of color or have created spaces for queer students, little to no effort has been made to best serve students at the intersection of these identities.

CAMPUS CHALLENGES AND QUEER STUDENTS OF COLOR

Queer students of color (QSOC) face numerous challenges on college campuses, yet little is known about their experiences (Russell, 2012). An expansive literature exists (Edgert, 1994; Palmer & Wood, 2011; Watson et al., 2002) about racism on college campuses and the challenges institutions have with retention and graduation rates of most students of color. Similarly, in the last decade, reports have discussed the challenges that queer students face on campus. Rankin, Weber, Blumenfeld, and Frazer (2010) conducted a national campus climate study, which showed that queer students were less likely to be satisfied with their experiences on campus, and more than one third of them strongly considered leaving their institution because of the hostile environments. Significantly, Rankin et al. (2010) found that the campus climate was improving for White-American gay and lesbian students but not for QSOC. Although this national climate study did include race as a factor, the quantitative study did not have a primary focus on the lived experiences of QSOC.

QSOC face potential victimization based on their racial/ethnic identity as well as their sexual orientation, gender identity, and/or gender expression. In many cases, the dual intersecting oppressions of race and queerness compound in dangerous and harmful ways (Balsam, Molina, Beadnell, Simoni, & Walters, 2011). Campus diversity centers focused on identity typically create a space for students of color. Some campuses have multicultural centers that allow or encourage students to self-segregate. Although this meets the needs of students for whom identity development tasks focus on a single identity, students exploring their multiple, intersecting identities may feel forced to choose one identity over another. LGBT campus centers are often critiqued for being White-centric, and multicultural centers are often critiqued for being heteronormative and cisnormative.

Negative experiences in the classroom compound the marginalization that QSOC face outside of the classroom. At predominantly white institutions (PWI) in particular, the burden of representation as a visible racial/ethnic minority and a potentially invisible queer minority may lead to negative impacts on educational outcomes (Narui, 2011). Some campuses have formed queer people of color (QPOC) student organizations and host regular conferences and events for QPOC students; however, most PWIs ignore QPOC students (Poynter & Washington, 2005). Institutions are able to classify themselves as PWI because of the availability of demographic information related to race/ethnicity. No standardized, parallel measure exists to measure the presence of LGBTQ+ identified students. The assumption is that most institutions are predominantly heterosexual and cisgender; students not in those populations are ignored or expected to only congregate in the small space designated as "LGBTQ friendly."

Campus climate data that specifically speak to the experiences of LGBTQ people of color is sparse (Rankin et al., 2010). Much of what we do know about violence and risk for harm toward LGBTQ people of color comes from outside of higher education. Research examining hate crimes shows that people of color and LGBTQ+ populations remain highly targeted and victimized. According to the National Coalition of Anti-Violence Programs (2013), LGBTQ people of color are still disproportionately affected by homicides toward LGBTQ people; 73% of all anti-LGBTQ homicide victims were people of color. Additionally, transgender people of color were 2.59 times more likely to experience police violence compared with White cisgender survivors and victims, and LGBTQ people of color were 1.82 times more likely to experience physical violence than White LGBTQ people (National Coalition of Anti-Violence Programs, 2013).

Explicit acts of hate, bias, and violence are complemented by the array and amount of microaggressions and microinvalidations that QPOC students face (Sue, 2010). Over time, these incidents send the message that racial, gender, and sexual minorities are less valued and invisible. For example, microinvalidations occur when transgender and multiracial identities are omitted from campus forms and data collection. Microaggressions toward marginalized populations have a direct impact on the mental health of their targets (Nadal, 2013).

OVERVIEW

This book seeks to: (a) contextualize the challenges that LGBTQ+ students of color face within diversity work in higher education institutions; (b) provide insight and reflection of the specific identity development patterns and needs of specific LGBTQ+ communities of color; (c) illuminate and describe the needs of LGBTQ+ people of color with regards to campus support systems, religious institutions, and mental health; (d) interrogate and explore intersectionality as a framework and provide emerging practices to move intersectionality from theory to practice; (e) discuss specific challenges of queer communities across the spectrum of gender identity and gender expressions; and (f) provide a list of foundational and emerging resources that speak to the needs of LGBTQ+ people of color on college campuses.

Although this book focuses on the intersections of race, sexual, and gender identities, we do recognize that many other identities will also take a role in shaping students' experiences. This book is a starting point to engage in conversations about the complexity of identities and is not a complete volume of all that can be discussed. We encourage people to take this work and push it further and examine the many experiences of students on college campuses.

In addition to the major challenges mentioned about hate crimes and campus climate, this book will discuss many other issues affecting QPOC in higher education. Parts of the book will discuss the complexity of identity development of QSOC. One chapter will focus on the spiritual lives of QSOC; race and religion are closely tied for many cultures, and LGBTQ communities have historically faced conflict (Moon Johnson, 2012). The relationship that QSOC have with local churches and campus student ministries can leave students feeling isolated as they attempt to potentially resolve, synthesize, or harmonize their religious, racial, and sexual identities (Moon Johnson, 2012). There is still a lack of discussion around other types of spirituality and how those fit within the lives of LGBTQ students.

Much of the discussion around QPOC is broad and generalizes all racial groups as if it is one unified community with the same challenges. Communities of color are diverse, and although they may all face racism, racism manifests itself in a variety of ways. For example, the impact of compounding racism and heterosexism on a queer-identified, cisgender Black man are distinctly different from those on a queer-identified, cisgender South Asian man, even if a triggering racist event is shared. These differences may be an effect of American anti-Blackness, the model minority myth, or other aspects of their lived experiences. It is crucial that we make space to create individual discussions by having chapters dedicated to Black queer students and Latinx queer students. We also aimed to have research focusing on Asian American queer students, South Asian queer students, multiracial queer students, and Native American queer students. However, there is still a drastic lack of research looking into the experiences of specific populations within QSOC communities. With the increasing number of international students on U.S. campuses, we will discuss the challenges that international LGBTQ-identified students face on U.S. campuses.

The conversations around LGBTQ people are often actually conversations about gay and lesbian people. We will intentionally create a discussion of how gender identity and expression intersects with race. Many campuses have gained a basic understanding of the needs of gay and lesbian communities, but the majority are drastically lacking in meeting the basic needs of transgender, genderqueer, and nonbinary people (Marine & Nicolazzo, 2014).

Other sections of this book will focus on the administrative roles of institutions of higher education and the challenges campuses face as they aim to serve the complex identities of students. The term "intersectionality" has been used often since Kimberle Williams Crenshaw coined the term in 1991, but little is actually known about how intersectionality moves from theory to practice on campus. A chapter discussing the philosophies, complications, and best practices on the concept of intersectionality is included. Following an in-depth discussion on intersectionality, the conversation will continue on to the role of student activism in the lives of QSOC. Campus changes often take place due to activists forming communities of color and/or LGBTQ+ communities; however, little is known about the impact it has on those students on the front lines who are sacrificing their time, emotions, and brilliance to make campuses more accepting, safe, and inclusive.

One of the major roles of identity-based student affairs educators (such as those in multicultural or LGBT centers) is to serve as mentors to students who are coming from historically disenfranchised backgrounds. These offices typically have as few as one or two staff members, so students must look to the larger campus community for mentorship. When QSOC look for mentors on campus, they are often left with limited options due to the lack of presence and visibility of QPOC faculty and staff members. To better understand the role that QPOC faculty and staff members play as mentors on campus, one must also consider the climate QPOC faculty and staff members experience on campuses around the country. A chapter will be dedicated to understanding the recruitment and retention issues campuses face as they consider racial, sexual, and gender identities of faculty and staff members.

The mental health needs of students around the United States should be a primary focus for any campus. However, marginalized members of communities are often at much higher risk for mental health issues and are less likely to receive the support they need (Chow, Jaffee, & Snowden, 2003). LGBTQ youth are at disproportionately higher risk of substance abuse (Marshal et al., 2008) and suicidal ideations (Bagley & Tremblay, 2000). A significant portion of this section will be dedicated to discussing the mental health services focused on QSOC. As each chapter concludes, a comprehensive list of resources and actions will be shared to ensure that campuses can easily access national resources committed to advocating QPOC.

WHO SHOULD BE READING THIS?

Every campus has QSOC, whether they are visible, organized, or actively seeking services. Many staff members working in LGBTQ centers are White and should continue to examine whether their spaces are safe and welcoming for students of color. Often White-American student affairs educators want to be antiracist; however, just "wanting" to combat racism is not enough. Intense learning, unlearning, and actions must be made and continue to be made to develop a welcoming environment. Multicultural, intercultural, diversity, and retention centers cannot focus only on the racial identity of students; students are navigating the complexity of many identities. How to confront transphobia and homophobia should be conversations had in centers focused on culture and identity. There is diversity within LGBTQ identity, and there is diversity within communities of color, so there is learning to be done even by those who identity as QPOC. The ideas QPOC have about each other cause strife within a deeply marginalized community, and the internalized oppression that many QPOC face needs ongoing attention and healing.

The conversations around identity and student development often happen in student affairs spaces; however, students face numerous microaggressions in the classroom, leaving them feeling excluded, misunderstood, and angry. Educators in the classroom should understand that it is no longer acceptable to isolate and oppress students. It is the job of all campus community members to continue to learn about marginalized populations; it is the responsibility of all campus members to shape the environments that we inhabit. This book is limited because it only focused on race, gender, and sexuality; however, it is a collection of works that will start a conversation and challenge people to expand their ideas of identity. Identity is complicated, and challenging racism, sexism, homophobia, transphobia, and any other form of oppression is an overwhelming task. This task, necessarily, does not fit into a single strategic area. However, it is a task worth prioritizing and making small strides toward making campuses safer places to live, learn, belong, and thrive.

REFERENCES

Ahmed, S. (2012). *On being included: Racism and diversity in institutional life*. Durham, NC: Duke University Press.

Ahmed, O., & Jundasurat, C. (2013). LGBTQ and HIV-affected hate violence in 2013. Retrieved from http://www.avp.org/storage/documents/2013_ncavp_hvreport_final.pdf

Bagley, C., & Tremblay, P. (2000). Elevated rates of suicidal behavior in gay, lesbian and bisexual youth. *The Journal of Crises Intervention and Suicide Prevention*, *21*(3), 111–117.

Balsam, K. F., Molina, Y., Beadnell, B., Simoni, J., & Walters, K. (2011). Measuring multiple minority stress: The LGBT people of color microaggressions scale. *Cultural Diversity and Ethnic Minority Psychology*, *7*(2), 163–174.

Chow, J. C.-C., Jaffee, K., & Snowden, L. (2003). Racial/ethnic disparities in the use of mental health services in poverty areas. *American Journal of Public Health*, *93*(5), 792–797.

Crenshaw, K. (1991). Mapping the margins: Intersectionality, identity politics, and violence against women of color. *Stanford Law Review*, *43*(6), 1241–1299.

Edgert, P. (1994, Spring). Assessing campus climate: Implications for diversity. *New Directions for Institutional Research*, *81*, 61.

Marine, S., & Nicolazzo, Z. (2014). Names that matter: Exploring the tensions of campus LGBTQ centers and trans* inclusion. *Journal of Diversity in Higher Education*, *7*(4), 264–281.

Marshal, M. P., Friedman, M. S., Stall, R., King, K. M., Miles, J., Gold, M. A., & Morse, J. Q. (2008). Sexual orientation and adolescent substance use: A meta-analysis and methodological review. *Addiction (Abingdon, England)*, *103*(4), 546–556.

Moon Johnson, J. (2012). *Beyond surviving: From religions oppression to queer activism*. Palm Springs, CA: Purple Book Publishing.

Nadal, K. L. (2013). *That's so gay!: Microaggressions and the lesbian, gay, bisexual, and transgender community*. Washington, DC: American Psychological Association.

Narui, M. (2011). Understanding Asian/American gay, lesbian, and bisexual experiences from a poststructural perspective. *Journal of Homosexuality*, *58*, 1211–1234.

Palmer, R. T., & Wood, J. L. (2011). *Black men in college: Implications for HBCUs and beyond*. New York: Routledge.

Poynter, K. J., & Washington, J. (2005). Multiple identities: Creating communities on campus for LGBT students. *New Directions for Student Services*, 111, 41–47.

Rankin, S., Weber, G., Blumenfeld, W., & Frazer, S. (2010). *State of higher education: For lesbian, gay, bisexual & transgender people*. Charlotte, NC: Campus Pride.

Russell, E. (2012). *Voices unheard: Using Intersectionality to understand identity among sexually marginalized undergraduate students of color*. Bowling Green, OH: Bowling Green State University.

Smith, D. G. (2015). *Diversity's promise for higher education: Making it work* (2nd ed.). Baltimore, MD: Johns Hopkins University Press.

Sue, D. W. (2010). *Microaggressions in everyday life: Race, gender, and sexual orientation*. Hoboken, NJ: Wiley.

Watson, L. W., Terrell, M. C., Wright, D. J., Bonner II, F. A., Cuyjet, M. J., Gold, J. A., Rudy, D. E., & Person, D. R. (2002). *How minority students experience college*. Sterling, VA: Stylus.

CHAPTER 2

INTERSECTIONALITY IN PRACTICE

Moving a Social Justice Paradigm to Action in Higher Education

Christian D. Chan, Adrienne N. Erby, and David J. Ford

Several disciplines have contributed to the development of intersectionality theory, as both a complex construct and a theoretical paradigm. Intersectionality continues to emerge and develop, as many of these disciplines formulate a diversity of perspectives around intersectionality constructs and tenets. In addition, the evolution of intersectionality in specific disciplines has created a significant interdisciplinary relationship that weaves the theoretical tenets together to enact social change. Historically, intersectionality takes a much more apparent presence in some disciplines (e.g., law, psychology, sociology) and continues its emergence in additional disciplines of application (e.g., higher education, business, counseling) to extend theory into action in social justice (Carbado, Crenshaw, Mays, & Tomlinson, 2013; E. Cole, 2009; Collins, 2010; Crenshaw, 1989, 1991; McCall, 2005; Warner, 2008). As intersectionality continues to evolve, it is imperative to operationalize the theory for application in both research

Queer People of Color in Higher Education, pp. 9–29
Copyright © 2017 by Information Age Publishing
All rights of reproduction in any form reserved.

and practice. However, the theory remains widely discussed in research to navigate the complexity of intersectionality as a construct (Bowleg, 2008; Clarke & McCall, 2013; Corlett & Mavin, 2014; McCall, 2005; Nash, 2008; Parent, DeBlaere, & Moradi, 2013; Warner, 2008; Warner & Shields, 2013), especially as intersectionality guides the construction of identity development and the exposition of social inequality. As numerous disciplines continue to wrestle with the challenge of developing a complex set of constructs in intersectionality, we describe the historical context of intersectionality, identify tenets of the overarching theory, and apply intersectionality to better understand the experiences of queer people of color (QPOC) in higher education.

INTERSECTIONALITY THEORY AS A LENS

Historical Context

When Crenshaw (1989, 1991) offered a critical lens to the invisibility and missing voices of women of color, she reinforced the major gaps of social justice movements apart from her own experiences. Namely, women of color were excluded from policy regarding people of color, in which sexism largely pervaded these discussions. In addition, women of color were also excluded from women's rights movements, which often reflected the voices of White women. In eliciting this information and observations, Crenshaw (1989) critiqued that political movements could not operate on a "single axis analysis" (p. 139) of antidiscrimination law. This message identified oppression as a multifaceted experience. The experiences of Black women were both unseen and unheard in the discourse of a political movement to advocate for their rights as Black women, despite efforts to attend to marginalization in the larger communities of Black people and women at large. The problem lies in the privilege within one category (e.g., race, gender identity). Consequently, Crenshaw (1989) challenged efforts to identify privilege when it exists on a single axis. The battle against discrimination formulates knowledge and experience from a group of mutually exclusive categories that ignore the plight of Black women. The resulting effect, however, is the increased oppression and marginalization that occurs for individuals operating within the framework of multiple marginalizations and, ultimately, a multiple minority individual.

Crenshaw (1989) argued that the failure to acknowledge this complexity was clearly reinforcement of the privilege that existed for individuals having a dominant status in one of the identification categories. In this context, the experience of Black women would largely remain nonexistent. Attempting to challenge sociopolitical structures, Crenshaw (1989) utilized her development of the theory to critically examine cases of law involving Black women and other women of color. In developing the theory, Crenshaw (1991) illuminated gaps in the perception of violence against women of color often masked by the construction of experiences based on mutually exclusive categories of social identity. Further, Crenshaw (1991) commented on the inequalities of sociopolitical structures failing to protect individuals living with a multiple-marginalized experience. This interaction precipitates a lack of resources and safety available to individuals suffering in these experiences but also develops ineffective knowledge about interventions in social inequality without a critical examination of intersecting categories of social identity. Institutions addressing inequality from a singular lens will largely offer resources and services to an entire marginalized group on the basis of one minority status (e.g., White women) but will fail to include resources for individuals marginalized within this group (e.g., women of color, immigrant women).

Evolution of Intersectionality Theory

As intersectionality theory continues to emerge in other disciplines, its evolution extends the theoretical tenets for applicability in specific disciplines. Consequently, the conceptualization of intersectionality continues to grow and change. Although Crenshaw (1989, 1991) initiated critical discourse of antiracist theory and feminist theory to illuminate the experiences of women of color, the representation of intersectionality across disciplines has expanded notions about identity development and social identity. As Crenshaw (1989, 1991) and Collins (1990) posited, intersectionality negotiates social identity as a multidimensional construct to validate the unique, lived experiences of individuals with multiple identities in a variety of domains (e.g., race, sexual/affectional orientation, gender, ability, socioeconomic status). Thus, identity development is not limited to the unilateral perspective, which research has historically used to understand social identity.

Emphasizing one identity over another can negate experiences connected to another identity, which is difficult to ignore as social identity processes operate in tandem (E. Cole, 2008, 2009; Parent, DeBlaere, & Moradi, 2013; Shields, 2008; Singh, 2013; Velez, Moradi, & DeBlaere, 2015). These social identity processes offer a way of knowing, making sense of experiences, and gaining critical consciousness about the manner in which institutions shape those experiences. In the context of social identity and cultural identity, the interplay between individual and context guide how individuals come to know and view the development and understanding of their own cultural identifications (e.g., Asian American, gay, middle class, able-bodied).

Although the salience of social identity may vary depending on context, the lived experience of multiple, intersecting identities is a more representative experience of human and identity development, given that individuals cannot necessarily compartmentalize their identities as silos. Moreover, there is an inherent communication of privilege from both sociopolitical movements and social structures to determine that individuals choose between their identities. Hegemonic social structures often emerge from groups holding the power and privilege with a major voice to reflect experiences as single categories. As Crenshaw (1989, 1991) had articulated, some sociopolitical movements mask as advocacy for the human rights of a marginalized group. More often, these same movements, however, fail to accurately represent the experiences of individuals living within the intersections, which leave the same groups without a voice in a sociopolitical movement or policy change. It assumes that some identities are less important and expendable. Instead of asking individuals to face the task of choosing an identity based on singular conceptions, researchers and scholars (Bowleg, 2013; Hurtado & Sinha, 2008; Mahalingam, Balan, & Haritatos, 2008; Singh, 2013; Szymanski & Sung, 2010; Velez et al., 2015; Viruell-Fuentes, Miranda, & Abdulrahim, 2012; Warner & Shields, 2013; Yim & Mahalingam, 2006) are integrating these multidimensional experiences creatively. More important, identifying intersectional experiences of social identity challenges and rearranges hegemonic norms about how social identity should be constructed and which social identities matter. E. Cole (2009) and Shields (2008) identified the role of the intersectionality perspective for identifying historically and institutionally underrepresented groups in research and scholarship. Eliciting information about underrepresented groups offers further ideas about the expansion of diversity in research. Additionally, reflecting on which groups have historically remained invisible, especially in the identification of their intersections, represents a microcosm of social inequality occurring at large.

This perspective offers a more meaningful image about understanding how categories of identification influence each other, especially categories operating from privilege and bias (E. Cole, 2009). To challenge mutually exclusive treatment of social identity categories, intersectionality represents social identities within individuals as interlocking categories representing an overarching system of privilege and oppression (Bowleg, 2008, 2012). With the advent of intersectionality theory, researchers, scholars, and practitioners can expand conceptualizations of social identity, including but not limited to race, ethnicity, sexual/affectional orientation, gender identity, social class/socioeconomic status, ability status, spirituality, age, and regional identity. The intersections among these identities lead to enhanced understanding about the identities excluded in specific examinations of social structures, policies, or contexts.

Trends in Intersectionality and Its Social Justice Lens

Intersectionality operates with foundations in social justice, as its origins emerge from the critical race theory (CRT) and feminist theory movements (Carbado et al., 2013). By creatively engaging complex understanding on the representation of intersectional identities and experiences, intersectionality theory draws on narratives identifying the manners in which individuals have been othered in their lived experiences on micro- and macrosystemic levels (B. Cole, 2009; Corlett & Mavin, 2014). Although these narratives and lived experiences can encounter results of discrimination at the actions of perpetrators (e.g., hate crimes, microaggressions), the theory extends concerns about social inequality to change policies and context affecting groups residing in the intersections of particular categories. It explicates power relations, where particular groups remain subordinated beyond commonly assumed groupings of minority (e.g., sexual minorities among women). Many of these minority groupings are predicated on power relations perpetuated by privileged groups in an institution or a context. The intersectionality framework functions as a method to disrupt stereotypes and deconstruct assumptions embedded within a sociopolitical structure, specifically because social location and subordination are often determined by individuals and groups in privileged positions. Considering these power relations, individuals marginalized along multiple identities often carry less power to determine their own decisions and outcomes—a challenge to individualistic values often tied to hegemonic power structures.

It is significant to note how Crenshaw (1991) defined and explicated various definitions of intersectionality in comparison with modern definitions of the theory's tenets. Using definitions from Crenshaw's (1991) article, Walby, Armstrong, and Strid (2012) identified structural intersectionality as "the intersection of unequal social groups" (p. 226), whereas political intersectionality refers to "the intersection of political agendas and projects" (p. 226). Connecting the Walby et al. (2012) angle on Crenshaw's (1991) analysis, structural intersectionality refers to the difference in how reform and social structures are experienced. Political intersectionality refers to the political philosophies in particular movements geared toward a single-axis framework, where groups are excluded on the basis of carrying more than one oppressed identity. In addition, Crenshaw (1991) developed the construct of "representational intersectionality," which defines cultural notions around particular groups living within their intersections (e.g., women of color) and how these groups are represented at large in relation to culture.

RELEVANCE FOR QPOC

Foundations of Identity

Identity development provides a central context necessary in understanding the experiences of QPOC, particularly within the context of social identity groups (e.g., race, gender identity, sexual orientation). Identity development within social identity groups must be understood in the sociopolitical context of privilege and oppression (Allport, 1954; Black & Stone, 2005; Erikson, 1968).

For queer-identified individuals, identity development is an active process involving initial awareness of difference in attraction, relational and/or sexual encounters, LGBTQ group socialization, forming an LGBTQ identity, and coming out to others (Barret & Logan, 2002). Models of sexual/affectional orientation identity development (Cass, 1979; McCarn & Fassinger, 1996; Weinberg, Williams, & Pryor, 1994) are generally linear in nature and describe initial questioning of one's sexual orientation from an assumed heterosexual identity. Similarly, individuals who identify as transgender often experience dissonance between their biological sex and gender identity at a young age (Beemyn & Rankin, 2011; Page & Peacock, 2013). Most children understand themselves as heterosexual/straight or cisgender, consistent with the socially constructed binaries assigned to sexual orientation and gender (Page & Peacock, 2013). Although many note feeling "different" early on, the understanding of that difference often does not come without active exploration culminating in identity achievement (Konik & Stewart, 2004).

Similarly, for racial minorities, an event or series of events results in awareness of one's racial identity (Atkinson, Morten, & Sue, 1998; Cross, 1978; Helms, 1995). Models of racial identity encompass (a) attitudes toward oneself, (b) attitudes toward others in the same minority group, (c) attitudes toward others in the dominant group, and (d) attitudes toward others in different minority groups. In early stages of identity development, little attention is paid to race, and the dominant White culture is assumed to be the norm, even the ideal. As racial minorities progress through these stages or statuses, they experience dissonance between the dominant White culture and the minority culture to which they belong, and they question the hegemony of the dominant group culture. Through active exploration of their own culture, racial minorities begin to develop a positive view of their culture and, conversely, a negative view of the dominant culture. Models of minority racial identity development typically culminate with an increased sense of balance, including a positive view of self as a cultural being as well as appreciation of other cultures, including the dominant group (Atkinson et al., 1998).

Despite many similarities in the minority identity development processes, several significant differences can impact the identity development process for racial minorities and queer-identified individuals. First, a queer identity drastically departs from the linear processes often associated with identity development toward a more fluid understanding of identity related to one's sexual orientation, gender, and gender identity (Levy, 2009; Rosario, Schrimshaw, Hunter, & Braun, 2006; Savin-Williams & Ream, 2007). Queer theory challenges the very nature of finite labels, linear development, and binary categories. Second, racial minorities have family and others with whom they can readily recognize as similar who can provide a sense of community. As such, QPOC may find strong familial/social support in developing a healthy racial identity but may find that support limited or entirely absent as they develop a queer identity (Chun & Singh, 2010). Because most queer-identified individuals are socialized in a heteronormative and cisgender culture and family context, they must forge their identities in relative isolation by comparison (Kus & Saunders, 1985). Last, the invisibility of a sexual minority identity can create a unique dissonance. A queer-identified person may be able to "pass" as heterosexual or as a cisgender man or woman; however, the burden of concealment, concern for safety, and continual task of "coming out" is ever-present. For QPOC, identity development is neither racial nor queer; rather, identity development is a multifaceted, dynamic, and fluid process of self-understanding as a QPOC.

Intersectional Invisibility

Models of social identity group development typically have a singular focus (e.g., race, sexual orientation). Thus, models of racial identity development may not fully convey the experiences of QPOC and vice versa in sexual or gender identity development. Consistently, both the conceptual and empirical literature (Purdie-Vaughn & Eibach, 2008; Sawyer, Salter, & Thoroughgood, 2013; Seng, Lopez, Sperlich, Hamama, & Reed Meldrum, 2012) highlight the need for a more multidimensional approach in understanding the experiences of QPOC.

Bowleg (2008, 2013) critiques the additive approach, in which experiences of oppression based on individual identities are explored in terms of cumulative cost (e.g., discrimination as a Latina, discrimination as a lesbian, and discrimination as a woman), thus the commonly used term "multiple jeopardy." The additive approach has an implicit assumption that these identities are disparate and separate. To separate these identities for a QPOC can result in a fragmented sense of self, in which one's experience is manipulated to fit a racial or sexual orientation prototype

(Purdie-Vaughn & Eibach, 2008). Belonging to multiple minority groups can create an experience of intersectional invisibility, including pressure to choose a primary identity group and marginalization within their respective social identity groups (Carbado, 2013; Purdie-Vaughns & Eibach, 2008). Although it is true that multiple minority identities can result in discrimination in multiple settings, intersectionality uses an "all" approach to understand oppression (e.g., discrimination as a Latina lesbian woman).

Focusing on the cumulative effects of oppression rather than the intersection of identities truncates individual experience and results in a contest of who experiences the greatest oppression (Purdie-Vaughns & Eibach, 2008). Further, the additive approach does not recognize the simultaneous presence of privileged and oppressed identity statuses. For example, a cisgender, gay-identified, Filipino man may experience discrimination and isolation in a largely heterosexual Filipino community and in a largely White LGBTQ community. The same Filipino, cisgender, gay man also has the benefit of privilege in a sexist and cisgender culture. Using an intersectionality lens results in more complete framing of experiences and identity within a complex layered social context.

Minority Stress and Resilience

Minority stress and resilience play an important role in understanding the experiences of QPOC. Minority stress is defined as the experience of the specific stressors related to one's identification within a minority group (Meyer, 2003, 2014). Research on race (Driscoll, Reynolds, & Todman, 2015; Kim, 2013) and sexual orientation (Burns, Kamen, Lehman, & Beach, 2012; Cochran, Sullivan, & Mays, 2003; Feinstein, Goldfried, & Davila, 2012) suggests that the LGBTQ community experiences a higher prevalence of mental health issues and greater health disparities compared with the dominant group. These negative outcomes provide a foundation for understanding the cost of minority stress. The minority stress model for LGBTQ individuals identifies four factors: (a) experience of prejudicial events and conditions, (b) anticipation of rejection or mistreatment, (c) invisibility and the need to conceal identity, and (d) internalization of societal stigma (Meyer, 1995, 2003). Research suggests that minority stress contributes to negative outcomes, including mood and anxiety disorders, sense of being a burden to others, suicidal ideation, and intimate partner violence (Baams, Grossman, & Russell, 2015; Burns et al., 2012; Edwards & Sylaska, 2013; Feinstein et al., 2012).

Given the pervasiveness of homonegativity and cisgenderism, it is not surprising to find that queer-identified individuals experience disproportionate rates of mental health issues and poorer health outcomes. Despite these significant challenges, QPOC often express a sense of strength associated with their identity, including freedom from traditional roles, opportunities to explore different experiences, forming strong social relationships, and enjoying personal growth (Bowleg, 2013; Bowleg, Huang, Brooks, Black, & Burkholder, 2003). Themes of resilience are often found in the literature (Bowleg et al., 2003; Breslow et al., 2015; Meyer, 2010) as QPOC embrace their identities and experiences. Thus, a more complete understanding of intersecting identities can be a powerful strength in developing a strong sense of self as a QPOC.

IMPLICATIONS AT MICROLEVEL

College students of color who also self-identify as lesbian, gay, bisexual, transgender, queer, questioning, intersex, and/or asexual (LGBTQQIA) or QPOC are multiply marginalized and subject to microaggressions because of racism and heterosexism (Balsam, Molina, Beadnell, Simoni, & Walters, 2011). Balsam et al. (2011) posited that members of this community may also experience racism within the LGBTQQIA community and heterosexism within racial/ethnic minority communities, specifically within their own racial/ethnic communities. QPOC who face microaggressions due to being a racial/ethnic and sexual minority are more prone to poor mental and physical health (Meyer, 2003). Because of LGBT minority stress and stigmatization, which includes experiencing microaggressions, racism from the LGBTQQIA community, and heterosexism from their own cultural group, the identity development of QPOC may be adversely affected. Heterosexism may account for differences in the timing and process of coming out between White members of the LGBTQQIA community and QPOC (Grov, Bimbi, Parsons, & Nanín, 2006). QPOC need to feel safe at institutions of higher learning and must be able to have positive experiences while feeling welcomed and included in their campus environments. These microaggressions may lead to perceptions of hostility in school settings (Smith, Allen, & Danley, 2007).

The College Environment

The college environment should be welcoming and inclusive of QPOC. Senior student affairs officers are responsible for creating this environment; they develop, articulate, and lead by a philosophy that supports the positive academic and psychosocial outcomes of queer students (Roper, 2005). Colleges and universities globally have committed to diversity and made it a ubiquitous word in their mission statements, strategic plans, student recruitment brochures, and university websites (Morrish & O'Mara, 2011). Although universities have marketed diversity, they have rendered queerness invisible. Sexual orientation is viewed as private, a lifestyle, and a choice. Thus, it is not part of the university's mission to enable students to realize difference. The language utilized in diversity mission statements must change to acknowledge real inclusion and empowerment of the queer persons in the university (Morrish & O'Mara, 2011). Ahmed (2007a, 2007b, 2012) reaffirmed the rampant disparity between diversity in practice and diversity statements. In response, Ahmed argued that practitioners can often fail to embody their diversity tenets, especially if they are not representative of a population. More often the language in diversity statements masks the stark realities of marginalization, oppression, and discrimination while misrepresenting the reality associated with a lack of inclusion. With universities rendering the queer identity invisible, QPOC are made to feel unwelcomed and not included because of their sexuality/sexual identity. Intersectionality may not be valued within the university population.

College Mental Health Professionals

Meyer (2003) posited that QPOC are more prone to poor mental health due to LGBT minority stress. College campuses have to be able to address the specific mental needs of QPOC, and college counseling centers and other college student personnel with counseling backgrounds have to be intentional in reaching QPOC. Mental health professionals should exude a deep level of empathy for QPOC. Smith and Shin (2015) found that having a greater level of empathy toward persons who experience heterosexism is critical toward interrupting systemic oppression. Neglecting to question essentializing stereotypes while committing the microaggression of exoticization—perceiving cultural groups to be fun and exciting and seeking ways to participate in the group by acquiring knowledge about their cultural artifacts (Nadal, Rivera, & Corpus, 2010)—leads to superficial understandings of discrimination. These superficial understandings have been associated with multicultural and diversity education (Andersen & Collins, 2007; Manning, 2009). Smith and Shin (2015) encourage helping professionals to adopt frameworks that bind racism and heteronormativity together, a framework aligned with the growing emphasis on social justice in the helping professionals. Therefore, human services providers become change agents instead of continually treating individuals for the damage done by systemic discrimination and exploitation (Smith & Shin, 2015). By doing so, mental health professionals on college campuses truly empathize with QPOC, are cognizant of the effects of racism and heteronormativity, and change the campus environment to make it more conducive for the expression of intersectionality.

College Student Personnel

College student personnel (faculty and staff) are also in a position to improve the campus climate for QPOC. Campus Pride rates campuses regarding their friendliness to students in the LGBTQQIA community (Morrish & O'Mara, 2011). It measures the presence of Safe Space programs, a LGBTQ Resource Center, Queer Studies programs, a LGBTQ alumni association, and transgender-inclusive facilities on campus. College student personnel can be change agents and advocate for these services on campus. Generally, these safe spaces have been exclusionary toward QPOC, and college student personnel have to be deliberate about ensuring that students in this population feel welcomed and included. According to di Bartolo (2015), transgender and gender nonconforming (TGNC) students of color are the least supported on our campuses despite being the most at risk for being marginalized. To support these students, campus mental health professionals should be trained to provide culturally sensitive services to TGNC students of color. Faculty members can create an inclusive learning environment by letting students introduce themselves and use their preferred names and pronouns. Various offices and residences on campus should be assessed for the inclusiveness of TGNC students, and one cannot assume that LGBTQ centers are inclusive spaces, especially for TGNC students of color (di Bartolo, 2015).

Advising

Career and academic advising for QPOC should also come from an empowerment model. Like other college student personnel, advisers must exude a deeper level of empathy, validate the intersectionality of being a QPOC, and be mindful of how racism and heteronormativity work in tandem. For example, they must be aware of the advising concerns (i.e., having a career role model of their own sexual orientation and are out at work, having support and encouragement of important persons in their lives, identity formation and expression, and facing prejudice and oppression) of QPOC and be aware of safe and inclusive spaces for curricular and co-curricular experiences (Nauta, Saucier, & Woodard, 2001; Palma & Stanley, 2002). Advisers must also have resources for internships and places of employment that include race/ethnicity and sexuality/sexual expression in their mission statements. If students disclose that they have experienced microaggressions due to being a QPOC, advisers should listen, validate their experience, and be able to refer them to the proper resource.

A MACROLEVEL PERSPECTIVE

Intersectionality in Higher Education Policy

Based on the multidimensional and transdisciplinary nature of intersectionality, there are a diversity of manners in which the intersectional experiences of individuals operate from a microlevel and apply to a macrosystem of policies, curriculum, and education. Intersectionality serves as the catalyst to question and challenge higher education practices to activate principles of social justice and equity for individuals living on the fringes of a system and multiple oppressions (e.g., sexism, racism, heterosexism, ableism, classism, genderism, colorism, ageism, colonialism). In the context of higher education, it is critical to identify the manners in which these multiple forms of oppression intersect. Otherwise, ignoring these interactions will bias the lens of individuals who operate in the privilege within their own minority groups. In fact, Nunez (2014) exemplified how intersectionality elicited information about the lack of Latino immigrant students' access to education. The study illustrated how creating transformative initiatives for each individual would counter story experiences about Latino immigrants' success in education, which would elucidate the lack of resources offered to Latino immigrants' educational experiences. A notable argument within Nunez's (2014) conceptual framework is the essence of multiple layers accounting for individualized experiences. As Nunez (2014) indicated, intersectionality examines beyond the microlevel to emphasize power relations among social categories, contextual understanding, and historical influence. Consequently, an analysis of services and policies within higher education requires a considerably comprehensive process to explore both present and historical patterns of marginalization. While Hankivsky (2014), Hankivsky et al. (2014), and Bowleg (2012) argued the development of policy analysis in health policy and public health, respectively, their perspective on intersectionality highly relates to the sociopolitical nature of higher education and the way in which institutions of higher education shape marginalized and multiply marginalized individuals.

At its core, intersectionality aims to develop and represent social justice tenets in larger social structures. Hankivsky et al. (2014) utilize this perspective specifically to formulate the basis for "Intersectionality-Based Policy Analysis" (IBPA) (p. 1). With the emergence of this framework, IBPA holds extensive weight in higher education to determine the stratification of social categories existing in student bodies and employee representation. IBPA focuses heavily on targeting structures that have historically contributed to oppression. In this inquiry, IBPA notes the difficulties of individuals falling into multiple minority groups, especially in the number of ways they have historically been invisible and often misrepresented. IBPA generated its components of critical analysis from an intersectionality foundation, with development of questions to critically analyze the problem and questions to formulate "transformative" change (Hankivsky et al., 2014, p. 3). Consequently, enacting change is tailored to the delivery of social justice principles and ideologies while working against inequities affecting a diversity of sociocultural dimensions. Generating an IBPA framework would necessitate inquiry from diverse viewpoints, where each member of a team analyzing a set of policies operates from his or her own professional experience, cultural values, and social identities. This framework utilizes a core principle of reflexivity to examine how privilege affects personal bias when critically analyzing a system's group or sets of policies.

As a particularly innovative contribution, Hankivsky et al. (2014) noted the challenge of operationalizing intersectionality and creating a meaningful praxis that moves beyond nebulous theoretical constructs. To arrive at a more critical analysis of policy, they propose a set of guiding principles and questions to examine reflexivity and social positioning. Examples of the values include "equity," "social justice," "intersecting categories," "multilevel analysis," "power," "reflexivity," and "time and space" (Hankivsky et al., 2014, p. 3). These guiding principles work in tandem with the questions woven into the analysis. Based on the IBPA framework from Hankivsky et al. (2014), some specific questions driving an IBPA framework include the following:

- What knowledge, values, and experiences do you bring to this area of policy analysis?
- How have representations of the "problem" come about?
- How are groups differentially affected by this representation of the "problem?"
- What inequities actually exist in relation to the "problem"?
- How will you know if inequities have been reduced? (p. 4)

Intersectionality in Higher Education Curriculum and Academia

As Jones, Kim, and Skendall (2012) indicated, personal identity development is also at the heart of explicating and living the intersectionality tenets. Many of these tenets are innately tied to the lived experiences of individuals constantly fighting, wrestling, negotiating, and making sense of their identities and the manner in which those identities are represented in a larger context. Most often these contexts manage to contain oppressive forces that reinforce the lack of representation around a marginalized identity. To bridge individual and context, there is a connection between the aspects of personal identity development, categorization of social identity, and context of social structures. In this lens, the personal becomes political. The categorization of social identity and its subsequent stratification affect the lived experiences of these personal identities. Through explicating this relationship between personal experiences of privilege and oppression and policies influenced by social structures, there is a rationale for the process of reflexivity, where individuals critically analyze their own social identity categories and the personal experiences of privilege and oppression tied to those identities.

As Walsh (2015) poignantly pointed out, personal experiences are a reflection of dominant and hegemonic institutional policies only catering to individuals within privileged groups. Walsh (2015) detailed personal experiences as a genderqueer woman, where she argued the inherent difficulty in reaching a status as a scientist in academia due to a dubbed presence as a feminist. Walsh (2015) critiqued the oppressive social structures because cisgender White men would immediately be accepted into academic circles as scientists. Any other form of knowing beyond the cultural lens of cisgender White male would represent a biased and subjective perspective. Walsh's (2015) perspective was born out of the critique in a social structure with encouragement to hire more faculty, scientists, and academics operating with marginalized experiences, especially when reducing to one category of marginalization only represents one set of perspectives and a reductionist view of feminism. Walsh's (2015) perspectives bring up several points that influence higher education policies about faculty representation and employment. Higher education institutions, particularly examples that carry several students and faculty of privilege, perpetuate systems of privilege, bias, and hegemony. Without an understanding of experiences that differ from a privileged norm, it is largely difficult to operate in a more inclusive environment with recognition for diverse viewpoints. Higher education institutions also run into more difficult challenges systemically, with supporting faculty and scientists coming from minority statuses, especially when an oppressed group is reduced to one category.

Meanwhile, Walsh's (2015) narrative is consistent with Bedolla (2014), who received negative feedback for trying to deliver her own lived experiences as a woman of color in political science academia. She was not accepted in those discursive spaces and received backlash at scholarly events. However, she channeled her experiences to create social change in academia and higher education through utilizing her own reflexivity as commentary for necessary changes in higher education. Bedolla (2014) noted the inherent challenge in particular groups with multiple minority intersections as lacking a "critical mass" (p. 450), but she observed that the ability to develop coalitions with a majority population was vital. Bedolla (2014) proposed coalitions that move across the multiple dimensions of cultural and social identity to create coalitions among faculty. In doing so, they would create representation for faculty across a diversity of identities and, subsequently, a diversity of ideologies, where the personal can become political. Each person would wish to create change on the basis of identifying oppressions in the coalitions. Bedolla (2014) also offered that oppression often operates in a competition of comparing which group has received more oppression historically or which oppression is worse. More important, Bedolla (2014) detailed the distinction between oppression and suffering, where oppression is often a function of structural inequality. She cautioned about the misconception that, although privileged individuals can experience suffering, their experiences do not necessarily constitute oppression.

Even more disturbing, some higher education institutions are without policies to protect and enact justice for victims of violence, rape, assault, or discrimination on the basis of a marginalized identity. For example, Calafell (2014) relayed her own experiences about how her institution had experienced confusion and lack of knowledge to address sexism and racism in confluence while she was a victim of sexual assault on multiple occasions. Although the university was unsure of how to handle such a process involving assault from an individual privileged in gender and race, Calafell (2014) explained how she received a slow process in resolving the issues and disputes around the assault and faced further isolation from her colleagues. Although Calafell's experience can account for a unique issue, which is not necessarily transferable to other experiences of mutually constituted oppression, the experience serves as an indicator of policies that do not necessarily reflect the navigation. In another account, Patton (2014) identified the reinforcement of hegemonic masculinity due to a homophobic stance on gender expression. In particular, Patton (2014) raised questions about the Appropriate Attire Policy at Morehouse College, where heterosexism and genderism pervaded despite its presence as a historically Black college and university serving men of color. There is an inherent challenge when faculty and students living as QPOC have difficulty negotiating for resources in an oppressive system because they are not offered the protections and proper supports as victims of interpersonal violence, discrimination, and oppression.

Several of these narratives describe issues on a more macrolevel perspective in higher education. Intersectionality teaches higher education professionals to utilize critical thinking differently by working through a diversity of narratives relevant to intersectional identities. In addition, the theory offers perspectives in how multiple minority statuses converge to relegate some individuals within a minority group to severe invisibility. These statuses also illuminate issues within the context of policy in higher education. Although it is common for unique lived experiences of QPOC to appear less frequently, the evidence from the empirical and conceptual literature details the constant invisibility in discriminatory experiences at the microlevel and the lack of protections and safety at the macrolevel—both serving as a function of the historical origins of hegemonic structures constructed by members of privileged groups.

CONCLUDING THOUGHTS

Intersectionality extends the critical thinking of scholars, researchers, and practitioners to move beyond the single axis of social categorization and social identity. Although the historical foundation of intersectionality grew in the law discipline and remained historically theoretical, its adaptation and application reach many more disciplines as a result of state-of-the-art research and a growing body of conceptual and empirical literature around the theoretical constructs. In fact, a movement is underway to delineate subcontent specializations within intersectionality due to the wide range of applicability and philosophical interpretation. As a result of the diverse interpretations and applications, numerous researchers are adapting this theoretical framework to enhance research methods that would creatively meet the lived experiences of marginalized individuals. Because the experiences of individuals living with multiple marginalizations or multiple minority statuses are often hidden, intersectionality proves to disrupt this pattern and norm while extending the voice to include those groups, such as QPOC.

In the context of higher education scholarship and practice, intersectionality represents a significant change in critical thinking, social justice, and advocacy. It operates with a social justice framework to take microlevel experiences and initiate social change across the meso- and macrolevels. Taking into account the lived experiences of QPOC, many students within this population are often left unseen and unheard due to the lack of services or policies reflecting their voices. Intersectionality further challenges practitioners to expand the notion of social identity in praxis because individuals cannot operate within a single axis of social identity. Most important, intersectionality challenges the nature of social inequality within social structures by taking reflexivity into account. As a wider audience reviews the constructs of intersectionality, this reflexivity process speaks to the forefront of embodying the social justice paradigm and changing context to meet the needs of multiple-marginalized individuals.

REFERENCES

Ahmed, S. (2007a). You end up doing the document rather than doing the doing: Diversity, race equality and the politics of documentation. *Ethnic and Racial Studies, 30*(4), 590–609.

Ahmed, S. (2007b). The language of diversity. *Ethnic and Racial Studies, 30*(2), 235–256.

Ahmed, S. (2012). *On being included: Racism and diversity in institutional life*. Durham, NC: Duke University Press. Retrieved from http://www.ebrary.com

Allport, G. W. (1954). *The nature of prejudice*. Reading, MA: Addison-Wesley.

Andersen, M. L., & Collins, P. H. (2007). Why race, class, and gender still matter. In M. L. Andersen & P. H. Collins (Eds.), *Race, class and gender: An anthology* (pp. 1–16). Belmont, CA: Wadsworth.

Atkinson, D. R., Morten, G., & Sue, D. W. (1998). *Counseling American minorities* (5th ed.). Boston, MA: McGraw-Hill.

Baams, L., Grossman, A. H., & Russell, S. T. (2015). Minority stress and mechanisms of risk for depression and suicide ideation among lesbian, gay, and bisexual youth. *Developmental Psychology, 51*, 688–696..

Balsam, K., Molina, Y., Beadnell, B., Simoni, J., & Walters, K. (2011). Measuring multiple minority stress: The LGBT people of color microaggressions scale. *Cultural Diversity and Ethnic Minority Psychology, 17*(2), 163–174.

Barret, B., & Logan, C. (2002). *Counseling gay men and lesbians: A practice primer*. Belmont, CA: Brooks/Cole.

Bedolla, L. G. (2014). How an intersectional approach can help to transform the university. *Politics & Gender, 10*(3), 447–455.

Beemyn, G., & Rankin, S. (2011). *The lives of transgender people*. New York, NY: Columbia University Press.

Black, L. L., & Stone, D. (2005). Expanding the definition of privilege: The concept of social privilege. *Journal of Multicultural Counseling and Development, 33*, 243–255.

Bowleg, L. (2008). When black + lesbian + woman ≠ black lesbian woman: The methodological challenges of qualitative and quantitative intersectionality research. *Sex Roles, 59*(5–6), 312–325.

Bowleg, L. (2012). The problem with the phrase *women and minorities*: Intersectionality—an important theoretical framework for public health. *American Journal of Public Health, 102*(7), 1267–1273.

Bowleg, L. (2013). "Once you've blended the cake, you can't take the parts back to the main ingredients": Black gay and bisexual men's descriptions and experiences of intersectionality. *Sex Roles, 68*(11–12), 754–767.

Bowleg, L., Huang, J., Brooks, K., Black, A., Burkholder, G. (2003). Triple jeopardy and beyong: Multiple minority stress and resilience among Black lesbians. *Journal of Lesbian Studies, 7*, 87–108.

Breslow, A. S., Brewster, M. E., Velex, B. L., Wong, S., Geiger, E., & Soderstrom, B. (2015). Resilience and collective action: Exploring buffers against minority stress for transgender individuals. *Psychology of Sexual Orientation and Gender Diversity, 2,* 253–265.

Burns, M. N., Kamen, C., Lehman, K. A., & Beach, S. R. H. (2012). Minority stress and attributions for discriminatory events predict social anxiety in gay men. *Cognitive Therapy and Research, 36,* 25–35.

Calafell, B. M. (2014). "Did it happen because of your race or sex?": University sexual harassment policies and the move against intersectionality. *Frontiers, 35*(3), 75–95, 207. Retrieved from http://search.proquest.com/docview/1636 560017?accountid=11243

Carbado, D. W. (2013). Colorblind intersectionality. Signs: Journal of Women in Culture and Society, *38,* 811–845.

Carbado, D. W., Crenshaw, K. W., Mays, V. M., & Tomlinson, B. (2013). Intersectionality. *Du Bois Review, 10*(2), 303–312.

Cass, V. C. (1979). Homosexual identity development: A theoretical model. *Journal of Homosexuality, 4,* 219–235.

Chun, K. Y. S., & Singh, A. A. (2010). The bisexual youth of Color intersecting identity developmental model: A contextual approach to understanding multiple marginalization experiences. *Journal of Bisexuality, 10,* 429–451.

Clarke, A. Y., & McCall, L. (2013). Intersectionality and social explanation in social science research. *Du Bois Review, 10*(2), 349–363.

Cochran, S. D., Sullivan, J. G., & Mays, V. M. (2003). Prevalence of mental disorders, psychological distress and mental health services use among lesbian, gay and bisexual adults in the United States. *Journal of Consulting and Clinical Psychology, 71,* 53–61.

Cole, B. A. (2009). Gender, narratives and intersectionality: Can personal experience approaches to research contribute to "undoing gender"? *International Review of Education, 55*(5–6), 561–578.

Cole, E. R. (2008). Coalitions as a model for intersectionality: From practice to theory. *Sex Roles, 59*(5-6), 443-453. doi: 10.1007/s11199-008-9419-1

Cole, E. R. (2009). Intersectionality and research in psychology. *American Psychologist, 64*(3), 170–180.

Collins P. H. (1990). *Black feminist thought: Knowledge, consciousness and the politics of empowerment.* New York and London: Routledge.

Collins, P. H. (2010). The new politics of community. *American Sociological Review, 75,* 7–30.

Corlett, S., & Mavin, S. (2014). Intersectionality, identity and identity work. *Gender in Management, 29*(5), 258–276.

Crenshaw, K. (1989). Demarginalizing the intersection of race and sex: A black feminist critique of antidiscrimination doctrine, feminist theory and antiracist politics. *University of Chicago Legal Forum,* 139–167.

Crenshaw, K. (1991). Mapping the margins: Intersectionality, identity politics, and violence against women of color. *Stanford Law Review, 43*(6), 1241–1299.

Cross, W. E., Jr. (1978). The Thomas and Cross models of psychological Nigrescence: A literature review. *Journal of Black Psychology, 4,* 13–31.

di Bartolo, A. N. (2015). Rethinking gender equity in higher education. *Diversity & Democracy, 18*(2). Retrieved from https://www.aacu.org/diversitydemocracy/2015/spring/dibartolo

Driscoll. M. W., Reynolds, J. R., & Todman, L. C. (2015). Dimensions of race-related stress and African American life satisfaction: A test of the protective role of collective agency. *Journal of Black Psychology, 41*, 462–486.

Edwards, K. M., & Sylaska, K. M. (2013). The perpetuation of intimate partner violence among LGBTQ college youth: The role of minority stress. *Journal of Youth and Adolescence, 42*, 1721–1731.

Erikson, E. H. (1968). *Identity: Youth and crisis.* New York: W. W. Martin & Company.

Feinstein, B. A., Goldfried, M. R., & Davila, J. (2012). The relationship between experiences of discrimination and mental health among lesbians and gay men: An examination of homonegativity and rejection sensitivity as possible mediators. *Journal of Consulting and Clinical Psychology, 80*, 917–927.

Grov, C., Bimbi, D. S., Parsons, J. T., & Nanín, J. E. (2006). Race, ethnicity, gender, and generational factors associated with the coming-out process among gay, lesbian, and bisexual individuals. *Journal of Sex Research, 43*(2), 115–121.

Hankivsky, O. (2014). Rethinking care ethics: On the promise and potential of an intersectional analysis. *The American Political Science Review, 108*(2), 252–264.

Hankivsky, O., Grace, D., Hunting, G., Giesbrecht, M., Fridkin, A., Rudrum, S., & Clark, N. (2014). An intersectionality-based policy analysis framework: Critical reflections on a methodology for advancing equity. *International Journey for Equity in Health, 13*(119), 1–16.

Helms, J. E. (1995). An update of Helms' White and People of Color identity models. In J. G. Ponterotto, M. J. Casas, L. A. Suzuki, & C. M. Alexander (Eds.), *Handbook of multicultural counseling* (pp. 181–198). Thousand Oaks, CA: Sage.

Hurtado, A., & Sinha, M. (2008). More than men: Latino feminist masculinities and intersectionality. *Sex Roles, 59*(5–6), 337–349.

Jones, S. R., Kim, Y. C., & Skendall, K. C. (2012). (Re-) framing authenticity: Considering multiple social identities using autoethnographic and intersectional approaches. *The Journal of Higher Education, 83*(5), 698–724.

Kim, M. (2013). Racial/ethnic disparities in depression and its theoretical perspectives. *Psychiatry Quarterly, 85*, 1–8.

Konik, J., & Stewart, A. (2004). Sexual identity development in the context of compulsory heterosexuality. *Journal of Personality, 72*, 815–844.

Kus, R. J., & Saunders, J. M. (1985). Stages of coming out: An ethnographic approach. *Western Journal of Nursing Research, 7*, 177–198.

Levy, D. L. (2009). Gay and lesbian identity development: An overview. *Journal of Human Behavior in the Social Environment, 19*, 978–993.

Mahalingam, R., Balan, S., & Haritatos, J. (2008). Engendering immigrant psychology: An intersectionality perspective. *Sex Roles, 59*, 326–336.

Manning, K. (2009). Philosophical underpinnings of student affairs work on difference. *About Campus, 14*(2), 11–17.

McCall, L. (2005). The complexity of intersectionality. *Signs, 30*(3), 1771–1800.

McCarn, S. R., & Fassinger, R. E. (1996). Revisioning sexual minority identity formation: A new model of lesbian identity and its implications for counseling and research. *The Counseling Psychologist, 24*, 508–534.

Meyer, I. H. (1995). Minority stress and mental health in gay men. *Journal of Health and Social Behavior, 36*, 38–56.

Meyer, I. H. (2003). Prejudice, social stress, and mental health in lesbian, gay, and bisexual populations: Conceptual issues and research evidence. *Psychological Bulletin, 129*(5), 674–697.

Meyer, I. H. (2010). Identity, stress, and resilience in lesbians, gay men, and bisexuals of Color. *The Counseling Psychologist, 38*, 442–454.

Meyer, I. H. (2014). Minority stress and positive psychology: Convergences and divergences to understanding LGBT health. *Psychology of Sexual Orientation and Gender Diversity, 1*(4), 348–349.

Morrish, L., & O'Mara, K. (2011). Queering the discourse of diversity. *Journal of Homosexuality, 58*(6–7), 974–991.

Nadal, K. L., Rivera, D. P., & Corpus, M. J. H. (2010). Sexual orientation and transgender microaggressions. In D.W. Sue (Ed.), *Microaggressions and marginality: Manifestation, dynamics, and impact* (pp. 217–240). Hoboken, NJ: Wiley.

Nauta, M. M., Saucier, A. M., & Woodard, L. E. (2001). Interpersonal influences on students' academic and career decisions: The impact of sexual orientation. *Career Development Quarterly, 49*(4), 352–362.

Nash, J. C. (2008). Re-thinking intersectionality. *Feminist Review,* (89), 1–15. Retrieved from http://www.jstor.org.proxygw.wrlc.org/stable/40663957

Nunez, A.-M. (2014). Employing multilevel intersectionality in educational research: Latino identities, contexts, and college access. *Educational Researcher, 43*(2), 85–92.

Page, A. D., & Peacock, J. R. (2013). Negotiating identities in a heteronormative context. *Journal of Homosexuality, 60*, 639–654.

Palma, T. V., & Stanley, J. L. (2002). Effective counseling with lesbian, gay, and bisexual clients. *Journal of College Counseling, 5*(1), 74–89.

Parent, M. C., DeBlaere, C., & Moradi, B. (2013). Approaches to research on intersectionality: Perspectives on gender, LGBT, and racial/ethnic identities. *Sex Roles, 68*(11–12), 639–645. doi: 10.1007/s11199-013-0283-2

Patton, L. D. (2014). Preserving respectability or blatant disrespect? A critical discourse analysis of the Morehouse Appropriate Attire Policy and implications for intersectional approaches to examining campus policies. *International Journal of Qualitative Studies in Education, 27*(6), 724–746.

Purdie-Vaughns, V., & Eibach, R. P. (2008). Intersectional invisibility: The advantages and disadvantages of multiple subordinate-group identities. *Sex Roles, 59*, 377–391.

Roper, L. D. (2005). The role of senior student affairs officers in supporting LGBT students: Exploring the landscape of one's life. *New Directions for Students Services, 111*, 81–89.

Rosario, M., Schrimshaw, E. W., Hunter, J., Braun, L. (2006). Sexual identity development among lesbian, gay, and bisexual youths: Consistency and change over time. *The Journal of Sex Research, 43*, 46–58.

Savin-Williams, R. C., & Ream, G. L (2007). Prevalence and stability of sexual orientation components during adolescence and young adulthood. *Archives of Sexual Behavior, 36*, 385–394.

Sawyer, L., Salter, N., & Thoroughgood, C. (2013). Studying individual identities is good, but examining intersectionality is better. *Industrial and Organizational Psychology, 6*, 80–84.

Seng, J. S., Lopez, W. D., Sperlich, M., Hamama, L., & Reed Meldrum, C. D. (2012). Marginalized identities, discrimination burden, and mental health: Empirical exploration of an interpersonal-level approach to modeling intersectionality. *Social Science Medicine, 75*, 2437–2445.

Shields, S. A. (2008). Gender: An intersectionality perspective. *Sex Roles, 59*(5–6), 301–311.

Singh, A. A. (2013). Transgender youth of color and resilience: Negotiating oppression and finding support. *Sex Roles, 68*(11–12), 690–702.

Smith, L. C., & Shin, R. Q. (2015). Negotiating the intersection of racial oppression and heteronormativity. *Journal of Homosexuality, 62*(11), 1459–1484.

Smith, W. A., Allen, W. R., & Danley, L. L. (2007). "Assume the position ... you fit the description": Psychosocial experiences and racial battle fatigue among African American male college students. *American Behavioral Scientist, 51*(4), 551–578.

Szymanski, D. M., & Sung, M. R. (2010). Minority stress and psychological distress among Asian American sexual minority persons. *The Counseling Psychologist, 38*(6), 848–872.

Velez, B. L., Moradi, B., & DeBlaere, C. (2015). Multiple oppressions and the mental health of sexual minority Latina/o individuals. *The Counseling Psychologist, 43*(1), 7–38.

Viruell-Fuentes, E., Miranda, P. Y., & Abdulrahim, S. (2012). More than culture: Structural racism, intersectionality theory, and immigrant health. *Social Science & Medicine, 75*(12), 2099–2106.

Walby, S., Armstrong, J., & Strid, S. (2012). Intersectionality: Multiple inequities in social theory. *Sociology, 46*(2), 224–240.

Walsh, R. J. (2015). XI. "Objectivity" and intersectionality: How intersectional feminism could utilise identity and experience as a dialectical weapon of liberation within academia. *Feminism & Psychology, 25*(1), 61–66.

Warner, L. R. (2008). A best practices guide to intersectional approaches in psychological research. *Sex Roles, 59*(5–6), 454–463.

Warner, L. R., & Shields, S. A. (2013). The intersections of sexuality, gender, and race: Identity research at the crossroads. *Sex Roles, 68*(11–12), 803–810.

Weinberg, M. S., Williams, C. J., & Pryor, D. W. (1994). *Dual attraction: Understanding bisexuality.* New York, NY: Oxford University Press.

Yim, J. Y., & Mahalingam, R. (2006). Culture, masculinity, and psychological well-being in Punjab, India. *Sex Roles, 55*(9–10), 715–724.

CHAPTER 3

COLLECTIVELY FEELING

Honoring the Emotional Experiences of Queer and Transgender Student of Color Activists

Paulina Abustan

INTRODUCTION

The everyday experiences, feelings, and emotions of queer and transgender students of color are often depicted to be isolated and individual
occurrences. This chapter brings attention to the critical need for educational leaders to recognize the lived experiences and emotions of queer
and transgender students of color not as singular events but as emotions
collectively lived and felt. Queer and transgender students of color *collectively
feel* together when issues that impact queer and transgender people of
color impact all of those who share these multiple, fluid, and complex
identities. Queer and transgender students of color *collectively feel* violence
when close to 90% of hate crimes directed toward LGBTQ people are
directed toward queer and transgender people of color (National Coalition
of Anti-Violence Programs, 2014). These students *collectively feel* the impacts
of institutional discrimination and violence when queer and transgender
students of color face disproportionate amounts of bullying from peers

Queer People of Color in Higher Education, pp. 31–56
Copyright © 2017 by Information Age Publishing

and high levels of school discipline from schoolteachers and administrators (Annamma, 2015; Burdge, Licona, & Hemingway, 2014; Ford, 2012; Mayo, 2014; Murray, 2011). Because queer and transgender people of color experience multiple forms of systemic oppression, which include racism, sexism, heterosexism, classism, ableism, and more (Alimahomed, 2010), researchers and activists seek to pay close attention to the lived experiences of queer and transgender people of color through the honoring of queer and transgender people of color voices, stories, and feelings. The purpose of this chapter is to recognize these feelings not as individual circumstances but as queer and transgender student of color activists *collectively feeling* together

Although previous researchers document the worldviews of queer and transgender people of color (Alimahomed, 2010; Bowleg, 2008; Linder & Rodriguez, 2012; Kanuha, 2013; Kumashiro, 2002, 2004; Martinez, 2014; Vries, 2015), little research focuses on prioritizing, validating, and honoring the collective emotional experiences of queer and transgender student of color activists. According to Ahmed (2004), "knowledge is bound up with what makes us sweat, shudder, tremble, all those feelings are crucially felt on the bodily surface, the skin surface where we touch and are touched by the world" (p. 171). Examining the *collective feelings* of queer and transgender people of color is critical when seeking to identify diverse knowledges and ways of knowing. Drawing from queer critical race feminist theory and through qualitative participatory action research observations, interviews, and focus groups, this study highlights the collective emotional experiences of queer and transgender student of color activists at a higher education institution and offers multiple recommendations to solving the everyday struggles that queer and transgender students of color face.

RESEARCH QUESTIONS AND METHODS

This study seeks to prioritize the emotional experiences of queer and transgender student of color activists when asking the questions: What are the overall collective emotional experiences of queer and transgender student of color activists at a higher education institution, and how do they embody and exemplify these everyday feelings? What do queer and transgender student of color activists think and feel about their professors, fellow students, campus resources, and communities, and how are these feelings rooted in histories and current systems of oppression and resistance?

It is critical for educators and administrators to uncover the lived and felt collective experiences of queer and transgender students of color activists in higher education due to the lack of research of queer and transgender students of color. Although previous scholars document the experiences of queer and transgender students and students of color leaders on college campuses (Kumashiro, 2002, 2004; Renn, 2007; Renn & Bilodeau, 2005;

Renn & Ozaki, 2010; Vaccaro & Mena, 2011), few researchers focus on the affective dimensions of emotional experiences connected to the overall collective experiences of queer and transgender student of color activists. This research follows affect scholars when heightening the criticality of documenting and analyzing the affect and emotions of queer and transgender student of color activists to be rooted in histories and systems of oppression and resistance.

Drawing from observations and the interview and focus group narratives of queer and transgender student of color activists, this study demonstrates the critical need for higher education administrators, educators, students, and community members to pay close attention to, affirm, validate, and honor the collective emotional experiences of queer and transgender student of color activists. Because educators and administrators often do not encourage the showcase of emotions and mental health in the classroom and university (Price, 2011), this study seeks to challenge the silencing of emotions and instead seeks to amplify the critical importance of *collectively felt* emotions. As affect scholars previously found, emotions are not singular events but instead are affective responses to historical and current systems (Ahmed, 2004; Berlant, 2011; Campbell & Sitze, 2013; Chen, 2012; Cho, 2007; Clough & Halley, 2007). For example, students are told not to write "I think" or "I feel" because educational systems privilege objective and rational minds and instead promote the silencing of emotions. This research illustrates the criticality of the affective politics of emotions to be rooted in collective histories and current situations produced by larger educational and societal structures.

Because emotional experiences are often suppressed and not purely individual, this study exemplifies the ways in which the emotional experiences of queer and transgender students should be seen and heard as collective experiences. This research follows the tenets of participatory action research when this study focuses on the collective emotional experiences of queer and transgender students of color. Because participatory action research transforms co-constructed theoretical research into collaborative action (Brydon-Miller, Kral, Maguire, Noffke, & Sabhlok, 2011), this research turns theory into collective action when it is intended to be presented to educational leaders, educators, students, and community members. The findings of this study aim to encourage educational leaders to implement recommendations to better support queer and transgender students of color at higher education institutions.

THEORETICAL FRAMEWORK

This study introduces queer critical race feminist theory, which draws from women of color feminism and queer of color scholars. Women of color feminists center the interconnected, inseparable, multiple, and fluid experiences of women of color, queer women of color, and those facing multiple forms of oppression and marginalization (Anzaldúa, 1987; Collins, 1990; Combahee River Collective, 1979; Crenshaw, 1994; Davis, 1983; hooks, 1981, 2000; Lorde, 1984; Moraga & Anzaldúa, 1981; Tumang & De Rivera, 2006). Queer of color scholars challenge queer theory, which often silences and/or minimizes the multiple systemic struggles of the military and prison industrial complex, poverty, homelessness, migration, and violence queer and transgender people of color encounter (Chavez, 2013; Ferguson, 2004; Grewal & Kaplan, 2001; Manalansan, 2003; Muñoz, 1999, 2009; Patton & Sanchez-Eppler, 2000; Perez, 2005; Puar, 2007; Rodriguez, 2003). I argue that queer critical race feminism draws its inspiration from women of color feminism and queer of color critique, along with the critical race, feminist, queer theory writings of Ahmed (2004, 2006, 2010, 2014), who illustrates the power of affective emotions challenging multiple forms of historical and current systemic discriminations. Queer critical race feminist theory centers collectively lived and felt emotions to be interconnected with the dynamics of race, gender, sexuality, class, and ability.

METHODS

This study took place during one academic semester. At the beginning of the semester, I facilitated individual interviews with each of the five participants who self-identify as queer and/or transgender student of color activists in higher education. With the five participants present, I hosted a focus group during the middle of the semester. At the end of the semester, I followed up with each of the five participants through individual interviews. All five participants were involved as leaders in a queer and transgender student of color campus organization. As a graduate student and self-identified queer woman of color activist, I knew all five participants previously through my involvement with the queer and transgender student of color campus organization. As an *outsider-within* researcher (Collins, 2004) who was an *outsider* to my participants as a graduate student and an *insider* to my participants as a queer student of color, I knew three of the participants for 2 years and two of the participants for 1 year.

OBSERVATIONS AND FINDINGS

Emotions

Ahmed (2010) discusses the ways in which emotions are *sticky* and become *stuck*. Certain emotions are associated with and oriented toward certain groups of people, items, and spaces because these emotions have been produced and reproduced over time (Ahmed, 2006). Emotions are

Table 3.1.   Participant Details

Name	Pronouns	Self-Identities	Years I Have Known Through the QTPOC Student Group
Raul	He/him	Working class undocuqueer Chicano	2 years
Tasha	She/her They/them	Working to middle-class multiracial Black-Cuban Queer gender fluid person of color	2 years
Usha	She/her	Middle-class student Asian American lesbian Vietnamese	2 years
Janelle	She/her	Multiracial Black with Chinese ancestry queer woman feminist womanist person of faith	1 year
Merissa	She/her	Multiracial Black bisexual woman	1 year

not individual and isolated occurrences when rooted in histories and current systems of oppression (Ahmed, 2004). Because emotions are affective responses to certain situations, people, things, and settings, I utilize queer feminist of color theory to analyze the emotional experiences my five self-identified undergraduate queer and/or transgender student of color activist participants shared with me during interviews and focus groups. Participants expressed their emotional and affective responses to interactions with students, educators, staff, campus spaces, student organizations, community members, family, and more. The following emotional themes were found throughout the 10 interviews and one focus group.

Depression and Anxiety

All five of the participants, pseudonym names used, expressed the emotional experiences of depression and anxiety. Raul, a self-identified working-class undocuqueer (undocumented and queer) Chicano, expressed the ways in which he and others around him constantly doubt their abilities to be successful students in a higher education institution. When dealing with these external and then internalized deficit messages rooted in histories and systems of discrimination toward his Chicano Latino communities, Raul experiences depression and turns to harming himself emotionally and physically. He struggles with negative perceptions of his undocumented, queer, and Chicano identities and communities. The predominantly White students he tutors question his abilities to teach the English language because of his accent and skin color. When applying for graduate school, Raul doubts any institution will accept him, but he refuses to be defeated. Raul states:

> Right now I'm in the process of applying for grad programs. I think there is no way I am getting accepted. Who am I? This person who speaks English with an accent. This person that went to a school where scores are really low. How dare this person be in academia? And it's more like you have to go back and be like "do I really belong here?" and stop asking questions. No, I belong.

Tasha, a self-identified working- to middle-class, multiracial, Black, Cuban, queer, and gender fluid person of color, shared the ways in which she/they were bullied when she/they were young. Tasha utilizes "she/they" pronouns due to her/their gender fluid identity. At times her/their gender presentation is feminine, whereas at other times her/their presentation is androgynous. Tasha explains how she/they were often teased about their physical appearance, race, and hair. During the beginning of college, she/they felt the need to dress overly feminine to hide her/their sexuality and gender identities. Although Tasha is now out and proud about her/their race, gender, sexuality, and class identities, she/they constantly struggle with internalized messages of self-hate, depression, and anxiety when other students often make fun of her/them. She/they feel(s) uncomfortable of her/their own Black skin due to her/their gender fluid identity. Tasha struggles with surfacing memories of bullying and sexual violence. Tasha shares:

> Lately, I've been crying until I can't cry anymore. There's a pain … feels like getting stabbed in the heart with a knife at the tip of my heart, almost like at the tip and it hurts so much where I can feel the knife in my back. That's how much it hurts.

Usha, a self-identified middle-class student and Asian American lesbian, discusses the ways in which she does her best to support her multiple friends contemplating or attempting suicide. Usha highlights the ways in which mental health is a huge issue for queers, people of color, and queer people of color. She experiences anxiety and grief when her friends attempt or commit suicide, and she emphasizes the importance of reaching out and being there for one another because many people, especially queer and transgender people of color who deal with multiple forms of discrimination, are silently struggling by themselves.

Usha declares:

> I've just been dealing with a lot of friends trying to take their life which is a way to cope and I want people to find different alternatives to cope with their feelings even if it is just talking to someone or going for a run or listening to music. They feel like they don't matter or something ... and they do. They think when they die it doesn't stop the world ... but it does stop the world for a lot of people.

Janelle, a self-identified multiracial Black with Chinese ancestry, queer woman, feminist, womanist, and person of faith, acknowledges mental health as a constant struggle that she deals with as a first-generation student struggling to pay the bills, assist her family, and make her family proud of her academic and career accomplishments. Along with worrying about finances and meeting expectations of her family, Janelle battles with constant anxieties of disappointing others around her merely for being who she is: a radical multiracial queer Black woman with opinions and no tolerance of any form of disrespect. She deals with the anxiety of reexperiencing microaggressions directed at her race, gender, sexuality, class, and faith on a daily basis.

Janelle expresses:

> I'm worried somehow, somewhere, I've offended someone or they are re-evaluating our relationship so that is something that makes me uncomfortable. I've been very uncomfortable within tiny groups of people who make jokes that are very racist or micro-aggressions towards me and that makes me uncomfortable. But that is everyday life.

Merissa, a self-identified multiracial, Black, bisexual woman, shares her story of attempting suicide exactly a year ago on the day I interviewed her. She discusses the ways in which she is feeling stronger and more connected today after surrounding herself with African American and queer communities that support all of her identities, experiences, and aspirations. She is less isolated and purposely seeks to get involved in African American and queer student organizations. She aims to reach out to others who may be feeling as hopeless as she felt a year ago.

Merissa states:

A year ago, I was so depressed because I ran away from my mom, and then my girlfriend and I broke up. It was like boom, boom. And so I felt like I went from having everyone to having no one. I felt very lonely and all of the normal signs and symptoms of depression and so I was wanting the pain to be over.

As previous scholars have documented, queer and transgender students, along with students of color, experience high rates of depression, anxiety, burnout, and hostility on college campuses (Kumashiro, 2002, 2004; Vaccaro & Mena, 2011). Because queer and transgender students are often underresearched and underrepresented in education and society, little attention is being paid to the emotional experiences of queer and transgender students. All five participants *collectively felt* emotions of anxiety and depression. Two of the participants shared how the queer and transgender student of color organization, of which they are leaders, purposely hosts meetings that discuss the mental health experiences of queer and transgender students of color. Their organization highlights the personal experiences of students experiencing self-harm, anxiety, depression, and suicide ideation. As activists, all five participants realize the importance of action and solidarity through community building, which demonstrates support for each other. The feelings of all five participants are not solely individual and isolated when their feelings connect with each other and greater queer and transgender communities of color. Although all five participants now realize their feelings are *collectively lived and felt*, they previously were not connected to groups that support them. All five participants continue to struggle to feel connected to those around them and to the overall communities of which they are a part or of which they want to be a part.

Stereotyped and Isolated

All participants shared the emotional experience of being isolated due to stereotypes. Usha discusses the ways in which her professors and friends assume her to be dating every single woman she hangs out with. She knows she is consistently being judged, thought of, and treated differently. Shah (1997) discusses the ways in which Asian American lesbian women are hyperinvisible and/or hyperexotified. Usha highlights the moment she felt hyperexotified and hypersexualized by her professor, who assumed her to be dating every single girl she spotted her with. Usha feels isolated because people who once viewed her to be invisible and nonsexual before she was out now hypersexualize her as an Asian American lesbian woman.

Usha describes:

> If it's a girl, she would assume that I'm dating them if I walk into the class
> with them at the same time. She would be like, "I don't want you dating our
> students. But if you are, you need to let me know." Yeah, I would be like, "I'm
> not … they're my friends," it's just like, automatically assumed.

Although she feels welcomed and accepted in the queer and transgender
student of color campus organization, Merissa elaborates how she cannot
express her true self with certain people. For example, she expresses how
her White mother does not understand her Black identity, her father does
not understand her gender and bisexual identity, and some of her friends
do not accept her bisexual identity. Many queer people do not accept her
bisexual identity, whereas many people of color challenge her Black identity. She feels the consistent need to defend and justify her identities and
does not completely feel accepted among her family and friends.

Merissa elaborates:

> My mom's side, which is the White side of my family, doesn't understand my
> race. Or my dad doesn't understand my gender. There is always someone
> who I have to explain myself or I don't feel like I'm completely understood.

Janelle shared her story of being mislabeled and stereotyped as the
angry Black feminist woman, in which several of her friends ceased talking
to her because she offended them in some way due to her politics when
she never intended to do so. Linder and Rodriguez (2012) highlight the
multiple ways in which women of color activists are often labeled as angry.
Women of color activists are on the constant defense of explaining and
justifying the validity of their multiple identities and experiences (Linder
and Rodriguez, 2012). Ahmed (2010) speaks of the figure of the feminist
killjoy who is often the "spoilsport" ruining conversations for people when
often discussing the politics of race, gender, and sexuality that others do
not wish to talk about. Janelle represents Ahmed's (2010) feminist killjoy
because she does not cater to other people's norms but instead expresses
herself fully, which includes her political opinions that then turn certain
people off.

Janelle illustrated:

> It makes me sad that someone would read or hear the things I've said and
> instead of them listening or trying to understand where I'm coming from …
> it's met with fear, hesitation, anger, disdain, or disgust. And that hurts me
> because even if they said something distasteful, which I'm sure they had, I
> don't meet them with that and it's like … it hurts more than anything and I

guess I get really melancholy and I just get really solemn and I just kind of … I guess my fire kinda dims a bit.

Tasha emphasizes how she/they intentionally surrounds herself/themselves among people who accept all of her/their identities and respect all of her/their communities. When people do not respect her/them, she/they feel isolated and are unable to connect with others around them. Ahmed (2010) highlights the ways in which queers become stereotyped as unhappy queers undeserving of love and happiness. Tasha emulates this unhappy queer trope when she/they do not connect with others when others do not seek to understand her/them.

Tasha shares:

I don't feel human. I feel a nothingness. Almost like I am existing and not living. I guess it affects when I am feeling uncomfortable it kinda affects how I am communicating with people or trying to connect with people. There is a lack of connection when that tries to happen.

Raul highlights the many moments he was ridiculed and stereotyped as the "angry student of color" in his predominantly White and heteronormative classes. Although he is not being angry and only sharing his perspectives, he is mislabeled as angry, and people automatically dismiss and do not listen to him. Being cast out to the margins, he becomes angry and begins to embrace the anger he feels. Although he is stereotyped and isolated, he does not feel alone thanks to queer woman of color feminist, Audre Lorde (1984), who assisted him in realizing his feelings of anger are valid.

Raul explains:

I embody anger. When I am uncomfortable, I feel like I cannot stay quiet. The communities I belong to have been quiet for too long. It's about being angry because people think you are being too angry. Your feelings are not valid.

All five participants discussed the ways in which they were mislabeled, stereotyped, and isolated. Some were stereotyped as passive or hypersexual, whereas others were read as unhappy and angry. It is important for educational leaders to pay attention to these emotional experiences because queer and transgender students of color are purposefully ostracized, isolated, and disconnected when others view them to be inferior. Queer and transgender students of color may begin to feel invisible or hypervisible when others have misguided perceptions and expectations of them. These false perceptions are rooted in histories of discrimination toward queer and transgender people of color. Feelings toward these queer and transgender student of color activists and the resulting isolation and disconnection these students experience are not isolated events but are instead an affective response to histories and current systems that perpetuate negative stereotypes of queer and transgender people of color.

Invisibility and Hypervisibility

Merissa conveys how she is often the only Black woman in her classes. She intentionally sits near the front of her class to make sure her opinions are heard by her professor and classmates. Merissa speaks of the multiple ways in which Black women are invisible in the classroom. Scholars document the ways in which Black women are purposefully not seen or perceived as angry or hypersexualized (Collins, 1990; hooks, 1981). Not only does Merissa struggle with simultaneous invisibility and hypervisibility of her Black woman identity, she reveals how her bisexuality is often erased. Although her father speaks of and asks questions regarding her boyfriends, her previous and current girlfriends are often unspoken of or referred to as friends. Those she is dating often make assumptions about her sexuality and misidentify her. The sexuality she self-identifies with is rarely embraced in its entirety.

Merissa gives an account of how others view her:

> They see me as straight or they see me as gay. They see me as one or the other. Especially when I'm talking to a girl, they think I'm gay. If I'm dating a guy, they think I'm straight. If I'm dating a guy or girl ... I'm still bisexual.

Before Usha presented herself with a masculine haircut and clothes, Usha noticed that an alarming number of people, friends, family, and acquaintances were unaware of her queer identity. Her sexuality was unseen because Asian American women are often stereotyped to be model minority, silent, and submissive women who cannot be queer (Shah, 1997). Now that Usha presents herself as masculine, her Asian American identity and sexuality become hypervisible, tokenized, and exotified. If her identities are not praised, they are put down and looked down on. Usha outlines her experiences and feelings as a simultaneously invisible and hypervisible Asian American lesbian:

> I think personally for me cuz I'm Asian and stuff, everyone here has been like "Oh my God, it's so rare to see a Gay Asian person," especially for a girl type of thing, and like they are super fascinated and ask me all sorts of questions. I totally don't mind, but there are people that are like "you are a disgrace to your family."

Raul often finds himself to be the one brown face in the sea of majority White faces or the one queer among many heteronormative-presenting people. Alimahomed (2010) speaks of the ways in which queer people of color are invisible or misrepresented in mainstream LGBTQ spaces and people of color spaces. Raul's brown skin is invisible when few validate his intellect and worth. His brown skin is hypervisible when anti-immigrant racist tropes circulate. His queer identity is often hypervisible among homophobic people of color spaces. Because mainstream LGBTQ spaces often are homonormative when mainly advocating for gay marriage and military inclusion agendas (Eng, 2010; Puar, 2007), Raul does not fit in and does not belong in these homonormative LGBTQ spaces when his politics go beyond marriage and military inclusion. Raul traces his feelings of invisibility and hypervisibility to spaces that do not accept his multiple and complex identities:

> Going to LGBTQ spaces where you are too brown to go in there. People look at you different. You're one of the few people speaking your languages and other people dismissing you. Not feeling good enough and going to spaces of color knowing you are the queer one.

Three of the five participants shared the ways in which they are often made to simultaneously feel invisible and hypervisible in multiple spaces, including classrooms, campus organizations, and family circles. These three participants' feelings of invisibility and hypervisibility are not isolated emotions when their emotions are rooted in historical and current systems that seek to interiorize and silence the fluidity and complexity of their queer of color identities. Queer of color scholars illustrate the contradictions and depth of diversity of queer of color identities (Ferguson, 2004; Manalansan, 2003; Perez, 2005). Issues that concern queer and transgender people of color move beyond the politics of marriage and military inclusion and instead are concerned with issues of the military and prison industrial complex, migration, poverty, hunger, gentrification, homelessness, lack of health care, scarcity of quality jobs with dignity, state-sponsored violence, and more (Clare, 2015; Hanhardt, 2015; Puar, 2007, Spade, 2015; Stanley & Smith, 2011). These queer and transgender student of color activists demonstrate their frustrations with others who are unable to accept their multiple and complex identities and their feelings of unbelonging in spaces that do not support multiple issue movements.

Frustration With the Lack of Intersectionality

Raul expresses his frustration with the lack of intersectionality on campus, especially among mainstream LGBTQ groups that do not proactively practice intersectionality in terms of embracing the multiple and fluid race, gender, sexuality, ability, and class identities and issues of queer and transgender people of color. Intersectionality, coined by Black feminist scholars, prioritizes the ways in which race, class, and gender experiences intersect and cannot be separated (Collins, 1990; Combahee River Collective, 1979; Crenshaw, 1994; Davis, 1983; hooks, 1981). Queer feminist scholars of color advocate for intersectionality when demonstrating the ways in which sexuality and ability cannot be separated from race, gender, and class discussions (Anzaldua, 1987; Lorde, 1984; Moraga & Anzaldua, 1981; Tumang & De Rivera, 2006). Raul reveals how he is disappointed with mainstream LGBTQ groups that often silence issues of race, gender, and class. Raul speaks of his impatience with mainstream LGBTQ groups ignoring the high murder rates of transgender women of color.

Raul calls to attention the lack of intersectionality on campus:

> Some of the women organizations are even better than our LGBT White groups. Recently, a women's organization did a tabling event remembering trans women of color who have been killed. Whereas, our LGBT folk were celebrating their pride week and their coming out events so I really appreciate the intersectional approach taken by other groups more than the LGBT spaces.

Tasha urges Black Lives Matter activists to not only focus on Black male lives but also the lives of Black women, including transgender and queer Black women. Queer of color scholars depict the numerous ways in which transgender and queers of color are often left out of race, gender, or sexuality conversations and movements (Chavez, 2013; Ferguson, 2004; Manalansan, 2003; Muñoz, 1999, 2009; Patton & Sanchez-Eppler, 2000; Puar, 2007; Rodriguez, 2003). Anzaldua (1987) and Bowleg (2008) emphasize the ways in which their queer women of color identities and communities should not be fragmented and separated. Tasha embodies multiple identities existing together and urges her/their Black community to accept the fluidity and complexity of multiple Black identities.

Tasha declares support for intersectionality:

> If we wanna build our community up, we cannot forget about the Black queer people of color. It's like saying Black Lives Matter but queers don't. You can't do that. If you're not down for all Black Lives, you're not down for Black Lives at all.

Two of the five participants discuss their frustrations with campus organizations and overall social movements that often support single-issue politics instead of advocating for multiple-issue politics and movements. Mainstream and predominantly White LGBTQ organizations were critiqued along with single-issue organizations and movements of color. Previous scholars document the ways in which queer and transgender people of color often do not belong or feel welcomed in single-identity or single-issue movements and spaces (Spade, 2015; Stanley & Smith, 2011). Although these spaces are necessary in bringing pride to often silenced and degraded identities and issues such as LGBTQ and Black movements, these queer and transgender activists illustrate the ways in which their frustrations with these spaces and movements is not an individual occurrence when their critiques of these spaces and movements is rooted in histories and current legacies of activism. For example, Chicana women often challenged the male-dominated and sexist attitudes of the Chicano Power movement (Blackwell, 2011). Black women and queer Black folks critique the ways in which straight Black male figures are honored and remembered as civil rights and Black Power movement leaders, with Black women, queer, and transgender people ignored. Asian Pacific Islanders and Native Americans are often left out of historical and current dialogues of social justice even when these groups are predominantly involved in activism. Driskill (2010) and Finley (2011) critique the ways in which Native Americans are often silenced in queer of color and Native scholarships and activisms. The two participants who feel disappointment toward spaces and movements situate themselves in ongoing movements that seek to challenge single-identity and single-issue politics. Calling for multiple identity and issue movements, these two participants call for the survival, healing, and pride of multiple identities and issues instead of forgetting and ignoring the power of intersectional identities and movements.

Survival, Healing, and Pride

Feelings of survival, healing, and pride were experienced differently and at different moments and spaces by three of the participants. Janelle specifically speaks to a poetry event hosted by her queer and transgender student of color organization as an event of survival, healing, and pride. I observed this event, in which two queer and two spirit Native people sang a traditional song in their Native language. Janelle found this event to be profoundly moving when witnessing people who struggle on a historical and daily basis for the survival of their race, gender, and sexuality identities, experiences, and practices. Driskill, Finley, Gilley, and Morgensen (2011) highlight the multiple ways in which queer Indigenous peoples continuously fight for the survival and revival of their cultures every day. Driskill (2010) speaks of the ways in which song is a form of activism when song is rooted in Indigenous practices of survival, community building, healing, and pride.

Janelle describes this moment of survival and healing:

A system was created to decimate who they are, where they come from, and take everything that belongs to them rightfully. And to have these people go up and be unapologetic and to share a bit of that with us, with me.... It was such a healing and beautiful moment.

Usha speaks of an all queer people of color panel hosted by a traditionally majority White LGBTQ student group I observed, in which predominantly White LGBTQ students listened to the lived experiences and perspectives of queer and transgender students of color. Usha describes this event as empowering to her because the majority of White LGBTQ student groups rarely feature queer and transgender people of color as speakers at their events. Alimahomed (2010) discusses the ways in which mainstream LGBTQ organizations often leave out queer people of color and queer people of color issues. An all queer and transgender people of color panel was a victory for Usha, evoking feelings of survival and healing.

Usha depicts this moment of healing and pride:

I thought that was a victory because everyone there was so focused and wanting to learn more. It was like them being taught. And they were taking down notes and like it was awesome to see.

Raul shares the pain he experienced when believing he was not smart when he was young. His feelings are not isolated and are rooted in systems of oppression that underfund Chicano Latino neighborhoods to keep schools and people in poverty and uneducated. These systems discriminate against English as a second language students when curriculums and tests do not support them. Martinez (2014) speaks of the ways in which the writings and intellectual contributions of women of color have been overlooked or discouraged. Resisting the erasure and silencing of women of color in academia, Martinez (2014) pushes women of color and queer women of color to write their stories, thoughts, and feelings as a form of liberation. After reading the numerous writings of queer people of color, Raul finds himself moving away from shame to having pride in his identities, with the goal of encouraging youth to find pride in their race, gender, sexuality, class, and ability identities to dismantle systems that seek to oppress them. The writings of women of color feminists, along with the writings of queer and transgender scholars of color, are healing for Raul because these writings assist him on his ongoing journey toward survival, healing, and pride. Raul shares how he did not always feel healing and pride toward himself and multiple communities.

Raul shares how his feelings of shame transformed to feelings of healing and pride:

> I came to this country at 10 and they made me take standardized tests after six months of being here and I failed them, all of them, because obviously I didn't know English and I also started hating my accent. After reading these works by queer people of color, I started seeing people like myself being published and it is something I can relate to and it helped me, again, to feel proud of the places that I come from, and not feel the shame that school systems have made me feel.

Three of the participants discuss their feelings of survival, healing, and pride when witnessing other queer and transgender people of color in positions of power. As Indigenous transgender and queer scholars share, song and dance is a form of healing, pride, and activism (Driskill, 2010; Finley, 2011). Grady, Marquez, and McLaren (2012) describe music and dance as healing for queers of color. Having the voices and perspectives of queer and transgender people of color amplified in campus spaces and academic writing is a form of empowerment for these participants. These feelings of survival, healing, and pride are not singular events when they are affective responses to educational and societal systems that often silence the multiple identities and issues of queer and transgender people of color. Scholars highlight how LGBTQ issues are silenced in schools (Endo & Millner, 2014; Murray, 2011; Mayo, 2014). Queer scholars of color illustrate how queer and transgender people of color identities and issues are silenced in the curriculum (Coloma, 2006, 2012; Kumashiro, 2002, 2004). The feelings of these participants are in solidarity with ongoing movements to include the transformational voices and perspectives of queer and transgender people of color in education and society. These queer and transgender student of color activists follow the traditions of Lorde (1984), who coins survival, healing, and pride for one's self and communities as deliberate acts of resistance.

Resistance

Feelings of resistance stirred among all participants who refuse the systemic marginalization of their race, gender, sexuality, class, and ability identities and experiences in different ways. According to Raul, resistance comes in the form of coming together as collective communities. Rodriguez (2003) highlights the concept of *Queer Latinidad*, in which people of color and queer people of color come together and build communities of support.

Raul depicts resistance as solidarity through community building:

> I think uniting, like right now in this room, all queer people of color, that never happens. I mean it does, but at our higher education institution it rarely happens, but it does happen.

Janelle envisions resistance as everyday survival in a world where queers and queers of color are more likely to be disciplined and pushed out of schools or murdered (Burdge et al., 2014; Ford, 2012; Mayo, 2014; Murray, 2011; National Coalition of Anti-Violence Programs, 2014). Women of color feminists illustrate the ways in which existence is a form of resistance as well as women of color and queer women of color loving themselves in a world that does not wish for them to love themselves (Lorde, 1984; Martinez, 2014).

Janelle illustrates resistance as existence:

> You existing is a form of resilience and healing. You existing in those spaces that might not initially or automatically include you as a whole person, you saying "this is who all of me is" will be healing for that community, for that space in itself.

Usha embodies resistance as being her authentic self and encouraging others around her to embrace their whole identities. Researchers such as Mayo (2014) and Murray (2011) argue for educational policies to support the whole identities of queer and gender-nonconforming students. Women of color and queer women of color feminists highlight the ways in which women of color and queer women of color experience a *mestiza consciousness* of simultaneously belonging and not belonging to multiple communities due to their multiple identities (Anzaldúa, 1987; Moraga & Anzaldua, 1981; Tumang & De Rivera, 2006). Usha resists the split of her multiple identities and seeks to be proud of her identities as a form of resistance.

Usha describes resistance as living authentically and unapologetically:

> I think being ourselves is resisting. Starting school here, I was like "No, I'm gonna wear girl clothes and hide behind all of this because I am not going to be judged and harassed." And then after spring semester, I was like "No, I don't really care anymore. I'm done hiding. I want a voice too."

Loving one's self and one's communities is a form of healing and resistance for three of the participants. These feelings and acts of resistance are not singular events when these feelings and acts are part of a collective and overall movement for queer and transgender people of color to resist institutions and systems that seek to silence and degrade those that deviate from White, heterosexual, cisgender, classist, and ableist norms. Embracing one's self and one's communities as multiple, fluid, and complex allows these participants to become the multiple-issue activists they are. They seek to build coalitions and strong communities of support for each other and those around them. Resisting silence, isolation, and self-hate is a form of resistance that demands for greater justice toward queer and transgender people of color marginalized in education and society.

Demanding Justice

During the focus group, Janelle, Merissa, and Raul envisioned an alternative university accepting of and advocating for queer and transgender people of color in education and society. Imagining alternative possibilities supports queer critical race feminist theory and participatory action research methodology because participatory action research seeks to transform theoretical research into action. Participants envisioned multiple student and community members demanding for justice and equity at the university level for queer and transgender students of color. The following demands were proposed which deeply connect to collective feelings, desires, and visions for justice.

Janelle imagines justice and equity through the institutionalization of queer of color leaders:

> Mandated cultural competence for leaders of LGBTQ organizations. Like there would be a quota of bringing people of color or queer people of color into these spaces regardless so they can push education.

Merissa envisions justice through queer of color speakers:

> Having a QPOC speaker series cuz Gender and Race Studies has a speaker series. All of these different departments have speaker series. If you could get these speakers and make it mandatory.

Raul calls for equity through increased financial support for queer students of color:

> I think it would be cool if they (the University) gives funding for queers of color to go to conferences, fund our research, and fund our communities and experiences instead of spending so much money on football. How about you fund your college students to do research?

During the focus group, these three participants imagined more university resources provided for queer and transgender students of color. Participants critiqued LGBTQ organizations on campus, academic departments, and the university itself. These activists *collectively feel* together when calling for increased attention toward queer and transgender students of color, who are often ignored and left out of academic conversations and financial funding. These participants envision the prioritizing of queer and transgender students of color. Collectively feeling together, the affective responses of demanding for justice are rooted in feelings of self-love and care for themselves and their multiple communities.

Self-Love and Care

Tasha, Janelle, and Raul spoke of their emotional and affective experiences with self-love and care. Women of color feminists prioritize the critical need for people to practice self-love and care (hooks, 1981; Lorde, 1984). Because relationships between queer people of color may result in violence due to histories and systems perpetuating queer people of color to practice hate toward themselves and their communities (Kanuha, 2013), it is important for queer people of color to develop and maintain thoughtful and caring relationships of love and support toward themselves and others. The participants demonstrated self-care in different ways, ranging from loving one's authentic self to finding supportive partners who cultivate self-love to being easy with one's self:

Tasha emphasizes:

Do you. Don't do anything you feel obligated to do. Do what you love.

Janelle shares:

My partner, he has taught me … he has helped me internalize self-love cuz even though my family has talked to me about self-love and esteem and confidence, I never internalized it enough.

Raul states:

Don't ever feel bad for taking time to take care of yourself. If you don't get the perfect A because you want an hour of extra sleep, that's fine. That's you taking care of yourself and that's okay.

These three participants express the ways in which feelings of self-love and care are crucial for queer and transgender student of color activists. Because queer and transgender people of color do not see themselves depicted in a positive manner in education and society, it is critical for them to love themselves and those around them in a world that attempts to silence and eliminate identities and issues central to queer and transgender people of color. To demand for justice and equity, these activists must continue to sustain themselves and those they love through self-love and care. Loving one's self and one's communities is a form of *collectively feeling* and collectively taking action to cultivate communities of support to sustain lifelong acts of activism.

Communities of Support

All participants defined communities as places where and people with whom they feel acceptance and support of their whole identities. It was evident that community is a place where the participants feel safe to be their authentic selves and support each other. According to the participants, community evokes feelings of security, open-mindedness, and the ability to share and validate personal and collective lived experiences.

Janelle illustrates:

I definitely would say I feel most comfortable now this year being part of our queer and transgender student of color organization. I definitely feel reassured. I feel safe from that judgment, from that initial judgment. That body language. The language and the verbal cues that indicate that the understanding has stopped. I feel safe from all of that prejudgment.

Raul describes:

I like the word familia. I think familia is not just your parents, grandparents, it can be friends, mentors, that you see as familia, because at the end of the day, you have those people who you have certain connections that are like family and it's necessary to remember that you do have family and you do have support systems with you.

Tasha explains:

When I'm in a safe space, when people care about who I am and the community as a whole ask questions, they are open instead of being closed off to me. That's when I'm definitely most comfortable.

Usha declares:

I really appreciate the discussions we have and stuff because we attack problems that are going on not just on campus, but personal stories, things that are happening in the community or in society. We talk about these things and I appreciate people feeling really comfortable when we get further into the discussion and everyone starts sharing.

All five of the participants are collectively feeling when they collectively define communities as places where and people with whom they are able to become their true and authentic selves without judgment and hesitation. Communities allow these activists to express their love for themselves and those around them. Ahmed (2006) discusses ways in which people become oriented toward certain people, places, and objects and argues how historically and currently society often orients and positions people against racialized and queered "others." The feelings of these activists are not isolated occurrences when these feelings are rooted in histories that seek to exclude racialized and queered "others." Affect scholars demonstrate the ways in which deserving and undeserving people and populations are created systems (Ahmed, 2004; Berlant, 2011; Campbell & Sitze, 2013; Chen, 2012; Cho, 2007; Clough & Halley, 2007). These queer and transgender student of color activists resist exile and exclusion through the creation of spaces in which they are worthy and deserving of support and love. In addition to seeking support and affirmation, these queer and transgender student of color activists seek mentorship and mentor others toward paths of self- and community love as forms of *collective feeling* and activism.

Mentorship

Last, emotional experiences of mentorship were key to all participants. All participants expressed their desire to mentor and be mentored by others. Because queer and transgender students of color are underrepresented in K–12 and higher education institutions as well as society at large, all participants expressed their appreciation of their mentors and desire to mentor others to love themselves and to not give up when life presents them with challenges. Raul recommends the following to his mentees:
Raul states:

> I wouldn't tell them it gets better. I will be real with them and tell them it is hard, but to remember that there is a bunch of people behind them just like them and us being in college can't forget where we come from and we have to be future mentors for other students who follow queer traditions of mentorship because that is something that has been very powerful about queer communities is our sense of mentorship because we usually might not have best ties with our biological families. I will just share with them that it is important to ask for help when needed but also remember that one day there will be people asking help from you.

Usha discusses the ways in which it is difficult to reach out but encourages people to reach out to each other. To Usha, mentorship is nonhierarchical and involves people being there to listen to and care for one another. Queer of color scholars illustrate the critical need for queer of color communities to support each other due to a lack of support from education and societal systems (Chavez, 2013; Ferguson, 2004; Manalansan, 2003; Muñoz, 1999, 2009; Patton & Sanchez-Eppler, 2000; Puar, 2007; Rodriguez, 2003).

Usha shares:

> I feel like sometimes it's hard for people to ask for help. So if you just constantly check up on everyone ... it doesn't matter if it's the happiest person on campus, they're usually the ones that are struggling the most so they are just trying to keep the face and not have people worry about them. So just asking everyone how they are doing ... try to hang out with everyone or just being there as much as you can. I feel like some people just need somebody, a friend to listen to, or keep their mind off something.

DISCUSSION AND RECOMMENDATIONS

The queer and transgender student of color activists expressed the following emotions: depression and anxiety, isolation due to stereotypes, invisibility and hypervisibility, frustration with the lack of intersectionality and acceptance of multiple identities, survival healing and pride, resistance, demanding justice, self-love and care, community building, and mentorship. Following queer critical race feminist theories and the scholarship of Ahmed (2004), I exemplify the ways in which these emotions are *collectively felt* when deeply rooted in histories and systems of oppressions. The emotions my participants experience are affective responses to institutionalized discrimination and trauma such as low-income and predominantly people of color neighborhoods and schools lacking financial resources and queer students of color lacking communities of support and mentorship due to the lack of queer of color representation in education and society.

My participants and I recommend that educational leaders, faculty, students, and community members:

- Learn about and accept the multiple, fluid, and complex identities and struggles of queer and transgender students of color.
- Institutionalize policies that seek to support queer and transgender students of color through queer of color visibility in curricula, educational leaders, faculty, staff, and speakers, along with recruiting and retaining more queer and transgender students of color.
- Allocate scholarships and grants to be awarded specifically for queer and transgender students of color.

- Create more spaces and moments for queer students of color to practice self-love, care, and healing.

CONCLUSION

Through a queer critical race feminist theoretical framework, I analyze the individual and collective emotional experiences of queer and transgender student of color activists to be rooted in histories and systems of oppression. Utilizing queer critical race feminist theory and participatory action research methodology, I co-construct my research with my participants as they co-create research purpose, questions, methods, methodology, and analysis with me. Input and feedback from my participants is encouraged, from formulating questions, to observations, to facilitating interviews and focus groups, to transcribing narratives, to analyzing key emotional themes. I encouraged my participants to contribute their insight throughout the research process as they shared with me possible theoretical frameworks, observations, and emotional themes I can explore. My research practices participatory action research methodology when it seeks to enact transformation and change of the oppressive systems that my participants and I encounter. With guidance from my participants, I seek to present the preliminary findings of my research to university leaders, faculty, students, and community members to move conversations and actions forward that seek to improve conditions for queer and transgender students of color.

REFERENCES

Ahmed, S. (2004). *The cultural politics of emotion*. New York: Routledge.

Ahmed, S. (2006). *Queer phenomenology: Orientations, objects, others*. London, UK: Duke University Press.

Ahmed, S. (2010). *The promise of happiness*. London, UK: Duke University Press.

Ahmed, S. (2014). *Willful subjects*. London, UK: Duke University Press.

Alimahomed, S. (2010). Thinking outside the rainbow: Women of color redefining queer politics and identity. *Social Identities*, 2, 151–168.

Annamma, S. A. (2015). "It was just like a piece of gum": Using an intersectional approach to understand criminalizing young women of color with disabilities in the school-to-prison pipeline. In D. J. Connor, J. W. Valle, & C. Hale (Eds.), *Practicing disability studies in education: Acting toward social change* (pp. 83–102). New York, NY: Peter Lang.

Anzaldúa, G. (1987). *Borderlands: The new mestiza la frontera* (4th ed.). San Francisco, CA: Aunt Lute Books.

Berlant, L. (2011). *Cruel optimism*. Durham and London: Duke University Press.

Blackwell, M. (2011). *Chicana power!: Contested histories of feminism in the Chicano movement* (1st ed., Chicana matters series). Austin: University of Texas Press.

Bowleg, L. (2008). When Black + lesbian + woman ≠ Black lesbian woman. *Sex Roles, 59*, 312–325.

Brydon-Miller, M., Kral, M., Maguire, P., Noffke, S., & Sabhlok, A. (2011). Jazz and the banyan tree: Participatory action research. In N. Denzin and Y. Lincoln (Eds.), *The sage handbook of qualitative research* (4th ed., pp. 387–400). Newbury Park, CA: Sage Publications.

Burdge, H., Licona, A. C., & Hemingway, Z. T. (2014). LGBTQ youth of color: Discipline disparities, school push-out, and the school-to-prison pipeline. [PDF document]. Retrieved from http://www.gsanetwork.org/files/aboutus/LGBTQ_brief_FINAL-web.pdf

Campbell, T., & Sitze, A. (Eds.). (2013). *Biopolitics: A reader*. London: Duke University Press.

Chavez, K. R. (2013). *Queer migration politics: Activist rhetoric and coalitional possibilities*. Urbana, IL: University of Illinois Press.

Chen, M. (2012). *Animacies: Biopolitics, racial mattering, and queer affect*. Durham, NC: Duke University Press.

Cho, G. M. (2007). Voices from the teum: Synthetic trauma and the ghosts of the Korean diaspora. In P. T. Clough & J. Halley (Eds.), *The affective turn: Theorizing the social* (pp. 151–169). Durham, NC: Duke University Press.

Clare, E. (2015). *Exile and pride: Disability, queerness, and liberation*. Durham, NC: Duke University Press.

Clough, P. T., & Halley, J. (Eds.). (2007). *The affective turn: Theorizing the social*. Durham, NC: Duke University Press.

Collins, P. H. (1990). *Black feminist thought: Knowledge, consciousness, and the politics of self-empowerment*. Boston, MA: Unwin Hyman.

Collins, P. H. (2004). Learning from the outsider within: The sociological significance of black feminist thought. *Social Problems, 6*, S14–S32.

Coloma, R. (2006). Putting queer to work: Examining empire and education. *International Journal of Qualitative Studies in Education* (QSE), *19*(5), 639–657.

Coloma, R. (2012). Homophobias: Lust and loathing across time and space. *International Journal of Qualitative Studies in Education, 25*(2), 212–215.

Combahee River Collective. (1979). A black feminist statement. In Z. Eisenstein (Ed.), *Capitalist patriarchy and the case for social feminism* (pp. 362–372). New York, NY: Monthly Review Press.

Crenshaw, K. (1994). Mapping the margins: Intersectionality, identity politics, and violence against women of color. *Stanford Law Review, 43*, 1241–1299.

Davis, A. (1983). *Women, race, and class*. New York, NY: Random House.

Driskill, Q. (2010). Doubleweaving two spirit critiques: Building alliances between native and queer studies. *GLQ: A Journal of Lesbian and Gay Studies, 16*(1–2), 69–92.

Driskill, Q., Finley, C., Gilley, B. J., & Morgensen, S. L. (Eds.). (2011). *Queer indigenous studies: Critical interventions in theory, politics, and literature*. Tucson, AZ: University of Arizona Press.

Endo, H., & Millner, P. C. (Eds.). (2014). *Queer voices from the classroom: A volume in research in queer studies*. Charlotte, NC: Information Age Publishing.

Eng, D. (2010). *The feeling of kinship: Queer liberalism and the racialization of intimacy.* Durham, NC: Duke University Press.

Ferguson, R. (2004). *Aberrations in black: Toward a queer of color critique.* Minneapolis, MN: University of Minnesota Press.

Finley, C. (2011). Decolonizing the queer native body. In Q. Driskill, C. Finley, B. J. Gilley, & S. L. Morgensen (Eds.), *Queer indigenous studies: Critical interventions in theory, politics, and literature* (pp. 31–42). Tucson, AZ: University of Arizona Press.

Ford, Z. (2012). Glsen releases new school climate report: 82 percent of LGBT students still encounter verbal harassment. Retrieved from http://thinkprogress. org/lgbt/2012/09/05/797501/glsen-releases-new-school-climate-report-82-percent-of-lgbt-students-still-encounter-verbal-harassment/

Freire, P. (1970). *Pedagogy of the oppressed.* New York, NY: Continuum.

Grady, J., Marquez, R., & McLaren, P. (2012). A critique of neoliberalism with fierceness: Queer youth of color creating dialogues of resistance. *Journal of Homosexuality, 59*(7), 982–1004.

Grewal, I., & Kaplan, C. (2001). Global identities: Theorizing transnational studies of sexuality. *GLQ: A Journal of Lesbian and Gay Studies, 7*(4), 663–679.

Hanhardt, C. B. (2013). *Safe space: Gay neighborhood history and the politics of violence.* Durham, NC: Duke University Press.

hooks, b. (1981). *Ain't I a woman: Black women and feminism.* Boston, MA: South End Press.

hooks, b. (2000). *Feminist theory: From margin to center.* Boston, MA: South End Press.

Kanuha, V. K. (2013). Relationships so loving and so hurtful: The constructed duality of sexual and racial/ethnic intimacy in the context of violence in Asian and Pacific Islander lesbian and queer women's relationships. *Violence Against Women, 19*, 1175–1196.

Kumashiro, K. (2002). *Troubling education: Queer activism and antioppressive pedagogy.* New York, NY: Routledge.

Kumashiro, K. (2004). *Restoried selves: Autobiographies of queer Asian-Pacific- American activists* (Haworth gay & lesbian studies). New York, NY: Harrington Park Press.

Linder, C., & Rodriguez, K. L. (2012). Learning from the experiences of self-identified women of color activists. *Journal of College Student Development, 3*, 383–398.

Lorde, A. (1984). *Sister outsider.* Trumansburg, NY: The Crossing Press.

Manalansan IV, M. F. (2003). *Global divas: Filipino men in the diaspora.* London, UK: Duke University Press.

Martinez, S. (2014). For our words usually land on deaf ears until we scream. *Qualitative Inquiry, 1*, 3–14.

Mayo, C. (2014). *LGBTQ youth and education: Policies and practices.* New York, NY: Teachers College Press.

Moraga, C., & Anzaldúa, G. (Eds.). (1981). *This bridge called my back: Writings by radical women of color.* New York, NY: Kitchen Table Woman of Color Press.

Muñoz, J. E. (1999). *Disidentifications: Queers of color and the performance of politics.* Minneapolis, MN: University of Minnesota Press.

Muñoz, J. E. (2009). *Cruising utopia: The then and there of queer futurity.* New York, NY: New York University Press.

Murray, O. (2011). Queer youth in heterosexist schools: Isolation, prejudice and no clear supportive policy frameworks. *Multicultural Perspectives, 4,* 215–219.

National Coalition of Anti-Violence Programs. (2014). National report on hate violence against lesbian, gay, bisexual, transgender, queer and HIV-affected communities released today: Multi-year trends in anti-LGBTQ hate violence and homicides continue [PDF document]. Retrieved from http://www.avp.org/storage/documents/2013_mr_ncavp_hvreport.pdf

Patton, C., & Sanchez-Eppler (Eds.). (2000). *Queer diasporas.* London, UK: Duke University Press.

Perez, H. (2005). You can have my brown body and eat it, too! *Social Text, 23*(3–4 [84–85]), 171–191.

Price, M. (2011). *Mad at school: Rhetorics of mental disability and academic life (Corporealities).* Ann Arbor, MI: University of Michigan Press.

Puar, J. K. (2007). *Terrorist assemblages: Homonationalism in queer times.* London, UK: Duke University Press.

Renn, K. A. (2007). LGBT student leaders and queer activists: Identities of lesbian, gay, bisexual, transgender, and queer identified college student leaders and activists. *Journal of College Student Development, 48*(3), 311–330.

Renn, K. A., & Bilodeau, B. (2005). Queer student leaders: An exploratory case study of identity development and LGBT student involvement at a Midwestern research university. *Journal of Gay & Lesbian Issues in Education, 2*(4), 49–71.

Renn, K. A., & Ozaki, C. C. (2010). Psychosocial and leadership identities among leaders of identity-based campus organizations. *Journal of Diversity in Higher Education, 3*(1), 14.

Rodriguez, J. M. (2003). *Queer Latinidad: Identity practices and discursive spaces.* New York, NY: New York University Press.

Shah, S. (1997). *Dragon ladies: Asian American feminists breathe fire.* Boston: South End Press.

Spade, D. (2015). *Normal life: Administrative violence, critical trans politics, and the limits of law.* Durham and London: Duke University Press.

Stanley, E. A., & Smith, N. (2011). *Trans embodiment and the prison industrial complex* (exp. 2nd ed.). Edinburgh, UK: AK Press.

Vaccaro, A., & Mena, J. A. (2011). It's not burnout, it's more: Queer college activists of color and mental health. *Journal of Gay & Lesbian Mental Health, 15*(4), 339–367.

Tumang, P. J., & De Rivera, J. (Eds.). (2006). *Homelands: Women's journeys across race, place, and time.* Emeryville, CA: Seal Press.

Vries, K. M. (2015). Transgender people of color at the center: Conceptualizing a new intersectional model. *Ethnicities, 15*(1), 3–27.

CHAPTER 4

QUEER FACULTY AND STAFF OF COLOR

Experiences and Expectations

Danielle Aguilar and Joshua Moon Johnson

Much of the literature around LGBTQ+ folks of color in higher education has focused on the student experience, and even here the literature is minimal. The current research leaves out a crucial population on college campuses: queer faculty and staff of color. We use the term "queer" to include people who do not self-identify as heterosexual and/or cisgender. On college campuses, most faculty and staff members are not only asked to perform the specific duties within their roles but also are expected to mentor students. Most institutions value having and recruit diverse faculty and staff members. However, once those faculty and staff members are recruited, little is known about their experiences. With emphasis being placed on the student experience, many times the continued development and support of faculty and staff are overlooked, which has more detrimental effects with people who hold multiple marginalized identities.

Considering the current conversations around diversifying faculty and staff at colleges and universities, it is important to understand the experiences of some of the most politically and socially vulnerable populations on

Queer People of Color in Higher Education, pp. 57–71
Copyright © 2017 by Information Age Publishing
All rights of reproduction in any form reserved.

campus. A commitment to diversifying faculty and staff members should go beyond recruitment and include retention and job satisfaction. As institutions examine the retention efforts of people of color on campuses, they need to look at identity more complexly and understand the implication of how people's identities intersect. This chapter focuses on the intersection of race, gender, and sexuality in the lives of faculty and staff members across the United States.

To know how queer faculty and staff of color experience the college or university, much research needs to be conducted. The following study was informed by past research on the experiences of faculty of color as well as LGBTQ faculty at colleges and universities. The purpose of this study is to highlight the lived experiences of queer faculty and staff of color at colleges and universities across the country. The following research aims to give voice to populations on college campuses that are often overlooked or marginalized and therefore provide insight on how to better support them. Our research questions aimed to explore any challenges that queer faculty and staff of color faced on their campuses, and if there were challenges, what resources supported and helped them address those challenges.

METHODS

To further understand the experiences of queer faculty and staff of color, qualitative interview methods were utilized. The 18 participants were given the option of telephone interviews or online open-ended questionnaires. After the first interview, follow-up questions were used to further clarify their experiences. Two separate researchers, Aguilar and Moon Johnson, conducted the interviews. The interviews took place over 18 months and included people from across the United States. The participants represented all regions of the United States and were located in rural, urban, and suburban campuses. The institutions the participants came from represented both public and private institutions and ranged in size from small liberal arts to large public research.

After all interviews were completed and transcribed, the researchers coded the interviews separately and then evaluated themes based on separate coding and past research. Both of the researchers identify as queer people of color and serve as staff members on university campuses. As instruments, their personal and professional experiences have effects on the study, and it is recognized as a limitation.

EXPERIENCES AT THE INTERSECTIONS

Through the participant interviews and a review of past research, this chapter will provide new knowledge about the experiences of queer people of color. Some of the participants shared experiences they felt were isolated to their racial identities, whereas others shared experiences that related to their gender and/or sexual identities. Although past research has related to these identities separate from one another, we will build on past research by culminating the chapter to addresses how multiple identities simultaneously affect a faculty or staff member's experience.

Faculty of Color

Although recruiting racially diverse faculty and staff at colleges and universities has been a longstanding goal, institutions have struggled to be successful. According to Turner (2002), campus efforts to diversify faculty is still among the least successful goals for college campuses. Kayes (2006) writes that this goal has fallen short because a dialogue is missing in the discussion of recruitment or not having a common understanding of prioritizing diverse hiring. Kayes (2006) further goes on to argue that "diverse candidate pools do not necessarily result in diverse hires because institutional, departmental, and search committee cultures can overtly or covertly undermine the goal of faculty/staff diversity" (p. 65). Although universities might state that they are committed to diversifying professional staff and faculty members, that commitment is empty without continuous dialogue and common understandings. Not only does that commitment to diversity fall short in recruitment and hiring but also in retention. As the participants in our study arrived to campuses and faced negative campus climate, they felt unsupported. Many of the participants expressed that their college or university had no institutional support group geared toward their identities. A more complex and well-rounded discussion of diversity needs to be had at all levels of the institution to both yield diverse candidates and retain and support those professionals once on campus.

The underrepresentation of faculty of color has been an ongoing challenge, and students recognize this. According to the National Center for Education Statics' Condition of Education report (2015), "of all full-time faculty in degree-granting postsecondary institutions, 79 percent were White, six percent were Black, five percent were Hispanic, and 10 percent were Asian/Pacific Islander" (p. 2). The study showed that American Indian/Alaska Native and multiracial faculty made up less than 1%. The study from the National Center for Education Statistics (2015) showed greater disparity when looking at full-time professors: "Among full-time professors, 84 percent were white (58 percent were white males and 26 percent were white females), four percent were Black, three percent were Hispanic, and nine percent were Asian/Pacific Islander" (p. 2). The study once again showed that American Indian/Alaska Native and multiracial faculty made up less than 1%.

Although a long-term goal of faculty diversification has existed, faculty positions are still overwhelmingly held by White Americans. Diggs, Garrison-Wade, Estrada, and Galindo (2009) conducted a small study of four scholars of color pursuing tenure. According to Diggs et al. (2009), the literature found that "issues of marginalization, racism and sexism can be manifested as unintended barriers to navigating the tenure process successfully" (p. 313). Diggs et al. (2009) also found that mentorship was crucial, especially for faculty of color pursuing tenure. Mentors and mentees do not need to share the same racial identity to be an effective mentoring relationship, but the mentor must have a high level of self-awareness. Based on the racial statistics of faculty members, it would not be easy for faculty members of color to have mentors who are the same racial identity. Steven, a participant in our study who identified as a Latino gay faculty member at a university in the Southwest, stated, "There are no other gay Latino males in our department and often time there are some moments of discomfort for topics of discussion." Steven went on to share that he felt the university made little to no effort to support him as a Latino faculty member. Based on his racial identity, he did not feel supported and often felt uncomfortable.

In Arnett's (2015) article, he interviewed prominent scholar Dr. Jerlando Jackson, and according to Arnett, "Dr. Jerlando F. L. Jackson argues that the burden of service can't come at the expense of academic productivity necessary for promotion" (p. 3). Meaning that faculty of color are automatically tapped to do diversity work on campus and mentor students, which can have a negative effect on obtaining tenure, and the cycle continues. Diggs et al. (2009) found that "The diversity work represented an additional load or cultural tax that faculty were paying in order to pursue tenure" (p. 322). Many of the participants within our study felt similarly. Because of their identity, they were automatically pinned to do diversity work or create affinity spaces for themselves and others. For example, Ben, a mixed-race queer administrator in Minnesota, stated, "I host a faculty and staff of color get-together because we often do not see each other." Although his role is in the multicultural office, the burden still fell on him to create a support group for faculty and staff of color. The group was started by an individual who saw the importance; therefore, there is no guarantee that this support group will continue once Ben leaves his position or the university.

Bower (2002) found that many faculty of color faced isolation, alienation, and overt discrimination by their peers and their students. Bower (2002) also found that some of the participants were consistently devalued and publically discounted in the workplace. Two of the participants in the study expressed being shut down by colleagues. Our findings were consistent with the literature. Corey, a Black gay administrator from New York, stated, "I get shut down or ignored because they don't think I know as much." Similarly, Selena, a queer Chicana staff member from Massachusetts, stated, "The white folks in the room speak over me and shut down my ideas." Corey attributed this treatment to his age, although he did express feeling tokenized as a person of color on campus. Conversely, Selena attributed her treatment to her identities as a queer Chicana because most of the pushback came from her White colleagues.

LGBTQ Faculty and Staff

Limited research has been conducted on the experiences of LGBTQ faculty and staff on college campuses. Rankin and Reason (2008) provided a solid definition of the concept of campus climate: "Climate as the prevailing standards, behaviors, and attitudes of people on campus, which are shaped by access and retention, research and scholarship, curriculum, group relations, university policies, and external relations" (p. 263). Unfortunately, the themes that emerged from the research on faculty of color are also similar to the research on LGBTQ faculty and staff. LGBTQ faculty and staff have also expressed similar concerns, such as harassment, isolation, and discrimination (Bilimoria & Stewart, 2009).

A study by Rankin (2005) found that "forty-one percent of the respondents stated that their college or university did not thoroughly address issues related to sexual orientation or gender identity" (p. 19). Rankin's (2005) research spanned 14 universities and surveyed 1,669 self-identified LGBTQ individuals. Within our study, we also found that participants did not feel like the institution was providing adequate support or education about the LGBTQ community. Johnny, a gay Native American administrator in Oklahoma, stated, "It is primarily very straight and little or no support for [the] LGBTQ community." Ines, a bisexual Latina staff and lecturer from California, felt that the university "Said the right things while microaggressing me and providing no support to my multiple identities." Faculty and staff members had expectations that the campuses would provide some types of support to LGBTQ faculty and staff members, but most were disappointed with how they were treated.

Bilimoria and Stewart (2009) conducted a study and found that science, technology, engineering, and mathematics (STEM) faculty chose to not be "out" or openly identify as LGBTQ to their colleagues. Our study supported Bilimoria's and Stewart's finding; Sandita, an Indian bisexual woman, expressed that she was not sure how safe it would be if she were out at work because she works with families and children. Several participants said they feared what would happen if they were "out." Conversely, some people openly identified as LGBTQ from the beginning of their term in their positions. For example, Erica, a Black queer woman in the South-east, stated, "I have been out from the beginning, but it hasn't been that welcoming for that identity, though not openly hostile." The experiences varied. Although some expressed positive environments for their LGBTQ identities, most reported the environments being uncomfortable, passively unwelcoming, and even hostile. Our findings supported past research that showed the negative climates that LGBTQ faculty and staff members faced. According to Rankin, Weber, Blumenfeld, and Frazer (2010), 81% of faculty and 82% of staff reported they experienced exclusionary, intimidating, offensive, or hostile conduct because of their sexual identity.

The research examining experiences of faculty and staff of color show many similarities as the research examining experiences of LGBTQ faculty and staff members. The experiences show how marginalized populations lack mentorship and the added burden of advocating for themselves and others in their communities, in addition to fulfilling their paid positions. Exclusive and hostile environments create obstacles with recruiting and retaining people of color as well as LGBTQ people. The research to this point has mainly focused on people of color or LGBTQ as isolated populations. These identities do not happen in isolation, and the experiences of queer faculty and staff of color are not fully known. We aim to take this conversation to a more complex level and better understand how race, gender, and sexual identity all intersect and affect institutions of higher education.

ISSUES FACED BY QUEER FACULTY AND STAFF OF COLOR

This study examining queer faculty and staff of color builds on the research of past scholars. This research project adds new complexities to the study of faculty and staff who are queer people of color (QPOC). The 18 participants came from diverse personal and professional backgrounds; however, consistent themes emerged. Due to the brevity of this chapter, we will focus on a few major themes: microaggressions, double burden, institutional support, lack of inclusivity, and limited views of diversity.

Microaggressions

According to Sue et al. (2007), racial microaggressions are brief and common occurrences that can be verbal, behavioral, or environmental indignities. These indignities, whether intentional or unintentional, create hostile, derogatory, or negative environments for people of color. Many of our participants shared their experiences with microaggressions. The acts ranged from being shut down, to intentionally not making eye contact, to verbal aggressions toeing the line of harassment. For example, Sandita, an Indian American bisexual woman working in North Carolina, mentioned that, during her interview process, the hiring supervisor asked whether she was married. Not only is this question a restricted question during the interview process, but Sandita also felt as if the hiring supervisor was assuming she was heterosexual. Unfortunately, the assumption of heterosexuality is common, especially if the individual does not fit societal stereotypes of gay or lesbian. For example, Elizabeth, a queer woman of color administrator in the South, wrote, "Many people do not assume I am queer because I don't look like a 'boy.'" Because of the stereotypical characteristics associated with being queer, anyone who does not fit into that category is automatically seen as heterosexual. For people like Elizabeth, that means constantly having to reiterate one's sexual identity, which can be taxing regardless of the campus climate. At each microaggressive assumption, the person has to decide to "come out" or just pass as heterosexual.

The binary between gay and straight still largely exists in society, which leaves bisexual, pansexual, or fluid people in complex situations. One participant in the study, Ines, is married to a man, and therefore many of her colleagues downplay or mock her bisexual identity. An example of mocking her bisexual identity was a colleague asking, "Who is the man in the relationship?" Comments such as these are rooted in heterosexism, the constant idea that a relationship must have man and a woman. Ines has even been asked inappropriate questions such as, "Do you have threesomes in your marriage?" Despite having reported the constant harassment at work, nothing was done by the institution to support Ines. Eventually, she had to leave her job due to the level of harassment.

Another participant in the study who goes by M had similar experiences. M, a gay Palestinian Arab staff member in the Midwest, and another staff member with the same ethnic background were continuously bullied by the supervisor and refused training that other colleagues were given. M subsequently left his position. Although leaving a job is an option for some, it is not an option for all. Some of our participants just mentioned sitting with the daily microaggressions. Catherine, a Black pansexual woman staff member in the South, explained, "[Discrimination] manifests way more blatantly and routinely. Often times I have to sit with the many microaggressions of the day—people don't understand how taxing and depressing it is to do that." For Catherine and many others in the study, the microaggressions were related to race, gender, and sexuality; therefore, the cumulative impact added up faster. Although microaggressions have a range of impact, the constant belittling or harassment is taxing on a person. Some cope by trying to ignore them, whereas others felt the only escape was to leave their position.

Double Burden

Many faculty and staff members are expected to take on mentorship roles with students as well as be engaged with other projects outside of their stated job responsibilities. For QPOC faculty and staff members, they are often expected to mentor all of the students of their racial background—because they are often the only ones in the department—as well as mentor LGBTQ students because they gravitate to them once they find out they openly identify as LGBTQ. In addition to mentoring, QPOC faculty and staff members are often expected to represent departments, advocate for marginalized groups, and lead all diversity initiatives. These faculty and staff members from historically marginalized communities hold the extra burden of "doing diversity work." For example, Serenity, a Black bisexual woman faculty member in Illinois, wrote, "Also naturally I'm beginning to get a lot of requests for services." Many faculty and staff may feel honored or want to support efforts related to diversity, but it has an impact on workload and work quality. Serenity later goes on to elaborate about the mixed messaging she gets from her colleagues: "I get a lot of feedback to hunker down, try to push through, and to not do anything but focus on my work." Serenity is on a tenure track in the sciences, and although she feels the need to be a part of the work on campus around race and queer issues, she was also advised to pay attention to her work. Serenity felt that if she continues to stray too far from her STEM faculty member duties, she might see the consequences within her ability to get tenured. Many QPOC faculty and staff members aimed to balance their work responsibilities while also trying to change the environments in which they worked. Serenity went on to say that she "constantly considers leaving this opportunity for a place that would be professionally worse but personally easier." Many QPOC faculty and staff made personal sacrifices to better their careers.

One participant named She, who is a Black lesbian administrator in the South, has worked to establish "the first Gay Straight Alliance along with numerous other educational forums, such as Gay and Greek, Standing in Our Truth, Black and Gay, and the Day of Silence" at her campus. She has only been at her institution for 3 years yet has established five initiatives to bring awareness to the LGBTQ community. Institutions benefit from the work that QPOC faculty and staff members do outside of their professional roles, but rarely are they compensated or rewarded for it. This situation is problematic because it leaves the onus on the one queer person to create support programs for the community as well as educate their institutions. It is no longer seen as an institutional issue but rather an individual issue, which leads to a lack in community resources and support.

Another burden that emerged from our study was tokenization. Ben shared his feelings with being tokenized as a queer mixed-race man. Erica also wrote, "My colleagues view me as an expert on LGBT issues ... though not sure if that's a good thing." Although it is great to get a perspective from an LGBTQ individual when creating an initiative, it adds an extra layer of stress to that individual simply because an assumption of expertise cannot be made just for being LGBTQ. QPOC faculty and staff had to be the spokespersons for several marginalized communities; this expectation creates unnecessary pressures and simplifies a person's identity to a category. These faculty and staff were not often seen as complexly as being both queer and people of color but usually one or the other depending on the situation.

Lack of Inclusivity

Campus climate is often talked about with regard to how students experience college; however, faculty and staff members often feel a lack of inclusion within the campus community. According to Rankin et al. (2010), many LGBTQ faculty and staff did not feel comfortable in their departments; they shared, "LGBQ faculty respondents (76%) were significantly less likely than LGBQ staff respondents (83%) to feel very comfortable or comfortable with their department/work unit climate" (p. 14). Although Rankin et al. (2010) did not specifically research queer faculty and staff of color, they did report several findings that showed QPOC people had much worse experiences on campuses.

Some of the participants from this study expressed not feeling fully included in campus spaces. If they went into a queer space, then their person of color identity was not fostered. If they went into a person of color space, thentheir queer identity was overlooked. Elizabeth stated, "I found that my queer identity is not supported in the ethnic/cultural groups to which I belong. The queer support group on campus currently does not have any people of color in leadership positions." Although Elizabeth was able to find community to support her identities, she was unable to find a support group that simultaneously took into account both her LGBTQ and racial identities. Serenity felt similar to Elizabeth: "Like much of my life, I feel between worlds ... not quite accepted in black communities, but not white; not quite accepted in the community, but not straight. I feel like I constantly don't belong anywhere." Much of Serenity's disconnection came from being interracially coupled with a bisexual cis-male. Although her partner was a main source of support in her life, their outward gendered appearance did not allow them to move through either LGBTQ or Black spaces easily. Serenity also mentioned that the communities were segregated, which is true for many rural and urban cities across the country. She went on to mention that the Black community has a lot of resentment toward the White community and therefore added the layer of burden when being in Black spaces because of her partner being White.

Another layer emerged for Elizabeth as she looked for spaces that were inclusive of her religious identity. Elizabeth mentioned the difficulty of finding belonging in a church that would fully accept her. She shared,

> It's a challenge trying to find a group where I feel comfortable with all of my identities. I certainly don't attend church, especially a Black one. If I did attend, I think I would feel more comfortable around the Quakers or Unitarians. It's sad but I think a lot of the churches in the community where I reside spew hatred.

Elizabeth had to sacrifice aspects of her community as she sought a community that understands and supports her religious, racial, and sexual identities. Another participant named She also felt similarly about religion. The university that She works at is religiously affiliated; moreover, She went on to say that one of her biggest challenges was due to "the strong religious affiliation with the Methodist church." Race and religion are closely tied together in U.S. culture, which can make it difficult to navigate when QPOC are looking for community. Additionally, it affects a person's work environment when someone is employed at a religiously affiliated institution. Navigating employment opportunities is already challenging for a racial and sexual minority, and eliminating all religiously affiliated institutions can stifle career success.

Institutional Support

The participants had a range of expectations for the institution regarding how they would be supported as LGBTQ faculty and staff of color. Most expected to encounter some challenges in the workplace because they were used to these issues in broader society. However, some expected institutions to create safe spaces, community support groups, trainings for other faculty and staff, and systems to report incidents. The expectations for these types of institutional support were rarely met. The lack of institutional support included people experiencing microaggressions and little being done to address it, not having a support group focused on either LGBTQ or historically marginalized racial identities, and financial assistance for programs to educate others. For example, Ally Cat, a gender-queer Korean American lesbian administrator in California, felt that the institution did not even financially support efforts to include LGBTQ students, much less faculty and staff members. Ally Cat stated, "One of the biggest challenges was funding. Students had to advocate getting LGBT funds, so we had to provide temporary funds." Although it can be seen as a victory because some funds were found, they were nervous because there was no guarantee that the university would continue funding LGBTQ programs on campus. Ally Cat also shared that she did not feel supported due to identity. Ally Cat went on to say that identity-based groups existed at the university, but nothing was designated for QPOC. Ally Cat was regularly frustrated in the workplace.

Most of the institutions did not have employee groups based on identity. Several of them did have LGBTQ groups, but those groups did not take race into consideration. Those with people of color employee groups did not consider LGBTQ identities. Serenity attends both Black and LGBTQ support groups but has found it difficult to fully bring up her identities and issues within each group. Serenity stated, "I just wish I knew a better way to merge the two because I find it difficult to talk about the issues of one identity with the other group." One could debate whether it is the institutions' responsibility to provide work support groups, but if these institutions espouse values to recruit diverse faculty, they should create systems to support them once they get there.

Although many institutions were found to not provide adequate support to LGBTQ people of color, many positive examples were discovered. For example, six of our participants expressed that their supervisor was their greatest sense of support at work. Brittany, a lesbian African American staff member from the South, said, "My supervisor. She is hands down one of the most affirming, smart, and empowering people I've ever met. I have never felt this supported personally or professionally." Selena also stated, "The first day I met him [her supervisor] and interacted with him, I knew I had found someone who would understand me." At any level of the profession, a supportive supervisor or colleague can make a big difference in job satisfaction, especially when it comes to being able to express one's identities. Another seven of our participants pointed to current colleagues as their greatest sense of support at work. Jamie, a Black lesbian staff member from Ohio, said, "I have some wonderful colleagues. Although most of them are not queer, I do feel supported." Supervisors and employees have the ability to understand the unique experiences of QPOC faculty and staff members and support them regardless of whether it is their identity.

Participants highlighted students as another form of support. Seven of our participants pointed to students as either their greatest sense of support at work or the most positive aspect of working at their institution. Although faculty, staff, and administration are there to support students, it seemed as if students were the motivation for some of the participants to work through the injustices they were experiencing. Ally Cat struggled with the university on multiple levels—limited funding for LGBTQ initiatives, low institutional support for queer faculty and staff of color, and a general lack of support by the institution or their supervisor—but Ally Cat still highlighted the students as the greatest sense of support at work. The participant named She, who struggled with the university's affiliation with the Methodist church, specifically named the LGBTQ students as part of her greatest sense of support at work. Similarly, Steven was having a difficult time being the only gay Latino in his department. He said, "The students in the classes have been so positive when I disclose my orientation. The students fostered an accepting environment." Although Steven was struggling to have conversations with colleagues, he found more comfort in disclosing his sexual orientation to his students. Using students as a support system is complex and can create confusing dynamics; however, many participants found safe and supportive environments with students in the workplace.

Some of our other participants found motivation to continue in their roles because they knew they served as role models and advocates for their students. For example, Brittany said, "I've been able to be a support for queer students, for students of color, in ways that I was supported as an undergrad." Brittany took much pride in the work she does and the support she has been able to give to her students that had helped her succeed as a student. Similarly, Jamie stated, "Having queer students of color see someone that looks like them and seeing their appreciation of that—being at the table (most of the time) to speak up for queer students." Both Brittany and Jamie found being a presence for students with similar identities was the most positive part of working at their respective institutions.

Limited Views of Diversity

In today's current cultural landscape and at institutions of higher education, the term "diversity" is a key word for a single identity, which is usually race but could possibly be gender or even sexual orientation. Several participants pointed to their frustration of the single identity view of diversity. Participants Jamie, Ben, and Catherine all had a similar experience despite being from different parts of the country and working at different types of institutions. Jamie and Catherine found that "diversity" at their universities meant race and ethnicity. Jamie said she often had to speak up when diversity only included race and ethnicity. She stated, "Yes I care about and support students of color, but that's not all diversity is." Catherine said that "diversity" at her university was simply a body count of racial diversity. In contrast, Jamie experienced his institution only highlighting LGBTQ issues as diversity; Jamie shared, "Yes, we are a really strong school on LGBT issues, but race is still an issue. It seems that they like folks of color as people but not as a group." Jamie highlights a critical point for him, which was when he realized that historically marginalized populations were not fully supported within their identities. He shared, "It can feel or seem as if they are merely tolerated, or worse, just a body count for the university."

Corey struggled to have her work community see her in more than just one simple way. She shared, "Trying to make sure they don't see me as the expert on all things POC [people of color]. I often have to remind people that I am gay, from a low-income background and other identities." When there is a lack of an intersectional framework, it may lead to the tokenization of a staff member. When people have to constantly remind others about their identities, it is taxing and they feel as though they are not fully seen for all that they bring. Erica had a similar experience of tokenization but could not figure out whether it was a positive or a challenge for working at the institution. Erica stated, "Their view of me as an expert on LGBT issues ... though not sure if that's a good thing." Tokenization often leads to this concept of expertise, which can be problematic in many ways. Not only does it put much of the onus on a single staff member, but it also becomes boxed in by the limitations of that staff member.

The participants in this study were vocal about the struggles they faced. Microaggressions were commonplace and made them feel unwelcomed, misunderstood, and even unsafe in hostile environments. In addition to being subtly excluded or attacked, they often felt a burden to advocate for marginalized students while also providing support spaces to other marginalized faculty and staff; these additional burdens made it hard to be successful in the jobs for they were being evaluated. As the QPOC faculty and staff faced challenges in the workplace, they expected the institutions to support them, and most of the time the institutions did not respond adequately with supporting QPOC faculty after bias-related incidents. Because some institutions did place a priority on diversity and moved it into discussion, our participants found the ideas of diversity were limited and simplistic. They often only focused on race and did not include an intersectional approach toward conversations, conflicts, or services. Given the number of challenges that QPOC faculty and staff members faced in this study, we will share recommendations.

RECOMMENDATIONS AND CONCLUSIONS

Because institutions aim to provide support systems and shift climates to better welcome queer faculty and staff of color, we offer the following recommendations based on the study:

- Policies: Analyze policies to ensure they are inclusive of people from gender, sexual, and racial minorities. Examine employee benefit options, including transgender-specific health care and antidiscrimination clauses.

- Conduct campus climate studies and include faculty and staff perspectives. Ensure that demographics allow intersectional analysis. Ensure that findings are shared with campus partners and made available to the campus community.
- Know community resources to support QPOC populations. Many participants stated that they found community resources as vital support systems.
- Engage in conversations of difference but do not make marginalized populations speak on behalf of all people in their identity groups.
- Provide trainings on race, gender, and sexual diversity to faculty and staff. Include trainings on recognizing and addressing microaggressions. Some of the participants stated that their supervisors and coworkers were the best support systems. Even well-intentioned colleagues need the knowledge to be affective allies.
- Create frameworks so employees can easily start identity-based groups. Provide human and financial resources.
- When search committees are being formed, provide adequate training on implicit bias, and review the importance of diverse candidates.

REFERENCES

Arnett, A. A. (2015, October). Diversifying higher ed still a challenge. *Diverse Issues in Higher Education.* Retrieved October 6, 2015, from http://diverseeducation. com/article/78225/

Bilimoria, D., & Stewart, A. J. (2009). Don't ask, don't tell: The academic climate for lesbian, gay, bisexual, and transgender faculty in science and engineering. *National Women's Studies Association, 21*(2), 85–103. Retrieved November 9, 2015 from http://muse.jhu.edu/journals/ff/summary/v021/21.2billimora.html

Bower, B. (2002). Campus life for faculty of color: Still strangers after all these years? *New Directions for Community Colleges, 118*, 79–87. Retrieved November 15, 2015, from http://files.eric.ed.gov/fulltext/ED467454.pdf#page=78

Diggs, G. A., Garrison-Wade, D. F., Estrada, D., & Galindo, R. (2009). Smiling faces and colored spaces: The experiences of faculty of color pursuing tenure in the academy. *Urban Review, 41*, 312–333.

Kayes, P. E. (2006). New paradigms for diversifying faculty and staff in higher education: Uncovering cultural biases in the search and hiring process. *Multicultural Education, 14*(2), 65–69. Retrieved December 27, 2015, from http:// files.eric.ed.gov/fulltext/EJ759654.pdf

National Center for Education Statistics. (2015). The condition of education. Retrieved April 19, 2017, from https://nces.ed.gov/programs/coe/pdf/ Indicator_CSC/coe_csc_2015_05.pdf

Rankin, S. (2005). Campus climate for sexual minorities. *New Directions for Student Services*, *111*, 17–23. Retrieved December 27, 2015, from https://www.gvsu. edu/cms4/asset/5D80BD51-996D-6AE0-B9D7668ADFEA7A31/ally_hand-outs_article_campus_climate_sexual_minorities_rankin_2005.pdf

Rankin, S., & Reason, R. (2008). Transformational tapestry model: A comprehensive approach to transforming campus climate. *Journal of Diversity in Higher Education*, *1*(4), 262–274.

Rankin, S., Weber, G., Blumenfeld, W., & Frazer, S. (2010). The state of higher education for lesbian, gay, bisexual, and transgender people. *Campus Climate*. Retrieved December 27, 2015, from http://www.campuspride.org/wp-content/ uploads/campuspride2010lgbtreportssummary.pdf

Sue, D. W., Capodilupo, C. M., Torino, G. C., Bucceri, J. M., Holder, A. M. B., Nadal, K. L., & Esquilin, M. (2007). Racial microaggression in everyday life: Implications for clinical practice. *American Psychologist*, *62*(4), 271–286. Retrieved September 13, 2015, from http://world-trust.org/wp-content/ uploads/2011/05/7-Racial-Microagressions-in-Everyday-Life.pdf

Turner, C. S. V. (2002). Women of color in academe: Living with multiple marginality. *The Journal of Higher Education*, *73*(1), 74–93. Retrieved December 3, 2015, from http://bern.library.nenu.edu.cn/upload/soft/0000/73.1turner%5B1%5D. pdf

CHAPTER 5

BELONGING TO MORE THAN ONE IDENTITY

The Quest to Integrate and Merge Latinx and LGBTQIA Identities

**Brittany J. Derieg,
Mario A. Rodriguez, Jr., and Emily Prieto-Tseregounis**

GROWING AND CHANGING POPULATIONS

Millennials—those who came of age in the beginning of the 21st century, are the most ethnically and racially diverse generation in American history, and they are on track to become the most highly educated. Latinx (also referred to as Latina, Latina/o, Hispanic, or Chicana/o depending on the author's specific meaning or geography) is the preferred term in this chapter so as not to reinforce the gender binary inherent in other labels. Latinx now make up nearly one in four children under age 18—closer to one in two for states such as Texas, California, and New Mexico—compared with one in six for the adult U.S. population (Patten, 2016). This finding is especially important for institutions of higher education to understand

Queer People of Color in Higher Education, pp. 73–85
Copyright © 2017 by Information Age Publishing
All rights of reproduction in any form reserved.

because Latinx have increased their college-going rate considerably in the last decade—from 54% in 2002 to 70% in 2012 (Snyder & Dillow, 2015). Latinas outpaced their male counterparts by a 13-percentage point margin (76% of those who graduated high school enrolled in some level of college, compared with 62% of men), with almost half enrolling in 2-year institutions (49%) as opposed to 4-year colleges (51%) (Excelencia in Education, 2015). An impressive 62% of those enrolled in community college did so in just two states—California and Texas (Excelencia in Education, 2013). With a growing young population of Latinx and their increasing potential to contribute to the U.S. labor force, improving the educational retention and success of this population is imperative.

In a 2013 report by the UCLA Williams Institute, 1.4 million (4.3%) U.S.-based Hispanic adults considered themselves to be lesbian, gay, bisexual, or transgender (LGBT). Using U.S. census data, this report also showed that Hispanic adults who identified as LGBT tended to be younger, were more likely to be a U.S. citizen, and were more likely to have completed a college degree than their heterosexual counterparts (Kastanis & Gates, 2013). As the number of Latinx entering higher education rises, so too does the number who identify as LGBT. Because students who identify with two or more subordinated identities (e.g., both Latinx and queer, or Latinx, queer, and female) do not usually fit in with the prototypes of any one of their respective groups, they often experience what is now recognized as *intersectional invisibility* (Purdie-Vaughns & Eibach, 2008). As explained by the original authors, Purdie-Vaughns and Eibach of Yale University, intersectional invisibility is "the general failure to fully recognize people with intersecting identities as members of their constituent groups. [It also] refers to the distortion of the intersectional persons' characteristics in order to fit them into frameworks defined by prototypes of constituent identity groups. (p. 5) …The struggle to be recognized or represented is the most distinctive form of oppression for people with intersectional subordinate-group identities. They face a continuous struggle to have their voices heard and, when heard, understood" (p. 7).

Despite the last decade's diversity initiatives and policy changes, college campuses still struggle to meet the needs of marginalized students. This situation is made all the more difficult when, for populations such as queer Latinx, almost no research considers *together* the impact and intersections of race, gender, and sexual orientation (Garcia, 2015). This chapter attempts to remedy this oversight, highlight relevant literature that can inform administrators, student affairs practitioners, and faculty, and make recommendations for practice and future research.

THE PROBLEM WITH LABELS

The Millennial generation is more than twice as likely to identify as multiracial than any other generation (Pew Research Center, 2015; Jones & Smith, 2001) and to reject other traditional social identity categories, such as those describing sexuality or gender. As the U.S. population has diversified, it has become more apparent that existing classification schemes (e.g., the five race/ethnicity categories of White, Black, Asian/Pacific Islander, American Indian/Alaskan Native, and Hispanic) fail to hold meaning for an ever-increasing portion of the population (Harris et al., 2015). According to the 2010 Census, more than 9 million people identified as belonging to two or more races, and more than 19 million people reported that they belonged to "some other race" outside the traditional five categories. Such identification was twice as common for those ages 18 or younger (Harris et al., 2015; Humes, Jones, & Ramirez, 2011).

This holds true for the Latinx population as well. Latinx are an incredibly diverse group, brought together by a shared language and common cultural practices but coming from many nations and backgrounds, each with distinctive political and economic histories. Although the three major Latinx subgroups in the United States are Mexican Americans, Puerto Ricans, and Cuban Americans, these subgroups are concentrated in different parts of the country, and the timing and causes of their family's immigration to the United States may differ. It is important to acknowledge that the diversity of this population complicates the literature's ability to make statements about the strengths and needs of Latinx as a unified group—and this complexity extends to the queer Latinx student population (Santiago-Rivera, 2003).

Just as census data show that the categories of race and ethnicity have begun to take on new meanings, so too have the traditional binary categories of gender. Although not yet largely accepted by the general public, modern theories of gender identification now interpret gender as a continuum, which recognizes that some people do not identify as either male or female or may identify as a mix of both, whereas others may identify with a specific gender but differ in ways that fall outside their culture's normative gender assumptions (Chiñas, 1995; K. Harris, 2015; Stryker, 2004). This fluidity also applies to sexual orientation, which can develop and evolve separately from one's gender identity and is of particular interest to this chapter.

As a note on nomenclature, in this chapter, the authors generally use the term "queer" as opposed to "gay" and "lesbian," or LGBTQIA to refer to all those sexualities and gender identities that fall outside heterosexual and binary gender categories. Categorical labels and acronyms that attempt to give a name to each identity, such as LGBT or LGBTQIA, are inherently exclusive to those identities not listed, but this does not mean that the term queer is without its problems. Despite its reclamation and use by the Gay Pride movement throughout the 1980s and 1990s ("We're Here, We're Queer, Get Used to It!") and its use in academia (e.g., queer theory, *queercrit* as an element of critical race theory), the term can still elicit a gut negative reaction from many, raising questions as to whether it can ever be effectively separated from its history of derogatory and derisive usage. That said, even the umbrella term "gay" is often avoided by queer people of color and many women because it is primarily associated with U.S. gay culture, which is to say the culture of middle-class White gay men (Almaguer, 1993). This makes sense in historical context because, despite the intense hostility that gay men and women faced across the country in the 1960s and 1970s, gay White men were in the best relative position to risk the dangers of going against gender and heterosexual norms. Emerging gay communities during this time became overwhelmingly White, middle class, and male-centered, and their collective position in society allowed them to create and shape the way the country saw this new gay identity. According to Almaguer & Carrasquillo (2012),

> The diminished importance of ethnic identity among these individuals, due principally to the homogenizing and integrating impact of the dominant racial categories which defined them foremost as white, undoubtedly also facilitated the emergence of gay identity among them. As members of the privileged racial group—and thus no longer viewing themselves primarily as Irish, Italian, Jewish, Catholic, etc.—these middle-class men and women arguably no longer depended solely on their respective cultural groups and families as a line of defense against the dominant group. Although they may have continued to experience intense cultural dissonance leaving behind their ethnicity and their traditional family-based roles, they were now in a position to dare to make such a move. (p. 264)

For queer people of color, however, most have never occupied such a privileged social space where they felt free to make their sexual identity their primary basis for their self-identity. For Latinx in particular, finding themselves socially disadvantaged by both class and race/ethnicity, undermining their family and cultural ties to accommodate U.S. gay culture is not an uncomplicated choice, especially considering the increased weight that family life, religion, and familial responsibility has in Chicanx and Latinx culture. Additional factors such as gender, geographic location, language, and degree of acculturation all further complicate the identity development and acceptance of queer Latinx in the United States. The implication is that queer Latinx men and women, as well as other racial minorities, do not navigate identities and labels in the same way as White Americans do, and even the umbrella term gay is saddled with implicit biases.

For Millennials today, presented with such a long list of conflicting and intersecting labels in the media and on college campuses, piecing together a cohesive identity can seem like quite the DIY project. The pressure to choose between one identity group over another can lead to valuing a part of one's identity while devaluing another (Tajon, 2009). As this chapter aims to illustrate, the identity development process for some groups can often be more complex than for others, and the traditional higher education model of creating dedicated advisors and spaces for students along racial/ethnic lines only (e.g., Chicano/Latino Student Center, African American Student Center) or along sexual orientation lines only (LGBTQIA resource centers) will increasingly miss the mark; individual student resource centers need to work together to intersect and embrace the spectrum of student needs if they are to be effective with this new generation of students.

On college applications across the Unites States, the conventional categories for race, gender, and sexual orientation are slowly being redrawn to be more inclusive and more reflective of the gray areas and intersections that exist in reality. In 2015, the University of California system added six choices for students when selecting their gender identity: male, female,; trans male/trans man, trans female/trans woman, gender queer/gender nonconforming, and different identity. In 2016, both the Universal College Application and the Common Application announced changes in their standardized application forms—which can be used at more than 600 colleges taken together—allowing students to disclose their gender identity in more detail. Across the country, practitioners are only just beginning to collect data on the number of students who identify as queer or gender nonbinary, a complex process given that many are reluctant to identify themselves on forms or applications their parents might see.

Despite how they might identify on admissions forms, students today are increasingly resistant to being defined by any one aspect of their identity. A queer Latinx, feeling that he or she does not fit in with the prototypical Latinx or queer person, may not benefit from either a Hispanic resource center or an LGBTQ resource center. This is not to say that we need a new, dedicated space for queer students of color on each campus because this too is an incredibly diverse group, and it is not to say that we need to chase the impossible goal of having dedicated student spaces for every combination of identities. Instead, existing student resource centers and staff should ensure they are not working with students in isolation. If a queer Latinx student is looking for support but is afraid to publicly visit the campus LGBTQ center, then staff at other centers should be available, visible, welcoming, and willing to collaborate as needed across units and departments. Staff should serve as a network of support rather than islands so as to not overwhelm any one person, department, or unit.

As more diverse students enter higher education, it behooves the institutions they attend to move away from student success models that rely on the predictive power of any one category (e.g., a single race or sexual orientation). Recent research has highlighted the ways that social categories previously considered to be mutually exclusive (e.g., Hispanic or White, male or female) are being recast as overlapping or continuous in recognition of the many individuals whose identities lie within the intersections of these conventionally binary distinctions (e.g., multiracial and transgender persons) (Kang & Bodenhausen, 2015).

CAMPUS CLIMATE FOR QUEER STUDENTS OF COLOR

Research from the past two decades demonstrates that many college campuses have been unwelcoming and even hostile toward their LGBT members. To address this concern, 155 four-year institutions across the Unites States have initiated structural changes, such as creating queer resource centers and safe-space programs, and provided institutional recognition to queer student groups (College Equality Index, 2016). In addition, many have revised or created queer-inclusive practices, such as domestic partner benefits or nondiscrimination policies. Others have launched queer-inclusive educational initiatives in staff orientations and sensitivity trainings for resident assistants and have integrated LGBT issues into the curricula. Yet even on some of these campuses, the climate reported by members of the queer community, especially queer students of color, continues to be less than welcoming (Tetreault et al., 2013).

Awareness of campus climate is integral to our understanding of the unique environmental factors present on each campus, which positively or negatively contribute to the success of queer students and queer students of color. Although the 1990s saw an explosion of campus climate studies, the practice has somewhat fallen out of fashion in recent years (Sanlo, Rankin, & Schoenberg, 2002). Shaun Harper, Executive Director of the University of Pennsylvania's Center for the Study of Race and Equity in Education, notes that even when he is called to conduct climate studies, their results are sometimes ignored—in part or in total—by administrations hoping to wish the problem away. In his December 2015 *Inside Higher Ed* article, "Paying to Ignore Racism," he goes on to say:

> I really want campus leaders to stop wasting their money and our time on climate studies they will never use.... We don't want to spend our time doing research for leaders who aren't seriously committed to equity, campus climate change and institutional transformation. We never exaggerate our findings; we instead commit ourselves to truthful representations of insights that people generously offer to us about the realities of race on campuses.

Choosing to ignore these realities won't make them less real. Eventually, colleges and universities will have to pay a much higher price for racism should their leaders choose to ignore our findings, no matter how harsh they seem.

Students of color will continually drop out in higher numbers (lost tuition dollars), faculty and staff members of color will keep leaving through a revolving door (higher turnover costs), and alumni of color will be considerably less likely to contribute financially to an institution they know to be racist (forfeited donations for institutional advancement) ... maintaining an institution's good reputation, authentically enacting diversity-related commitments espoused in mission statements and elsewhere, and leading with integrity is priceless. (para. 12–14)

The irregular approach to campus climate surveys in the past decade is unfortunate because they can provide valuable baseline data on the experiences of and attitudes about queer people, students of color, perceptions of campus diversity, and gaps in service (Renn, 2010; Sanlo et al., 2002). In addition to informing resource allocations for student affairs units, these surveys also serve a symbolic function within the institution—signaling to queer students, students of color, disabled students, and other marginalized members of the campus community that their experiences matter to the university. Of course, this faith will only carry a campus so far—action must ultimately follow.

Renn (2010) notes in her article about LGBT and queer research in higher education, "Studies of campus climate generally focus on three areas: (a) perceptions and experiences *of* LGBT people, (b) perceptions *about* LGBT people and their experiences, and (c) the status of policies and programs designed to improve the academic, living, and work experiences of LGBT people on campus" (p. 134). What this statement is missing is the need to explore LGBT identities as they intersect with race, cultural expectations, and gender identity, which each add a significant layer of complexity as student affairs professionals attempt to make meaning from the responses in relation to campus culture. Without this information, practitioners may miss hearing from significant segments of the student population and may mistakenly attribute incidents of hate and bias as resulting from isolated pockets of racism, sexism, or homophobia, when the reality is much more nuanced. Similarly, LGBT faculty, staff, and administrators of color are also affected by negative attitudes and behaviors resulting from a poor campus climate, which can limit their ability to achieve their career goals or mentor or support students.

So what does the literature say about best practices to address these negative campus climates for queer students, queer students of color, and queer Latinx in particular? Garcia (2015) and Rankin (2010) suggest that interventions fall into three categories:

1. institutional support and commitment to a campus that is openly welcoming to queer students of color;
2. recruitment and retention of openly queer students, faculty, and staff of color; and
3. attention to student life, including social outlets, housing, and safety.

Examples of best practices in these types of programs include development of "safe zone" programs (Draughn, Elkins, & Roy, 2002), inclusion of queer people and queer people of color in the mainstream curricula (Rankin et al., 2010), creation of residence life or resource centers focused on their unique needs and issues (Herbst & Malaney, 1999), creation and implementation of antidiscrimination policies, and creation and implementation of rapid response systems to record and address the needs of students who have experienced violence and harassment on campus (Rankin et al., 2010). Faculty scholarship that includes diverse perspectives and methodologies surrounding issues of social justice and advocacy should be invested in because this both supports the mission of higher education and also illustrates to students the importance of these areas (Rankin & Reason, 2005). What is critical here is that these measures do not default to focusing on predominately White LGBT students because this only reinforces the prototypical view of queer college students and does little to reduce the feelings of isolation and "otherness" that many queer Latinx report experiencing.

SUPPORT FOR QUEER STUDENTS OF COLOR

Queer people of color are more likely than White queer people to conceal their sexual orientation or gender identity to avoid harassment (Rankin, 2005). In a 2010 study of more than 5,000 queer students, faculty, and staff at colleges and universities across the United States, Rankin also found that queer respondents of color were more likely than their queer White counterparts to indicate race as the basis for their harassment, but that sexual identity remained the primary risk factor for harassment for both groups. Queer students reported experiencing higher rates of harassment than queer faculty and staff respondents, although queer faculty respondents were the most likely to attribute their harassment to their gender identity (Rankin et al., 2010).

In response to a campus climate survey of 14 institutions, many queer respondents commented that they did not feel comfortable being "out" in venues where straight people of color were predominant, and they also felt out of place in predominately White LGBT settings (Rankin, 2005).

Unquestionably, there is a need to address the lack of campus support for queer Latinx and queer students of color. Rankin (2006) also asserts, "Our understanding of campus climates must, therefore, incorporate differences based on social identity group memberships" (p. 112).

One of the most important student services a college or university can provide is accessible, visible support for its students (Gloria et al., 2005). Academic Affairs departments and Student Affairs have each supported increased awareness and sensitivity in and out of the classroom regarding queer students and, separately, students of color. What is not yet visible on college campuses is support for students who identify as both queer and of color. Perceptions of supportive environments reinforce positive learning and social outcomes for students, especially with respect to issues of racial understanding (Flowers & Pascarella, 1999; Whitt et al., 2001).

Of importance to note is the research of Gloria, Castellanos, Scull, & Villegas (2009), which examined coping mechanisms described by Latino males in college. This research found that the least used coping mechanism for Latino males in the study was that of seeking professional advice. This finding held true for those students experiencing incidents of a negative campus climate, cultural misfittings, questions of identity or sense of self, gender roles, familial obligations, and/or lack of finances to persist in higher education. In several of these areas, the pressures that Latino men reported were distinct from their female counterparts. Latino men more often reported feeling obligated to financially support the needs of their families, creating undue stress as they attempted to negotiate the expected familial roles. These stressors also apply to queer Latinos. The tendency to avoid seeking professional help or advising creates an "If we build it, they will come" mindset at institutions with regard to opening Latinx and/or queer student support centers. Campuses must be proactive, and center directors must work across campus networks with student organizations, faculty, financial aid staff, housing and student life staff, and academic advisers if they hope to successfully reach those queer students of color who might otherwise be left to struggle on their own.

DOCUMENTING PROGRESS

Predicting or calling for new directions in LGBT and queer research in higher education requires knowledge of what exists and an analysis of what is needed to advance theory, research methods, and educational practice. The previous sections of this chapter provide an overview of what exists and gestures toward what is needed. Here we highlight the need to build on existing work to inform the next decade of serving students of color and supporting research in higher education.

Although campus climate studies are no longer on the cutting edge of research focused on issues related to queer students and students of color in higher education, they remain a key tool in the work of what Mayo (2007) described as "attempting to make those institutions more accountable to LGBT members" (p. 80). For campuses that have evaluated their campus climate (i.e., soliciting feedback from students as well as faculty and staff), surprisingly few have conducted follow-up studies to compare progress (if any) since their initial campus climate reports (Renn, 2010). Following a decade in which hundreds of institutions put in place nondiscrimination policies, domestic partner benefits, and LGBT campus resource centers, it is critical that campuses reexamine the experiences of those in their campus communities. To assist with this process, an impressive increase has occurred in the number of available web-based standardized tools with which to carry out these studies, and their use provides researchers with the ability to compare data across campuses.

Critically and longitudinally analyzing the experiences of student groups, with an eye toward intersectional identity expression, can highlight and inform those practices and resources that are effective at supporting the student experience and student success and those that are not. Changes in the experiences and satisfaction of faculty and staff may be harder to assess because they were likely not as well documented in the first place, but each plays a large part in the overall expression of campus climate (Renn, 2010).

CONCLUSION

Queer students of color are still struggling for an equitable voice in higher education and increased visibility by administrators. Even in 2016, fewer than half of the states in the United States provide legal protection in schools regarding harassment based on sexual orientation (ACLU, 2016). Even in those that do, queer students of color are not guaranteed a supportive or an inclusive climate; their needs are often just as overlooked, and their experiences are mischaracterized according to their race or ethnicity or by their first-generation status, socioeconomic status, or gender.

In her 2005 article, "Campus Climates for Sexual Minorities," Rankin provides a summary of what a campus would look like if it has embraced the challenges of meeting the needs of queer students of color:

> In the transformed institution, heterosexist assumptions are replaced by assumptions of diverse sexualities and relationships, and these new assumptions govern the design and implementation of all institutional activities, programs, and services. Transformative change demands committed leadership in articulating both institutional goals and policies. New approaches

to learning, teaching, decision making, and working in the institution are implemented. (p. 22)

The authors of this articles sees the need for new research approaches to address the experiences and needs of queer Latinx and other students who identify with two or more subordinated identities. At the same time, large-scale studies of campus climate are needed that both inform practice and, through their use of fluid and inclusive identity categories, signal to the marginalized members of the campus community that their experiences have value and should be heard.

Future researchers and authors looking to analyze student outcomes and create predictive models should acknowledge the unique challenges that queer students of color face when it comes to racism, heterosexism, and lack of general support structures for this population. For administrators and student affairs practitioners, student services need to allow students to receive help while protecting their anonymity, and resources need to be readily accessible, highly visible, and interconnected so as to take advantage of the diversity of experiences and backgrounds of their staff. Last, to create welcoming environments and offer safe spaces maintained by positive reinforcement and support, administrators, faculty, and staff in higher education need to be more aware and sensitive to the intersectionality and complexity of students' lived experiences (Garcia, 2015), engaging in listening (in both practice and research) to understand the discourses of others instead of listening to argue against or dismiss them.

REFERENCES

ACLU. (2016). Non-discrimination laws: State by state information. Retrieved June 15, 2016, from https://www.aclu.org/map/non-discrimination-laws-state-state-information-map

Almaguer, T. (1993). Chicano men: A cartography of homosexual identity and behavior. *The Lesbian and Gay Studies Reader*, 255–273.

Almaguer, T., & Carrasquillo, M. L. (2012). Gay Latino studies: A critical reader (review). *MELUS: Multi-Ethnic Literature of the US*, 37(1), 228–230.

Chiñas, B. (1995). Isthmus Zapotec attitudes toward sex and gender anomalies. In S. O. Murray (Ed.), *Latin American male homosexualities* (pp. 293–302). Albuquerque: University of New Mexico Press.

College Equality Index. (2016). *List of colleges with a LGBT center*. Retrieved June 20, 2016, from http://www.collegeequalityindex.org/list-colleges-lgbt-center

Draughn, T., Elkins, B., & Roy, R. (2002). Allies in the struggle: Eradicating homophobia and heterosexism on campus. *Journal of Lesbian Studies*, 6(3–4), 9–20.

Flowers, L., & Pascarella, E. (1999). Cognitive effects of college racial composition on African American students after 3 years of college. *Journal of College Student Development, 40*(6), 669–677.

Garcia, L. F. (2015). Documenting the experiences of gay Latinos in higher education through the use of Testimonio. Retrieved from http://repository.usfca.edu/cgi/viewcontent.cgi?article=1296&context=diss

Gloria, A. M., Castellanos, J., Lopez, A. G., & Rosales, R. (2005). An examination of academic nonpersistence decisions of Latino undergraduates. *Hispanic Journal of Behavioral Sciences, 27*(2), 202–223.

Gloria, A. M., Castellanos, J., Scull, N. C., & Villegas, F. J. (2009). Psychological coping and well-being of male Latino undergraduates sobreviviendo la universidad. *Hispanic Journal of Behavioral Sciences, 31*(3), 317–339.

Harper, S. (2015, December 10). Paying to ignore racism. *Inside Higher Ed.* Retrieved from https://www.insidehighered.com/views/2015/12/10/colleges-should-stop-paying-money-ignore-racial-problems-essay

Harris, K. (2015). *Disrupting the binary: A space for gender diversity* (Dissertation, Diploma for Graduates). Retrieved from http://hdl.handle.net/10523/6374

Harris, B., Ravert, R. D., & Sullivan, A. L. (2015). Adolescent racial identity self-identification of multiple and "other" race/ethnicities. *Urban Education*, 0042085915574527.

Herbst, S., & Malaney, G. D. (1999). Perceived value of a special interest residential program for gay, lesbian, bisexual and transgender students. *NASPA Journal, 36*(2), 106–119.

Humes, K. R., Jones, N. A., & Ramirez, R. R. (2011). Overview of race and Hispanic origin: 2010. U.S Census Bureau. Retrieved from http://www.census.gov/prod/cen2010/briefs/c2010br-02.pdf

Jones, N. A., & Smith, A. S. (2001). *The two or more races population: 2000* (2010 Census Brief). Washington, DC: U.S. Department of Commerce, Economics and Statistics Administration, U.S. Census Bureau.

Kang, S. K., & Bodenhausen, G. V. (2015). Multiple identities in social perception and interaction: Challenges and opportunities. *Annual Review of Psychology, 66*, 547–574.

Kastanis, A., & Gates, G. (2013). *LGBT Latino/a individuals and Latino/a same-sex couples.* Retrieved June 5, 2016, from http://williamsinstitute.law.ucla.edu/wp-content/uploads/Census-2010-Latino-Final.pdf

Mayo, C. (2007). Queering foundations: Queer and lesbian, gay, bisexual, and transgender educational research. *Review of Research in Education, 31*, 79–94.

National Center for Education Statistics (2013). Retrieved from https://nces.ed.gov/pubs2015/2015011.pdf

National Center for Education Statistics (2015). Retrieved from https://nces.ed.gov/pubs2016/2016014.pdf

Pew Research Center. (2010, February 1). Millennials: Confident. Connected. Open to change. Retrieved June 6, 2015, from http://www.pewsocialtrends.org/files/2010/10/millennials-confident-connected-open-to-change.pdf

Pew Research Center. (2015, June 11). Multiracial in America. Retrieved from http://www.pewsocialtrends.org/2015/06/11/multiracial-in-america/

Patten, E. (2016.) *The nation's Latino population is defined by its youth*. Washington, DC: Pew

Purdie-Vaughns, V., & Eibach, R. P. (2008). Intersectional invisibility: The distinctive advantages and disadvantages of multiple subordinate-group identities. *Sex Roles, 59*(5–6), 377–391.

Rankin, S. R. (2003). *Campus climate for gay, lesbian, bisexual and transgender people: A national perspective*. National Gay and Lesbian Task Force Policy Institute.

Rankin, S. R. (2005). Campus climates for sexual minorities. *New Directions for Student Services*, 17–23.

Rankin, S. R. (2006). LGBTQA students on campus: Is higher education making the grade? *Journal of Gay & Lesbian Issues in Education, 3*(2–3), 111–117.

Rankin, S. R., & Reason, R. D. (2005). Differing perceptions: How students of color and white students perceive campus climate for underrepresented groups. *Journal of College Student Development, 46*(1), 43–61.

Rankin, S. R, Weber, G. N., Blumenfeld, W. J., & Frazer, S. (2010). *2010 state of higher education for lesbian, gay, bisexual & transgender people*. Charlotte, NC: Campus Pride.

Renn, K. A. (2010). LGBT and queer research in higher education: The state and status of the field. *Educational Researcher, 39*(2), 132–141.

Sanlo, R. L., Rankin, S., & Schoenberg, R. (2002). *Our place on campus: LGBT services and programs in higher education* (pp. 33–40). Westport, CT: Greenwood Press.

Santiago-Rivera, A. (2003). Latinos values and family transitions: Practical considerations for counseling. *Counseling and Human Development, 35*(6), 1–12.

Snyder, T. D., & Dillow, S. A. (2015). *Digest of Education Statistics 2013. NCES 2015-011*. Washington, DC: National Center for Education Statistics.

Stryker, S. (2004). Transgender studies: Queer theory's evil twin. *GLQ: A Journal of Lesbian and Gay Studies, 10*, 212–215.

Tajon, M. M. (2009). Identity development of Latino gay men. *Dissertations & Theses. 128*. Retrieved from http://aura.antioch.edu/etds/128

Tetreault, P. A., Fette, R., Meidlinger, P. C., & Hope, D. (2013). Perceptions of campus climate by sexual minorities. *Journal of Homosexuality, 60*(7), 947–964.

Whitt, E., Edison, M., Pascarella, E., Terenzini, P., & Nora, A. (2001). Influences on students' openness to diversity and challenge in the second and third years of college. *Journal of Higher Education, 71*, 172–204.

CHAPTER 6

(RE)FRAMING FAITH

Understanding and Supporting Queer Students of Color and Faith in Their Search for Meaning

Chris Woods

In thinking about how to support queer students of color in college, the conversation about the impact of faith on their identity development is often left underexplored and underserved. For many queer students of color, religion and faith are intrinsically tied to the ways in which they think about other aspects of their identities, such as racial identity, ethnic identity, and gender identity and expression. This chapter seeks to explore the ways in which queer students of color navigate faith identity in college and how professionals on college and university campuses can better support and understand this population.

Faith often serves as a point of contention, as well as a source of support for queer students (Love, Bock, Jannarone, & Richardson, 2005). The contention arises when external forces, such as families, peers, places of worship, religious texts, and religious figures, position faith in opposition to queer identity. For many students of color, faith provides a sense of belonging and source of internal support, especially as these students navigate challenging environments both inside and outside of higher

Queer People of Color in Higher Education, pp. 87–107
Copyright © 2017 by Information Age Publishing
All rights of reproduction in any form reserved.

education institutions (Stewart, 2010; Strayhorn, 2011; Watt, 2003). For queer students of color, navigating queer identities within and outside communities of color can often be isolating and lonely experiences, especially when there is a lack of visible role models and services to support them both on and off campus (L. Patton, 2011; Strayhorn, 2011; Strayhorn, Blakewood, & DeVita, 2010; Strayhorn & Scott, 2011). Little research in higher education has focused on trying to bridge a gap of understanding about the unique experiences of queer students of color and faith. To better understand the unique needs of this population, I conducted a study of the lived experiences of eight lesbian, gay, bisexual, queer, and questioning people of color and faith at a large predominantly white institution in the Midwest. This study revealed that, in the process of making meaning of their multiple and intersecting identities, the contention among their faith, sexual orientation, and racial identities challenged these students to (re) frame their faith to make space for their identities to coexist.

FRAMING MULTIPLE IDENTITIES

As I examined the ways in which queer students of color and faith make meaning of their multiple and intersecting identities, a number of theoretical frameworks were employed to guide the literature and methodological choices used to inform this study. The theoretical frameworks that informed this study include the Model of Multiple Dimensions of Identity (MMDI; Jones & McEwen, 2000) and its future iterations (Abes, Jones, & McEwen, 2007), college student meaning-making (Baxter Magolda, 2001, 2008, 2009), and intersectionality (Crenshaw, 1991).

Jones and McEwen's (2000) MMDI emerged from their research on a diverse sample of 10 college women to understand how their identities have impacted their experiences in college. The MMDI is a conceptual model that captures identities within a moment in time and context. This model includes a sense of self that is separate from but informed by identities that circle around the core in varying proximities. These proximities, which often depend on the context that surrounds the individual, refer to the level of salience these identities have for people. This model highlights how multiple identities holistically encompass a person, despite levels of salience, and are situated within a social context that can shift and change.

Baxter Magolda's (2001) theory of meaning-making provides a framework for how students come to understand their relationship to their identities and how that relates to their environment. Baxter Magolda (2001) describes meaning-making as a process of external to internal self-definition, where students create their own knowledge and understanding about themselves. The meaning-making process includes Baxter Magolda's (2008) theory of self-authorship, which is how students understand themselves in a way that is not mediated solely by outside influences. Some of these outside influences include but are not limited to family, peers, authority figures, religious institutions, cultural expectations, and the media. To achieve self-authorship, Baxter Magolda (2008) describes three components: trusting the internal voice, building an internal foundation, and securing internal commitments. This process of self-authorship is often triggered by what Baxter Magolda (2009) describes as moments of cognitive dissonance, or "the crossroads" (p. 629). The crossroads are moments when what we previously believed to be true is challenged by something presented to us that is contradictory to that previous truth. In these moments, students can begin to think about things differently or continue to believe what they believed before. The process of integrating or rejecting what is previously known or believed and creating a new understanding or belief sparks self-authorship.

Abes, Jones, and McEwen (2007) explored the relationship between multiple identity theory and meaning-making in their reconceptualized MMDI (R-MMDI). The same conceptual model as the MMDI (Jones & McEwen, 2000) is used, but the R-MMDI incorporates the ways in which contextual influences are mediated by a meaning-making filter that parses through information that would influence one's understanding of identity. The meaning-making filter can exist in various degrees of openness depending on how individuals process information as it relates to their multiple and intersecting identities.

Although the MMDI and R-MMDI consider multiple identity development and the ways in which identity interfaces with the environment, their models do not explicitly capture how larger structures of power, privilege, and oppression impact how one makes meaning of their multiple and intersecting identities. Crenshaw's (1991) theory of intersectionality emerged from her legal work around how narratives about violence against women often failed to capture the experiences of women of color. In her groundbreaking work, Crenshaw (1991) challenged people to think about multiple identities simultaneously and how these identities interact within systems of power, privilege, and oppression. As it relates to queer students of color and faith, intersectionality becomes critical in thinking about how participants exist within college environments and social contexts that do not always value or acknowledge their experiences and identities, which is the landscape where they must make meaning.

WHAT WE KNOW ABOUT QUEERS STUDENTS OF COLOR AND FAITH

The literature surrounding the experiences of queer students of color and faith in higher education is sparse. Some research has made mention of the intersections of racial identity, sexual orientation, and faith identity, but few have centered research on queer people of color and faith in higher education. However, research in higher education has explored the intersections between faith identity and sexual orientation, between racial identity and faith identity, and between sexual orientation and racial identity.

Students of Color and Their Faith

Much of the research on the intersections of racial identity and faith identity talked about the ways in which faith and spirituality are integral to how students of color find purpose and meaning in their lives, even when they are not formally involved in religious community (Stewart, 2010). When students of color are involved in religious or faith-based campus groups predominantly comprised of people of color, faith can be a source of community building and can increase their sense of belonging, especially in the context of a predominantly white institution (PWI) (Strayhorn, 2011). A sense of connection to a higher power helps many students of color develop resilience to cope with negative messages around their multiple identities (Strayhorn, 2011; Watt, 2003).

Queer Students and Their Faith

Although faith identity can be a source of resilience and support for students of color, research on queer students' experiences with faith was more complicated. Love et al. (2005) brought together faith and sexual orientation identity development models to better understand the experiences of lesbian and gay students. They found that these students often lacked "role models and visible socializing experiences" (p. 194) to help them in their LGBTQ identity development. Additionally, faith identities became challenging to navigate because religious institutions and texts created environments where participants felt unwelcomed. Participants who reconciled their faith and sexual identities were able to draw strength from their spiritual lives, maintain a faith in God, and develop confidence in being out as gay or lesbian. Unfortunately, the researchers also found that participants who were not able to reconcile these identities did not feel comfortable being open about their sexual orientation and/or faith identities depending on the context they were in, compartmentalized their identities, and avoided spirituality. The process of faith for LGBTQ students is more fluid and nonlinear, with a variety of situations and experiences that shift the way one thinks about faith and sexual orientation (Abes, 2011). In her study of Jewish lesbians, Abes (2011) discovered that faith identity is an area that becomes more self-authored over time and context, whereas lesbian identity becomes more integrated into one's other multiple identities.

EXPERIENCES OF QUEER STUDENTS OF COLOR

The literature on queer students of color revealed that racial identity is often more salient, whereas LGBTQ identity is often a more personal process (L. Patton, 2011; Patton & Simmons, 2008). In the historically Black college and university (HBCU) context, queer Black students shared feeling isolated and lonely in not being able to express their sexual orientation (L. Patton, 2011). These feelings of isolation, in addition to overt homophobia in the form of physical violence and verbal assaults, are contradictory to feeling supported in their racial identity at an HBCU (Strayhorn & Scott, 2011). Within a PWI context, queer students of color struggle with a lack of support both on and off campus in their racial and sexual identities, specifically a struggle to identify a sense of belonging on campus and feeling unsupported in LGBTQ identity development at home (Strayhorn, 2012; Strayhorn et al., 2010). Similar to the research on queer students and faith, the research on queer people of color in higher education described the lack of role models and visibility that reflects their experiences (Patton & Simmons, 2008; Strayhorn & Scott, 2011). Much of the research on queer students of color in HBCU and PWI settings described a feeling of being multiply oppressed by their racial identity, sexual orientation, and, for some, gender identity/expression (Patton & Simmons, 2008; Strayhorn, 2012; Strayhorn, Blakewood, & DeVita, 2010; Strayhorn & Scott, 2011).

Experiences of Queer People of Color and Faith

Given the gaps in higher education research that explicitly focus on the experiences of queer students of color and faith, I looked to research within related fields of counseling and sociology for themes as it relates to these intersections of identities. Garcia, Gray-Stanley, and Ramirez-Valles (2008) found through a life span study of LGBTQ Latinx people that little more than 60% of LGBTQ Latinx people in their study left the Catholic faith in adolescence and adulthood in search of LGBTQ-affirming faith environments or became religiously unaffiliated. For those who did stay in the Catholic Church, they saw their sexual orientation and faith identities as separate from one another. This need to compartmentalize religious identity and sexual identity serves as a tactic to maintain involvement in faith and racial communities (Pitt, 2010). The desire to maintain relationships in religious communities is heightened by the fact that many communities of color understand faith and race as intrinsically connected with the idea of family including biological and spiritual members (De La Torre, Castuera, & Rivera, 2010).

The research in higher education about the intersections of faith identity, racial identity, and sexual orientation has looked at these identity categories separately or paired two of these identities together. The research tells us that a contention exists for queer students of color and faith when the research shows that queer students struggle to feel affirmed within the context of many faith institutions, whereas many students of color find a sense of support in faith communities. Although some participants in the aforementioned studies made mention of their experiences as queer students of color and faith, little research is focused on the experiences of queer students of color and faith and how they navigate the contentions between their identities. Therefore, I conducted a study that explored how queer students of color and faith navigate the complex relationship between their identities and the contexts these students navigate.

THE STUDY

I utilized a constructivist epistemological framework and a grounded theory methodology for this study. Constructivism (Crotty, 1998) as an epistemological framework situates meaning as being constructed as participants engage with their social contexts. In this particular case, the social contexts that surrounded participants played a critical role in the meaning they made of their multiple identities. Additionally, constructivism assumes that social contexts are constantly changing, which allows for multiple realities to emerge for participants as they engage with the world around them over time (Charmaz, 2006). Utilizing a grounded theory methodology, I was able to identify an emergent theory that is reflective of the experiences of the people being studied through a rigorous process of drawing meaning directly from participants' individual and collective experiences (Jones, Torres, & Arminio, 2006). A constructivist, grounded theory approach was well suited to this study because it offered a way to explore how queer students of color and faith made meaning of their multiple and intersecting social identities that was grounded in the experiences of participants and situated within the social contexts they make meaning of on a daily basis.

Participants

The participants were eight undergraduate students attending a large PWI in the Midwest. More information about the participants, including their pseudonyms, can be found in Table 6.1.

Table 6.1.   Summary of Characteristics of Study Participants (Pseudonyms Used)

Name	Age (y)	Gender	Sexual Orientation	Race/ Ethnicity	Faith
John	20	Male	Gay	Hispanic/ Mexican	Spiritual
Zeek	20	Male	Gay	Latino/ Puerto Rican	Methodist
Mike	20	Male	Gay	Asian/ Filipino, Spanish, and Chinese	Roman Catholic
Dynea	19	Female	Gay	Black	Christian
Raj	21	Male	Gay	South East Asian/ Indian	Muslim
Christopher	20	Male	Gay	African American	Christian/ Unitarian Universalist
Nick	19	Male	Straight/ "Questioning"	Black/ Zambian	Christian
Kevin	22	Male	Gay	Asian/ Chinese	Christian

Participants were recruited through purposeful sampling methods (Morse, 2007). Consistent with these methods, data were analyzed throughout the collection process to achieve saturation, which would ensure that enough data had been collected that could paint the fullest picture of the experiences being explored (Jones, Torres, & Arminio, 2006). A majority of the participants emerged from outreach to a variety of racial identity-based student groups, LGBTQ student groups, and multicultural student services at this institution. Given the difficulty in accessing queer students of color and faith in a PWI context, snowball sampling was utilized to increase diversity in the sample, especially with those who may not have disclosed their sexual orientation to others (M. Patton, 1990). Despite rigorous sampling methods, the sample size lacked in the areas of gender, religious, and sexual orientation diversity, with most participants identifying as gay men from a Christian background. Additionally, a number of students discontinued participation in the study given the personal nature of the topic and were not included in the final study.

Data Collection

Data were collected through a semistructured interview protocol that asked participants a series of open-ended questions about their experiences as queer students of color and faith and how they came to understand their identities and the relationship between these identities. The open-ended nature of the questions provided opportunities for me as the researcher to better understand how each individual made meaning of his or her experiences and tailor any additional questions to the participants' own needs. To assess for meaning-making, Baxter Magolda and King (2007) describe the ways that researchers are required to be attentive and flexible to participants and adapt to anything that may arise during an interview. It became important for me as a researcher to leave room for reflective space, which allows participants to think, feel, and speak to derive their own meaning from open-ended questions, rather than the researcher guiding participants in a particular direction.

Data Analysis

I utilized a constant comparative approach (Charmaz, 2006) to analyze data. This approach involves comparing different participants with one another, comparing a single participant to him or herself at different points during the interview, comparing different experiences, and comparing multiple categories to one another (Jones, Torres, & Arminio, 2006). This process helps to identify strong codes that lead to the construction of a single theory that speaks to all participants' experiences. This process also allows for gaps to be identified in the data that would lead to further sampling or an acknowledgment of the unique ways in which a participant does not conform to an emergent theory. At the conclusion of data analysis, member checks were conducted to ensure that my interpretations reflected how participants made meaning of their experiences.

EXPLORING HOW QUEER STUDENTS OF COLOR (RE)FRAME FAITH

As participants shared their stories, they described challenges in reconciling the intersections of their racial identity, faith identity, and sexual orientation at one point or another in their lives. A number of external factors contributed to the ways in which participants came to understand the relationship between their multiple and intersecting identities. The following themes emerged from the interviews as external influences, messages, and experiences that contributed to how participants made meaning of their identities: (a) identity salience, (b) importance and role of family, (c) messages about LGBTQ people, (d) role models with a "different story," and (e) coming to identify as LGBTQ. It was discovered that participants, in making meaning of their experiences, (re)framed their faith to make space to reconcile contentions presented to them in the intersections of their racial identity, faith identity, and sexual orientation.

Identity Salience

Participants were asked to complete an inventory of their social identities and asked which were more or less salient. All eight participants shared that race was one of the most salient identities for them for a number of reasons. Race was an identity where they felt most different in a PWI setting. Furthermore, experiences of racism before and during college, strong connections to their racial backgrounds, and other challenges they have faced served as a daily reminder in the PWI setting of their racial difference. Some participants experienced shifting relationships to racial identity as a salient identity over time. It was not until Kevin, an international student from China, went to college that he understood himself as having a racial identity, specifically one that made him different from his surroundings. Nick immigrated to the United States from Zambia in high school and became aware of race after multiple negative experiences of being targeted as a black person in his small Midwestern town.

All participants, except for one, identified sexual orientation as their most salient identity. Nick identified as straight, but was in the process of questioning same-gender attractions he had. For the majority of the other participants, sexual orientation was an identity that makes them different from others and impacted their relationships with people and how people chose to relate to them, in both positive and negative ways. Many participants described always feeling a sense of difference from others in their attractions to people who fall outside of heterosexual relationships.

Unlike racial identity and sexual orientation, faith identity was only salient for three out of the eight participants: Raj, Mike, and Nick. Nick was highly involved in a Christian community on campus, including attending services and Bible studies regularly. Mike and Raj described the ways in which their faith backgrounds, Roman Catholic and Muslim, were intrinsically connected to their racial/ethnic background and, therefore, were incredibly salient. Although faith was not as salient for all of the participants, many of the participants described the ways in which their faith was informed by experiences being raised in religious communities that were also connected to their racial/ethnic backgrounds. When race, sexual orientation, and faith were considered together, racial identity served as an added layer of complexity to the area of strong contention in the participants' meaning-making process: faith identity and sexual orientation. The way participants came to understand their race, sexual orientation, and faith were mediated by messages from family, communities, and peers.

Importance and Role of Family

All eight participants described having strong relationships with their families. Families served as a source of support and an emotional foundation. However, as participants developed their identities over time, some families showed support for their development as queer students of color and faith, whereas other participants felt explicit or implicit lack of support from their families, specifically as it related to expectations that families had around race, gender, and sexual orientation. Zeek, who was not out to his parents as gay, described the ways in which going to college and developing his identities as a queer person of color and faith changed the way he thought about his and other people's identities. He shared that, "since I have a bigger voice now, it has led to more problems, because now I have formed my own opinion, and [my father] has his opinion and we sometimes butt heads." Zeek's sense of a "bigger voice" led to tension between him and his father, who Zeek described as sharing openly homophobic and transphobic statements in response to media and public figures. When Zeek decided to confront his father, he was met with an ultimatum: "If you don't like it, then you can move out." Zeek described the ways that these kinds of messages about LGBTQ people ultimately led him to not disclose his sexual orientation to his family, for fear that he would break that crucial relationship. Regardless of how supportive families were, specifically around their sexual orientation, all participants described how maintaining relationships with their families were critical to their success in college, even if that meant not openly identifying as queer.

Messages About LGBTQ People

As participants came to understand their sexual orientation, they encountered a number of messages about LGBTQ people. Three of the participants experienced ongoing bullying around their gender expression, specifically femininity, and perceived sexual orientation that pushed them to think about their own relationship to LGBTQ identity at a younger age. As mentioned before, Zeek was the only participant who experienced overtly negative messages about LGBTQ people from his family. The majority of participants experienced silence around LGBTQ issues and identities. Raj described the ways in which LGBTQ identities were a taboo subject in his Indian and Muslim communities at school and home:

> I have been to Bangladesh and India a couple of times and homosexuality is something that is not really acknowledged, which is interesting because hijras are. In their minds, you are either straight person or [hijras] and that is the way they have always seen it. I am sure there are homosexuals as defined by us, but they are just on the down low. Even if they are [homosexual], they are still seen as straight, because they have sex with their wives. The mentality is just different.... If I were to come out as gay to them, I think there would just be confusion.

In a Bangladeshi and Indian context, Raj saw the complete lack of existence of LGBTQ people in those spaces, not including hijra. The lack of acknowledgment of LGBTQ identities in this context does not offer space for LGBTQ people to experience their identities openly and build communities.

Many of the participants shared the ways that silence and lack of messages contributed to an environment where they did not feel comfortable speaking about LGBTQ identities, including their own. Additionally, seven out of the eight participants came from a Christian background, where they heard many religiously affiliated messages through Biblical references that were positioned as anti-LGBTQ. Christopher, being raised in a socially progressive environment that included many visible LGBTQ people and families, was the only participant who experienced overtly positive and affirming messages about LGBTQ people, which was one of many contributing factors that led Christopher to develop a strong sense of identity as a queer person of color and faith before coming to college. Christopher's experience with positive and visible LGBTQ people and families, along with a number of other participants, shows the positive impact that role models can have for queer students of color and faith.

Role Models With a "Different Story"

In addition to Christopher, only two participants had experiences with positive role models who provided a counternarrative to the negative messages and stereotypes about LGBTQ people. John described the ways in which technology served as a medium for him to find role models. Through listening to and engaging with the LGBTQ podcast community, John was able to identify positive LGBTQ role models from all sorts of backgrounds and careers, which created a positive outlook on his own future and allowed him to expand his understanding of what LGBTQ identities and communities included. The lack of mentors or role models made it challenging for some participants to connect to their LGBTQ identity. In exploring his sexual orientation, Nick sought out the LGBTQ community to find others he could relate to, but after attending LGBTQ student organization meetings and events, he found that the negative stereotypes he had heard about LGBTQ people were true, making him feel a sense of disconnect from being able to identify as something other than straight. Some participants, such as Raj, strived to be a positive role model for LGBTQ people, especially LGBTQ people of color, to support them in their identity development. Raj grew up being bullied because of his perceived sexual orientation associated with his feminine gender expression. In coming into his own identities, Raj strived to be a role model that he never had growing up so that those who are bullied can see that there are things to look forward to and people who are here for them.

Coming to Identity as LGBTQ

The participants described various relationships to the concept of "coming out" as LGBTQ. For many participants, coming out to every-one was not an end goal or a feasible possibility because of a variety of factors related to racial communities they come from, familial expectations needing to be upheld, financial dependence on family members, and the desire to maintain a sense of connection to religious communities. Some participants identified as bisexual before identifying as they did at the time of the interviews. Raj and Dynea described bisexuality as offering a space for their friends and peers to adjust to their same-gender attractions in a way that was not as definitive as simply identifying as gay. The pressure to conform to identity boxes and the difficulty to explain himself pushed Zeek to identify as gay, although he described his sexual orientation as more fluid than gay. Others, such as Christopher and John, identified as gay at an earlier age because of their access to positive support systems such as families and role models. Participants like Raj, Christopher, and John began to explore their sexual orientation at a young age, which influenced the complexity and nuanced understanding of their intersecting identities they brought to the study.

One aspect of all participants' processes of identifying as LGBTQ involved racism they experienced in the LGBTQ community, including instances of microaggressions or bias in dating, exoticizing participants' bodies and identities, and the visible lack of representation of people of color in LGBTQ communities at their institution. Raj even described the LGBTQ community as lacking a familial and community-oriented nature in the way that his racial/ethnic community prioritized connectedness.

Kevin described the ways in which he first experienced racial discrimination and difference through his involvement in the LGBTQ community at his college. His experiences in LGBTQ student groups and events made him feel different and excluded in some of these spaces. All of these experiences highlight the ways that sexual identities are situated within messages from other identities, such as gender expression and racial identity.

(Re)framing Faith

All of the aforementioned messages, families, role models (or lack thereof), and experiences contributed to the ways in which participants understood their identities and experiences as queer people of color and faith. All participants described experiencing various degrees of contention between their faith and sexual orientation at the time of the interviews or at some point in their lives. To reconcile their queer and faith identities, with their racial identity in mind, all participants had to (re)frame their faith. (Re)frame is used in this way because faith identity was initially framed for each participant through families, religious communities, peers, and so on. However, when faced with the contention that came with trying to reconcile their identities as queer people of color and faith, they were forced to (re)frame their faith in a way that is unique to their own process of making meaning of their experiences and different from the messages they received around their faith. All participants described the ways in which their faith served as a source of values, emotional support, or, as John described, "creates hope." Although faith was a source of support for all participants, many described the ways in which their faith also served as a source of contention.

Of all the participants, Mike seemed to struggle the most with navigating how to reconcile his sexual orientation with his faith and racial identities. In response to a question about how he navigated the intersection between his faith and sexual orientation, he shared:

> That's the one thing I haven't been able to reconcile yet, and I have been trying to for the last few years because they are both really important to me. And I am starting to just leave it, like I am both of them and they don't need to make sense with each other as long as I can be okay with being both of them at the same time, but it still gets to me every once in a while … I feel like there's a way to make them work but I haven't been able to find it yet. Even if I did make it work, I would have to be bending the rules because it's very basically said in Roman Catholicism that being gay is incompatible if you're [gay], but you don't act on it. But if you act on it then they can't go together. And I do act on it so that's where the problem lies…. It hasn't been a problem outside of me, but it has been a problem inside of me.

Mike acknowledged that he could make the contention between his faith and sexual orientation work and for him to be "both of them," but he was held back by messages from the Roman Catholic Church, which say that you cannot act on same-gender attractions or you would not be abiding by Church teachings. He was the only participant who expressed struggles with the contention between his faith and sexual orientation at the time of the study.

John, who was raised in a Mexican household with traditional Catholic roots, described a significant moment when he realized the need to embrace his gay identity, despite the messages he was hearing from his faith community:

> We had to go on a retreat where they locked us in a church the whole day. I don't know how the conversation started, but I started talking about my experiences as a gay person and how I feel unsafe in the church setting and I got really emotionally and really deep but every one of my classmates around me were really affirming about it. Right after that discussion, we all went into the church for another discussion and the guy who was leading that small group discussion came up to me and was like "Oh I used to identify as gay but then I found the church and found God" and your typical ex-gay messages and I was like … for me that was a very enlightening moment. I don't want to be you when I grow up because I find my identity so powerful and important to me that I'm not going to throw it away to fit into another group … or not throw it away, which I never intended to, but adjust it to fit into another box that I didn't want to be a part of to begin with. So, for me that was a very interesting experience that very much lit up my gay identity and made me realize that I'm fabulous.

After this experience, John actively rejected his faith and embraced his gay identity as his most salient identity, which he saw as two separate and irreconcilable identities. However, in moving to a PWI context in college, John became more connected to his racial identity, which he saw as intrinsically tied to his faith through things such as prayer and self-reflection, going to church with family, and praying to spiritual and religious icons such as the saints. Although raised Catholic, John began to identify as spiritual as a middle place between the positive experiences with faith in his Mexican home and the messages he perceived to be negative in his church retreat experience. Spirituality offered a space for John to achieve a more authentic sense of connection to all of his identities as a queer student of color and faith in a PWI setting.

Unlike the negative role model experience that John shared, Dynea's positive role model experience with her woman pastor in her small Black Church provided a model for which Dynea could be a queer woman of color and faith:

The fact that she is a woman preaching the Word, I felt like God accepts you no matter who you are or where you come from. I was like, "If she's a woman being a pastor...." I am sure somewhere in the text it says that's not supposed to be. The fact that I'm gay and a Christian, even though it is not supposed to be, has to be accepted.

Dynea's pastor, in facing her own adversity within the Black Church as a pastor, created an alternative message for Dynea that was different from the negative messages that Dynea had heard about LGBTQ people in the Black Church. Although Dynea's pastor did not identify as LGBTQ, Dynea was able to resonate with her pastor's experience of being marginalized in her faith community around her gender and being accepted as a leader in her community. Her pastor's resilience created a message that allowed Dynea to resolve contention among her faith identity, sexual orientation, and racial identity.

Nick identified a unique way to (re)frame his faith in a way that made space for his same-gender attraction. Despite the fact that he identified to everyone as straight, Nick described the way in which his faith and same-gender attraction reconciled internally for him:

It is cool because I have seen communities talking about the sinfulness and that sucks, but I have seen God use [same-gender attraction] in cool ways. There was a guy who was Atheist last year who I saw at church and eventually brought to Bible study. He was in my Physics class. I remember specifically seeing him at church, because I found him attractive. Like "Oh, he's a good looking guy!" Then I saw him at church and thought, "Hey! There's that guy again!" Other people in my class I didn't remember except for the good-looking guys and girls. It is cool how God is using this to bring someone like him into the faith ... I even remember the guy who brought me to Real Life (Bible Study) was a really good-looking guy. I met him at Church. He asked me to get dinner with him one time. I remember thinking that I liked him a lot because he was really attractive and affirmed in his faith. God's using [same-gender attraction] in cool ways, even when my friends look it at as evil. God still used it to bring people to the faith and for me to be where I am right now.

In these particular instances, Nick described the ways in which his same-gender attraction actually had purpose beyond the physical. In the way Nick made meaning of these experiences, God used Nick's attraction to men as an opportunity to bring him and others closer to believing in God. Nick saw his same-gender attraction as divinely inspired and, therefore, purposeful and positive contributions to his salvation and the salvation of others, despite the negative messages he heard against LGBTQ people. His story highlights one of the many unique ways in which queer students of color and faith (re)frame their faith to make meaning of their individual experiences and embrace the intersections of their identities.

IMPLICATIONS FOR FUTURE RESEARCH

In conducting the research for this study and as the literature review and theoretical frameworks suggest, I found myself having to pull from a variety of sources to gather prior research and developmental models that could reflect the experiences of queer students of color and faith. This study highlights the need for more identity development research to continue to challenge monolithic narratives of queerness, experiences of people of color, and faith identity. However, as the student populations we serve continue to diversify and demand resources from their institutions, there is a significant need for intersectional approaches to identity development research that is situated in power, privilege, and oppression.

The theoretical frameworks and identity development research used for this and many other studies on marginalized communities on college and university campuses is often grounded in research with a majority of white paradigms, populations, and research subjects, which we shift and rework to fit the needs of students of color. Additionally, this research is often focused on a singular lens on identity development, with little to no attention paid to multiple identities. For example, researchers such as Cass (1979) and D'Augelli (1994) are regularly evoked to ground any research on LGBTQ students, although their work included a largely white sample and focused on a singular lens on gay student identity development. A truly intersectional, anti-oppressive framework would dismantle the need to ground our research using these dominant frameworks and create frameworks situated in community needs and rhetoric.

Intersectionality and other critical identity frameworks have been used more recently in student affairs literature to situate student development theory within a framework that takes into consideration marginalized and underrepresented experiences in college and the ways in which colleges and universities reflect and often contribute to larger structures of power, privilege, and oppression that exist in society (Abes & Kasch, 2007; Pizzolato, 2003; Torres, 2009; Torres & Hernandez, 2007). However, more work can continue to be done in this area. Additionally, Jones and McEwen's (2000) MMDI has undergone a recent reconceptualization that integrates intersectionality. The Intersectional MMDI (I-MMDI) captures how individuals make meaning of their multiple identities within multiple systems of power, privilege, and oppression within a snapshot of time and context (Jones & Abes, 2013).

A number of limitations and gaps of this study provides opportunities for future research. Future research need to include non-Western faith identities of queer students of color and faith. Additionally, research needs to explore gender diversity within the experiences of queer students of color and faith, including but not limited to the unique experiences of women of color and faith and more dedicated research for transgender and gender-nonconforming students of color and faith.

IMPLICATIONS FOR PRACTICE

The findings of this study, in addition to professional experience working with queer students of color and faith in LGBTQ and multicultural affairs, have led to a number of implications for professional practice to better build environments, programs, services, and staff members that can better support this population of students.

Building Community for Queer Students of Color and Faith

Study participants were asked a final question about how they navigated their sense of belonging and community as queer students of color and faith. Students described feeling the need to pick and choose the identities that are most salient for them at any given moment to identify communities they can relate to because campus spaces are often designed around singular constituency spaces with few cross-sections. Campuses may have a group for queer and trans students of color (QTSOC), but these spaces should include discussions around faith that can offer space for QTSOC who identify with faith currently, previously identified with faith but no longer do, and were raised in religious communities to make meaning of their experiences. However, the onus for these conversations should not be solely on QTSOC spaces but should be integrated regularly into conversations and programming we provide for our students.

Programming and Services for Queer Students of Color and Faith

The programming and services we provide around queer students of color and faith identities are critical to providing opportunities for role models and visible representatives that reflect this population. When there are not individuals on campus who reflect these identities and experiences, outsourcing programs, lectures, faculty, and others can introduce and reinforce the importance of conversations about queer people of color and faith. These types of programming and services should be offered by LGBTQ student services (if applicable), multicultural affairs, faith-based services on campus, academic departments, and other offices serving students. Given that many campus spaces and services are designed or structured as single-constituency spaces, campus collaboration is critical among: LGBTQ services providers and faith-based services on campus and in the community; multicultural affairs, LGBTQ and faith-based services on campus; and LGBTQ student groups, people of color student groups, and faith-based student groups, which may require advisors to these groups to lead the charge of bringing these communities together to address their diverse and sometimes conflicting needs, interests, and viewpoints.

Rather than one-off programs about queer and faith identities, a series of programs and services focused on queer and trans identities and faith identities can be introduced. Although these spaces may benefit white students looking to explore these identities, it is important to center QTSOC voices and perspectives in conversations about religion and faith. In addition to bringing speakers, artists, faith leaders, and activists who can speak to these experiences, it is important to introduce a diverse array of religious and spiritual traditions that we often do not acknowledge on college campuses and society at large, including but not limited to Islam, Buddhism, paganism, African traditional and diasporic (e.g., santeria, and vodou) religions and spiritualities, and indigenous religions and spiritualities. Developing a queer and trans-inclusive faith guide of resources on campus, off campus, and online for queer and trans people of faith should also include people of color-inclusive/centered resources and places of worship in your area that also account for religious and spiritual diversity.

(Re)framing Our Dominant Narratives

To create these spaces, professionals in higher education also have to engage in self-work around the experiences and needs of queer students of color and faith. This includes challenging the dominant narrative of coming out, which does not work for all students because of a variety of cultural, religious, and contextual reasons. Deeper education and research around these topics are suggested for professionals to develop a greater comfort in speaking about and creating spaces around these topics. Consistent with intersectionality (Crenshaw, 1991), supporting queer students of color and faith in their search for meaning requires that we do not essentialize the students we work with and that we (re)frame our own monolithic narratives about the experiences of queer students of color and faith.

Professionals can challenge the tendency to essentialize and support queer students of color and faith by creating environments where students can share their stories and make meaning of their own experiences, rather than creating our own narratives of who they are and what they should do based on what we think we know. Additionally, intersectionality asks us to actively work toward dismantling the systems that further alienate, isolate, and oppress queer students of color and faith through the services and programs we offer. Hopefully, this study provides a framework for the ways in which the multiple identities of queer students of color and faith are situated within larger structures of power, privilege, and oppression both on and off campus that impact how these students make meaning of their experiences.

REFERENCES

Abes, E. S. (2011). Exploring the relationship between sexual orientation and religious identities for Jewish lesbian college students. *Journal of Lesbian Studies*, *15*(2), 202–225.

Abes, E. S., & Jones, S. R. (2004). Meaning-making capacity and the dynamics of lesbian college students' multiple dimensions of identity. *Journal of College Student Development*, *45*(6), 612–632.

Abes, E. S., Jones, S. R., & McEwen, M. K. (2007). Reconceptualizing the model of multiple dimensions of identity: The role of meaning-making capacity in the construction of multiple identities. *Journal of College Student Development*, *48*(1), 1–22.

Abes, E. S., & Kasch, D. (2007). Using queer theory to explore lesbian college students' multiple dimensions of identity. *Journal of College Student Development*, *48*, 619–636.

Baxter Magolda, M. B. (2001). *Making their own way: Narratives for transforming higher education to promote self-development*. Sterling, VA: Stylus.

Baxter Magolda, M. B. (2008). Three elements of self-authorship. *Journal of College Student Development*, *49*(4), 269–284.

Baxter Magolda, M. B. (2009). The activity of meaning making: A holistic perspective on college student development. *Journal of College Student Development*, *50*(6), 621–639.

Baxter Magolda, M. B., & King, P. M. (2007). Interview strategies for assessing self-authorship: Constructing conversations to assess meaning making. *Journal of College Student Development*, *48*(5), 491–508.

Cass, V. C. (1979). Homosexual identity formation: A theoretical model. *Journal of Homosexuality*, *4*, 219–235.

Charmaz, K. (2006). *Constructing grounded theory: A practical guide through qualitative analysis*. Thousand Oaks, CA: Sage.

Crenshaw, K. (1991). Mapping the margins: Intersectionality, identity politics, and violence against women of color. *Standford Law Review*, *43*, 1241–1299.

Crotty, M. (1998). *The foundations of social research: Meaning and perspective in the research process.* Thousand Oaks, CA: Sage.

D'Augelli, A. R. (1994). Identity development and sexual orientation: Toward a model of lesbian, gay, and bisexual development. In E. J. Trickett, R. J. Watts, & D. Birman (Eds.), *Human diversity: Perspectives in people in context* (pp. 312–333). San Francisco, CA: Jossey-Bass.

De La Torre, A. M., Castuera, I., & Rivera, L. M. (2010). *A la familia: Conversation about our families, the Bible, sexual orientation and gender identity.* Washington, DC: Human Rights Campaign Foundation. Retrieved April 24, 2017, from http://www.thetaskforce.org/static_html/downloads/release_materials/tf_a_la_familia.pdf

Garcia, D. I., Gray-Stanley, J., & Ramirez-Valles, J. (2008). "The priest obviously doesn't know I'm gay": The religious and spiritual journeys of Latino gay men. *Journal of Homosexuality, 55*(3), 411–436.

Jones, S. R., & Abes, E. S. (2013). *Identity development of college students: Advancing frameworks for multiple dimensions of identity.* San Francisco, CA: Jossey-Bass.

Jones, S. R., & McEwen, M. K. (2000). A conceptual model of multiple dimensions of identity. *Journal of College Student Development, 41*, 405–414.

Jones, S. R., Torres, V., & Arminio, J. (2006). *Negotiating the complexities of qualitative research in higher education: Fundamental elements and issues.* New York, NY: Routledge.

Love, P. G., Bock, M., Jannarone, A., & Richardson, P. (2005). Identity interaction: Exploring the spiritual experiences of lesbian and gay college students. *Journal of College Student Development, 46*, 193–209.

Morse, J. M. (2007). Sampling in grounded theory. In A. Bryant & K. Charmaz (Eds.), *The SAGE handbook of grounded theory* (pp. 229–243). Thousand Oaks, CA: Sage.

Patton, L. D. (2011). Perspectives on identity, disclosure and the campus environment among African American gay and bisexual men at one historically Black college. *Journal of College Student Development, 52*(1), 77–100.

Patton, L. D., & Simmons, S.L. (2008). Exploring complexities of multiple identities of lesbians in a Black college environment. *Negro Educational Review, 59*(3–4), 197–215.

Patton, M. Q. (1990). *Qualitative evaluation and research methods.* Newbury Park, CA: Sage.

Pitt, R. N. (2010). "Still looking for my Jonathan": Gay black men's management of religious and sexual identity conflicts. *Journal of Homosexuality, 57*(1), 39–53.

Pizzolato, J. E. (2003). Developing self-authorship: Exploring the experiences of high-risk college students. *Journal of College Student Development, 44*, 797–812.

Stewart, D. L. (2010). Knowing God, knowing self: African American college students and spirituality. In T. L. Strayhorn & M. C. Terrell (Eds.), *The evolving challenges of Black college students: New insights for policy, practice and research* (pp. 9–25). Sterling, VA: Stylus.

Strayhorn, T. L. (2011). Singing in a foreign land: An exploratory study of gospel choir participation among African American undergraduates at a predominantly White institution. *Journal of College Student Development, 52*(2), 137–153.

Strayhorn. T. L., & Scott, J. A. (2011). Coming out of the dark: Black gay men's experiences at historically Black colleges and universities. In R. T. Palmer & J. L. Wood (Eds.), *Black men in college: Implications for HBCUs and beyond* (pp. 39–53). New York, NY: Routledge.

Strayhorn, T. L., Blakewood, A. M., & DeVita, J. M. (2010). Triple threat: Challenges and supports of Black gay men at predominantly White campuses. In T. L. Strayhorn & M. C. Terrell (Eds.), *The evolving challenges of Black college students: New insights for policy, practice and research* (pp. 85–104). Sterling, VA: Stylus.

Torres, V. (2009). The developmental dimensions of recognizing racist thoughts. *Journal of College Student Development, 50,* 504–520.

Torres, V., & Hernandez, E. (2007). The influences of ethnic identity on self-authorship: A longitudinal study of Latino/a college students. *Journal of College Student Development, 48,* 558–573.

Watt, S. K. (2003). Come to the river: Using spirituality to cope, resist, and develop identity. *New Directions for Student Services, 104,* 29–40.

CHAPTER 7

INTERNATIONAL LGBTQ STUDENTS ACROSS BORDERS AND WITHIN THE UNIVERSITY

Hoa N. Nguyen, Ashish Agrawal, and Erika L. Grafsky

INTRODUCTION

In this chapter, we focus on the experiences of international lesbian, gay, bisexual, transgender, and queer (LGBTQ)-identified students at U.S. universities. International LGBTQ students are underrepresented and understudied. They may share similarities to queer people of color, given the intersectionality of their racial, ethnic, sexual, and gender identities. However, their international statuses and lived experiences as sojourners—temporary travelers in a foreign land—generate critical differences in their narratives and identity development. Minimal research informs how international LGBTQ students in U.S. higher education navigate their multiminority statuses. Therefore, our first aim is to review the literature on international LGBTQ students and their identity development. We also present a contextual background to support a global understanding of LGBTQ issues and cultural sensitivity. Our second aim is to discuss how on-campus communities can be more welcoming and inclusive of

Queer People of Color in Higher Education, pp. 109–122
Copyright © 2017 by Information Age Publishing

international LGBTQ students. Finally, we share our personal struggles and successes in creating an international LGBTQ student organization, called AcrossBorders@VT, on the Virginia Tech campus.

A REVIEW OF THE LITERATURE

The United States continues to be the top choice of location for study abroad. The Institute of International Education (IIE) Open Doors Report, which tracks trends in study abroad experiences, found an 8% (66,408 students) increase of international students enrolled in the 2013/2014 academic year compared with the previous year (Institute of International Education, 2014a). This enrollment amounted to 886,052 international students, a record high for the United States. Given that more international students are enrolled in the United States than any other country, and this number is only increasing, it is important to consider the needs of international students.

International LGBTQ Rights

International students in the United States originate from more than 220 countries (Institute of International Education, 2014b). Despite the number of countries of origin, a disproportionate ratio originates from China, India, South Korea, and Saudi Arabia. None of these countries provides legal recognition of same-sex marriage or protection against discrimination and victimization of LGBTQ people. In Saudi Arabia, it is illegal for men and women to behave like or wear clothing of the opposite sex, and consensual sexual activity with someone of the same sex is punishable by flogging or even death (Bureau of Democracy, Human Rights, & Labor, 2013c). Countries such as China and South Korea do not criminalize consensual same-sex activities between adults, but the lack of legal protection against hate crimes and workplace discrimination forces LGBT communities and organizers to avoid openly identifying as LGBT out of personal protection (Bureau of Democracy, Human Rights, & Labor, 2013a, 2013b). On December 11, 2013, India's Supreme Court reinstated an anti-sodomy law from British rule that had been previously repealed in 2009, which criminalizes same-sex intercourse.

Understanding these structures of institutionalized discrimination is important. For instance, neighboring countries within the same region may have different laws and values regarding LGBTQ people. Furthermore, the statuses, rights, and social acceptance of LGBTQ persons vary from country to country. We should be careful not to paint any country with too broad a brush, which may risk making assumptions about the level of acceptance that international LGBTQ students have been exposed to in their countries of origin. In recognizing our own ethnocentrism, we should be careful not to adopt a binary view about Western and Eastern cultures and avoid associating one as being better than the other. Ultimately, no one country could say that it has been able to grant full equal rights and privileges to LGBTQ people.

It may be more helpful to adopt a view where levels of acceptance in various countries exist along a spectrum and depend on the social positions of each LGBTQ individual. We use the term "social positions" to acknowledge the various privileges and oppressions that international LGBTQ students experience (Brown, 2009). An upper class, transgender, pansexual student from Canada may certainly hold different social positions, and along with that different experiences of privilege and oppression, than a lower class, cisgender, gay student from Brazil.

Challenges of Being an International LGBTQ Student

International LGBTQ students face a double barrier, where they feel isolated among other international students because of their sexual and gender identity and isolated among their LGBTQ students because they are international (Valosik, 2015). They may also struggle with developing relationships in the United States partially because of differing cultural standards, values, dating, intimacy, and ideas around friendships (Herbert, 2003). Oba and Pope (2013) proposed four major challenges that international LGBTQ students face:

1. They may not have focused on their sexual identity development before coming to the United States and are now navigating that process while trying to find a sense of home in the United States;
2. They may have trouble disclosing to friends in the United States and at home because of contrasting cultural definitions of friendship;
3. They may not have learned about sexual risks, safe sex practices, and sexually transmitted disease prevention, and they may also struggle with access to physical and mental health care in the United States; and
4. They may encounter the challenge of repatriation, particularly if they are returning to a nonaffirmative environment.

Pope, Singaravelu, Chang, Sullivan, and Murrays (2007) echoed the four challenges noted by Oba and Pope (2013) and acknowledged a few additional issues, including communication, cultural taboos, and experiences of students who are just starting to question their identities. According to these scholars, a safe space to discuss these concerns is critical. Valosik (2015) suggested that nurturing a safe space is important for international LGBTQ students who experience a set of needs different from domestic LGBTQ students. Other concerns included language barriers, cross-cultural adjustment, safety and danger, visa and immigration issues, and the impact of family, culture, media, politics, and religion (Herbert, 2003).

Tang (2007) suggested that global LGBTQ issues should be a part of Western college curriculum. Further, Pope et al. (2007) suggested that educational institutions hosting international students should tackle LGBTQ issues at new student orientation and provide counseling and social support resources from the start of their entrance into U.S. colleges. They provided a sample brochure with information about the LGBTQ culture in the United States and on campus and community resources for international LGBTQ students. They emphasized how counselors should seek to understand their own bias regarding LGBTQ identities.

Pope et al. (2007) discussed a great framework for counseling international LGBTQ students, one that addressed cultural taboos, feelings of isolation, students in the questioning phase, and how the college institution can help. We agree that counselors should examine their cultural biases when working with sexual and/or gender minorities from various cultural backgrounds. Counselors, lecturers, and other staff members interacting with international students should receive training in how to be culturally sensitive and affirmative of diverse sexual orientations and gender identities.

Cultural Values and Norms

A conversation about cultural values and norms is salient for international students, especially when their culture of origin significantly differs from their host culture. In one article, Quach, Todd, Hepp, and Doneker Mancini (2013) specifically focused on Chinese gay, lesbian, and bisexual students and how the cultural value of filial piety influences sexual identity development. They argued that Western models of sexual identity development do not highlight the importance of family values, honor, and expectations, all of which are salient in Chinese culture (Quach et al., 2013). Depending on how much they ascribe to certain cultural values, international students may feel pressure to conceal their sexual identities by marrying and having a family as a way to continue the family bloodline, follow the cultural norm, and meet family expectations. This experience may be similar for students from more collectivist and family-oriented cultures.

Individualism has been used to describe a value that places more importance on a person's individual and immediate family needs. In contrast, collectivism reflects a value of placing the group needs above those of individuals and their immediate family (Hofstede, 1980). In one study, researchers problematize our binary assumptions about individualistic versus collectivistic cultures by showing how EuroAmericans were not necessarily more individualistic than Latinos or African Americans, nor were they less collectivistic than Koreans and Japanese (Oyserman, Coon, & Kemmelmeier, 2002). They also reported that only Chinese individuals showed a higher tendency to be less individualistic and more collectivistic among Asian cultural groups (Oyserman et al., 2002).

Herbert's (2003) study did not focus on students from one country but rather explored the experiences of lesbian, bisexual, and queer students from multiple countries: England, Japan, Taiwan, Spain, Malaysia, Zimbabwe, Yugoslavia, Indonesia, and Costa Rica. Her participants all identified as female, and thus she looked specifically at cultural messages about gender. However, because the study focused on sexual identity development, she did not recruit gender minorities. The international students in her sample felt more freedom to express their sexual identity in the United States but experienced more racism, discrimination, and struggles with different cultural norms (Herbert, 2003).

Heteronormativity were common themes in Tang's (2007) study on international gay and lesbian students and Yang's (2015) study, which focused on Chinese international LGB students. Yang's (2015) study addressed acculturation for LGB students from China and applied two versions of the Model of Multiple Dimensions of Identity (MMDI) formation: the Reconceptualized MMDI (R-MMDI), which takes a self-authorship lens; and the Queer MMDI (Q-MMDI), which takes a queer theory lens. These identity models are the few that take an integrative and a holistic perspective on identity development. These models have yet to be tested with international LGBTQ students from different cultures.

Identity Development and Coming Out

Scholars suggest that sexual orientation development models are not culturally sensitive (Quach et al., 2013). Derived from an understanding of sexual identity in the United States, it is no surprise that these models for examining sexual identity will be United States-centric. The focus on the disclosure of sexual and gender identity for international students needs to be situated in their cultural contexts. Most Western models for identity development involve the coming out process, where individuals disclose their sexual and/or gender identity. International students may disclose later in life or never at all depending on beliefs about sexual orientation and gender identity, as well as the legal statuses of each in their country. Cultural narratives that are homophobic and legal policies that criminalize sexual and gender identity or do not provide protection against victimization and discrimination may also be obstacles for coming out.

In addition, identity models focus on individual processes and do not take into account the significance of family relationships. Quach et al. (2013) suggested that family values of filial piety may influence Chinese GLB students to sacrifice their own wants and desires for the sake and well-being of their families. Therefore, the pursuit of identity development that risks family honor and threatens the family's place within the cultural community may conflict with these deeply held family values.

Another potential obstacle of coming out for international LGBTQ students is the risk of losing not only the support of their family but also their cultural community if they choose to disclose. At the same time, they risk not feeling fully accepted in the LGBTQ community in the United States because of their cultural differences. In such a case, disclosing may feel like a trade-off, and deciding either way (to disclose or conceal) is a lose-lose situation. Further, disclosure may not seem necessary when one is not in a significant relationship with an intimate partner. There may be little reason to disclose their sexual and/or gender identity to others, including family, when the perception or reality is that they are single.

Limitations in the Literature

One limitation is the lack of empirical research on this topic. Most of the research on international LGBTQ students was derived from dissertations and theses. Published papers on this topic have been theoretical and exploratory. There is also a deficit in papers specifically about international status and transgender issues. Most empirical studies on international students chose to focus on sexual orientation because the researchers did not want to conflate sexual and gender identities. They also acknowledged that trans-identities are grouped under the LGBTQ umbrella, but these experiences have a set of unique problems. This notion is clearly exemplified when certain countries, such as Iran, legalize transitions for trans-identified individuals but do not legalize same-sex marriage. This does not insinuate that life for transgender individuals who decide to transition in Iran is necessarily better. In each country, a uniquely complex context needs to further explored, beyond what the law says. Some countries may be more open and understanding to sexual orientation than gender identity.

Another critique of the literature is the oversimplification of international LGBTQ students' identities. Although intersectionality is acknowledged in the literary scholarship, international LGBTQ students' identities are discussed like an equation, where LGBTQ plus international status amounts to the lived experiences of these individuals. It is a slippery slope when we try to untangle the threads of multiminority statuses. This is apparent in the previously mentioned cultural and sexual identity models that treat identity development like layers of an onion, when there is not such a clear partition of "layers" among sexual, cultural, subcultural, and any of the other gender, ethnic, religious identities, and so forth. Thus, it is critical to remind ourselves of the old-age wisdom, "The whole is greater than the sum of its parts."

OUR INITIATIVES: ACROSSBORDERS@VT

In this section, we will discuss our experiences of starting and running a student group, called AcrossBorders@VT, to provide support for international LGBTQ students at Virginia Tech and cater to their unique needs. Virginia Tech is a land-grant university located in Blacksburg, Virginia, with more than 30,000 full-time students. In the fall of 2010, more than 2,300 international students studied at Virginia Tech. Five years later, in the fall of 2015, 3,573 international students attended the school, with approximately 60% of them being graduate students and 40% undergraduate students (Cranwell Student Center, 2015).

The need for creating a space for international LGBTQ students at Virginia Tech was felt by some of the students in the beginning of the fall 2014 semester, and the group was created in November 2014 by Hoa Nguyen and Ashish Agrawal. We will discuss some of the unique needs of international LGBTQ students that we felt needed to be addressed through a specialized group, our efforts in the past year to provide a more inclusive and supportive stay for international LGBTQ students at Virginia Tech, the challenges faced by us in our journey, and the future strategies needed to reach out to and better support more international LGBTQ students at the university.

Unique Needs of International LGBTQ Students

As noted in the previous sections, international students constitute a minority group in U.S. universities. Although we have discussed what the literature has found on the unique needs of international LGBTQ students, this section focuses on the needs that we saw from our personal experiences with AcrossBorders@VT, which have similarities to the research while also adding more specifics. Like any other minority group, the needs of international students are different from others, and special attention is required to address those needs.

However, the minority status of international students is not only overlooked at U.S. universities but is also conflated with other minority groups based on gender, race, and ethnicity. Although from a U.S. perspective, international students can be put into those groups based on their genders and race, they might not have the lived experiences of being a part of that minority in the United States. For example, although Ashish might be identified as a person of color by many in the United States, he does not relate to the issues facing people of color in the country because he was born in India and moved to the United States to pursue graduate studies. He never faced discrimination based on his skin color in his native country and hence cannot easily identify with the experiences of people of color here.

International students come from a diverse set of cultural backgrounds and hence have a different worldview toward the world and life. Because of the cultural variations, the way they communicate with others and forge relationships also varies. As a result, they find it difficult to forge relations with U.S. students. This situation is further exacerbated by the fact that many international students do not have English as their first language and grew up in environments where English was not the mode of everyday communication. As a result, they find it difficult to communicate their thoughts, feelings, and ideas when they are in the United States.

While the LGBTQ support groups at the Virginia Tech campus advocate for issues such as unisex bathrooms, inclusive classroom environments, workplace protections, and recognition as minority students, many international students struggle with coming out to their friends in the United States and their families back home. Consequently, the needs of these students are not met by most of the LGBTQ support and resource groups on campus. In contrast, students who come from countries that are more advanced than the U.S. in terms of LGBTQ rights do not find relevance in the kind of activism that on-campus LGBTQ groups are doing. These unique needs of international LGBTQ should be given special attention, and AcrossBorders@VT strives to address these needs.

Before we discuss what AcrossBorders@VT has accomplished in the past year, our plans in the coming years, and our challenges, it is important to clarify that we are not trying to suggest that all countries other than the United States share the same or similar culture. We have noted that different countries are at different places in terms of legal and social acceptance of LGBTQ-identified people. The idea behind creating a group for all the international students is that, despite coming from diverse cultures, international students share the similar experience of being LGBTQ-identified in a cultural setting that is different from their native culture. The international status also leads to some of the same legal challenges (e.g., visa, immigration issues) for all the international students regardless of the countries of their origin. These similarities in their experiences can be used as the convergence point to bring them together so they can provide support to one another.

AcrossBorders@VT: Our Goal and Activities

The biggest aim for us while creating AcrossBorders@VT was to create a safe space for international LGBTQ students at Virginia Tech and other university affiliates. Confidentiality was a key component of this safe space because, although some members were visible in the LGBTQ community, other members did not want to openly identify their sexual orientation and/or gender identity. We expand on this issue below. Another component of the space was acceptance and openness to all sexual, gender, ethnic, and cultural identities. We addressed this issue by creating a group of international LGBTQ students, both physically and online. We organized individual and group meetings with international students who identified as LGBTQ. In those meetings, we discussed the issues they are facing and the ways we as a group can support one another. We also created an e-mail address and a Facebook group so that people could engage in online conversations and discuss issues outside the meetings.

Privacy and Personal Support

One of the considerations we had while creating the group was the privacy and confidentiality of the members. As noted earlier, cultural stigmas are associated with identifying as an LGBTQ person in many cultures. Therefore, we did not want to create a situation where any student could be ostracized through association with our group. To maintain the privacy and confidentiality of our members, we mostly met in-person for dinners or lunches at restaurants or someone's house. Also, people were notified of these meetings through private messages. Similar, we made the Facebook group secret, which meant nobody could see the group until they were invited by someone to be a part of the group. We still follow the same model of organizing meetings and forming an online community of international LGBTQ students in which members support one another. The support that we try to provide to the AcrossBorders@VT members is not limited to meetings and discussing issues. We aim to foster friendships with others and help one another in any need, be it academic, personal, or related to one's sexual or gender identity. Also, because many members are not out, it gives them a space and a group of people with whom they can be comfortable while being themselves.

Raising Awareness

Apart from working with LGBTQ-identified international students at an individual level, we have also been trying to raise awareness about LGBTQ issues in various countries. We have been closely working with the Intercultural Engagement Center (IEC) at Virginia Tech to incorporate a module called International 101 to their existing SafeZone program. The SafeZone program at Virginia Tech aims to increase awareness among the members of the Virginia Tech community about the needs and issues of gender and sexual minorities and to create an inclusive environment for all. The new module focuses on LGBTQ issues in different countries and highlights the unique needs of international LGBTQ students in the United States. Also, it highlights considerations that U.S. LGBTQ-identified students need to make while traveling abroad for study or research. The module was first piloted in the spring of 2015 and was then offered as part of the SafeZone curriculum once each in the spring and fall of 2015. We have been continually improving the content of the module based on the feedback we received during the past two offerings.

In the spring of 2016, members Ashish and Yen applied for Virginia Tech's Diversity Scholar Program to increase our visibility on campus. Diversity Scholars develop projects, events, and activities that make a difference through transformative dialogue and advocacy. The program provides support and space for students wishing to implement projects, such as mentorship programs, cultural exhibits, networks, support groups, keynote presentations, campaigns, and other projects, which can create change. We were accepted into the program, joining a group of students who were also passionate about diversity and inclusion.

Partnerships With Other Student Organizations

We have also partnered with other student groups and organizations on campus to make them more inclusive of the needs of international LGBTQ students and organize events together. Partnering with other groups on campus not only helps us share resources but also increases our visibility. Hence, we have been able to better support international LGBTQ students and reach out to many through other LGBTQ groups on campus. We collaborated with the Queer Grad Professional and Allies (QGPA) group at Virginia Tech to participate in the International Street Fair (ISF) at Virginia Tech in April 2015. The ISF is aimed to showcase the cultures of different nations. During the street fair, we distributed material related to LGBTQ awareness in different countries to the students and faculty. We connected with the Cranwell International Center (CIC), the resource center for international students at Virginia Tech, to reach out to international students during the new student orientation. The CIC has helped us send out information about AcrossBorders@VT to students through their weekly newsletter.

FUTURE PLANS

In this section, we will discuss some of the upcoming initiatives. These initiatives are aimed at reaching out to more students by either directly contacting them or increasing our visibility at the university and national levels. One of our plans is to translate some of the coming out resources from English into other languages such as Mandarin, Taiwanese, Korean, Vietnamese, and Hindi. Given that the parents and family members of many international students are not well versed in English, it becomes difficult for them to educate their families about the issues faced by LGBTQ-identified people. There is lack of educational material on LGBTQ issues in many languages. In some cases, family members might not even know what it means to be an LGBTQ person. Having resources in a language that can be understood by them is helpful to educate them about LGBTQ identities and the issues faced by LGBTQ-identified people. Although the aim is to create these resources in as many languages as possible, we have picked five at this moment because we could only find people who could translate resources for us in these five languages.

Another initiative we plan to work on for the next year is reaching out to international students by getting directly involved with students groups from different countries at Virginia Tech. The idea is to conduct workshops and SafeZone training sessions with students from one particular country so that we can address the LGBTQ climate in that particular country and connect with more students. In November 2015, Ashish attended the annual Out in Science, Technonology, Engineering, and Mathematics (oSTEM) conference and talked with people about the work done by AcrossBorders@VT. Our initiatives were well appreciated, and many people were keen to start a similar group at their respective universities. Next year we plan to attend more such conferences and spread the word about our work through more formal presentations and paper publications. This chapter also serves the purpose of raising awareness about our work.

Challenges

The biggest challenge we face in running AcrossBorders@VT is not being able to connect with and attract many international LGBTQ students. Even if we reach out to them, some do not want to attend our meetings or engage in our activities. Low student turnout is a result of many factors. First, a stigma is associated with queerness. As noted earlier, students do not want to come out or associate themselves with any queer group because of the stigma associated with queerness in many cultures. Second, they might be afraid that if others, including their friend, know about their association with a queer student group on campus, they might be ostracized. This is especially salient for international students because being closer to a friend from their native country at the university is an important way in which they remain connected to their own culture. Third, students might shun the sexual or gender minority part of their identity and focus solely on their studies.

Although funding for events and initiatives has not been a major challenge for us yet, we have been able to raise money at the ISF and collaborated with other campus organizations to use their funds. However, we envision that funding might be a constraint in the future when we plan to attend conferences and hire people to translate resources for us. Funding has been an issue because we are not a registered organization with the university, and hence we are not eligible to get university funds.

CONCLUSIONS

Educators and practitioners can help address international LGBTQ students' unique needs by being culturally sensitive, aware of issues relevant to their experience, and knowledgeable of resources that could be helpful to them. We included a shortened list of resources (Appendix) that may be helpful for international LGBTQ students and those working with them. This list is by no means exhaustive, but it is a beginning place for international LGBTQ students to seek information and support. Our experiences with AcrossBorders@VT show that much more work needs to be done regarding the advocacy of LGBTQ rights cross-culturally. As the world continues to become more connected, we hope that it also becomes more open and safe for LGBTQ people regardless of their culture and countries of origin.

APPENDIX

International LGBTQ Resources

- This website shows which university campuses across the United States have LGBT Student Centers: http://lgbtcampus.org/lgbt-map

- International Gay and Lesbian Human Rights Commission is an international advocacy organization that offers country-specific information.
- International Lesbian, Gay, Bisexual, Trans and Intersex Association (IGLA) is an international advocacy organization with regional chapters: Asia, Africa, Europe, the Americas, and the Caribbean. Look at the member listings of each regional chapter to find LGBT organizations in specific countries.
- Amnesty International is an international human rights organization. Check out their country listings to find information about human rights violations against LGBT individuals in specific countries.
- International Lesbian, Gay, Bisexual, Transgender and Queer Youth and Student Organization is an international organization uniting LGBTQ organizations serving youth and students. Check out their member listing for organizations in specific countries.
- GlobalGayz is a website collecting travel stories about LGBT life internationally; it is an excellent source of information on GLBT life abroad.
- Rainbow Special Interest Group of NAFSA: Association of International Educators is a website with culture-specific information of international students, useful resources and readings for campus organizations, and links to other organizations.
- Questions about LGBT students who are applying for a student visa and their partners: http://travel.state.gov/content/visas/english/study-exchange/student.html
- Wikipedia has a list of LGBT rights organizations organized by country and region.

REFERENCES

Brown, L. S. (2009). Cultural competence: A new way of thinking about integration in therapy. *Journal of Psychotherapy Integration, 19*(4), 340–353.

Bureau of Democracy, Human Rights, and Labor. (2013a). *Country reports on human rights practices for 2013: China.* U.S. Department of State. Retrieved from http://www.state.gov/j/drl/rls/hrrpt/humanrightsreport/index.htm?year=2013&dlid=220350

Bureau of Democracy, Human Rights, and Labor. (2013b). *Country reports on human rights practices for 2013: Korea, republic of.* U.S. Department of State. Retrieved from http://www.state.gov/j/drl/rls/hrrpt/humanrightsreport/index.htm?year=2013&dlid=220350

Bureau of Democracy, Human Rights, and Labor. (2013c). *Country reports on human rights practices for 2013: Saudi arabia.* U.S. Department of State. Retrieved from http://www.state.gov/j/drl/rls/hrrpt/humanrightsreport/index.htm?year=2013&dlid=220350

Cranwell Student Center. (2015). *2015 fast facts: International students.* Retrieved from http://www.international.vt.edu/assets/docs/2015-fast-facts.pdf

Herbert, M. L. (2003). *Beyond the borders: Sexual identity development for lesbian, bisexual, queer international students* (Doctoral dissertation). Retrieved from Proquest Dissertations and Theses Database: http://search.proquest.com.ezproxy.library.wisc.edu/docview/305237589?accountid=465

Hofstede, G. (1980). *Culture's consequences.* Beverly Hills, CA: Sage.

IGLA, the International Lesbian, Gay, Bisexual, Trans and Intersex Association. (2014). *Lesbian and gay rights in the world.* Retrieved from http://old.ilga.org/Statehomophobia/ILGA_Map_2014_ENG.pdf

Institute of International Education. (2014a). International student enrollment trends, 1948/49-2013/14. *Open Doors Report on International Educational Exchange.* Retrieved from http://www.iie.org/opendoors

Institute of International Education. (2014b). International student totals by place of origin, 2012/13- 2013/14. *Open Doors Report on International Educational Exchange.* Retrieved from http://www.iie.org/opendoors

Oba, Y., & Pope, M. (2013). Counseling and advocacy with LGBT international students. *Journal of LGBT Issues in Counseling, 7*(2), 185–193.

Oyserman, D., Coon, H. M., & Kemmelmeier, M. (2002). Rethinking individualism and collectivism: Evaluation of theoretical assumptions and meta-analyses. *Psychological Bulletin, 128*(1), 3–72.

Pope, M., Singaravelu, H. D., Chang, A., Sullivan, C., & Murray, S. (2007). Counseling gay, lesbian, bisexual, and questioning international students. In H. D. Singaravelu & M. E. Pope (Eds.), *A handbook for counseling international students in the United States.* Alexandra, VA: American Counseling Association.

Quach, A. S., Todd, M. E., Hepp, B. W., & Doneker Mancini, K. L. (2013). Conceptualizing sexual identity development: Implications for GLB Chinese international students. *Journal of GLBT Family Studies, 9*(3), 254–272.

Tang, S. (2007). Gay and lesbian international students. Retrieved from http://search.proquest.com.ezproxy.lib.vt.edu/docview/304718873/fulltextPDF/87ECDBEF401D48EDPQ/1?accountid=14826 (ProQuest Dissertations Publishing, MR26402).

Valosik, V. (2015). Supporting LGBT international students. *International Educator, 24*(2), 48–51.

Yang, J. (2015). Conceptualizing the college experience of LGB international students from China. Retrieved from http://search.proquest.com.ezproxy.lib.vt.edu/docview/1695807110?pq-origsite=summon&accountid=14826 (ProQuest Dissertations Publishing, 1590925).

CHAPTER 8

"FUN AND CAREFREE LIKE MY POLKA DOT BOWTIE"

Disidentifications of Trans*masculine Students of Color

T. J. Jourian

Men and masculinities studies in higher education, as well as emergent scholarship on the experiences of trans* college students, have been expanding in recent years. Both strands have significant gaps that in combination reify the gender-binary, hegemonic masculinity, and singular nonintersectional narratives that leave trans*masculine students of color largely absent from our literature and our consciousness as higher education scholars and practitioners. A phenomenological study investigated how trans*masculine college students understand, define, and adopt a masculine identity, and how their various and salient intersecting identities inform their masculinities. Out of 19 total participants in the study, 11 identified as trans*masculine people of color. This chapter highlights their stories and experiences of resilience, resistance, and reconstructions of racialized (trans*)masculinities.

The pathways are intentionally titled *(trans*)masculine* rather than either *trans*masculine* or *masculine*. The presence of *trans** in the pathways' names honors the role that the students' trans*ness played in informing their conceptions and experiences of gender. The parenthetical disruption between *trans** and *masculine* allows for two understandings to be made: (a) that these pathways are possibilities for all types of masculine people, not just trans*masculine individuals; and (b) that for these students, trans*ness and masculinity are not necessarily always integrated and fused but might exist independent of each other in certain contexts.

By centering trans*masculine students of color and their understandings of masculinity, this chapter advances an intersectional and a transformative investigation of masculinity from the perspective of those who figuratively and/or literally move across genders. Doing so validates trans* students' lives, perspectives, and resilience. Such validation is important if we are to improve trans* students' sense of belonging, involvement, persistence, and academic success on campus, and shift the oppression that trans* students face on hostile campuses. Additionally, such a unique perspective offers all of us much in the pursuit of liberatory gendered and raced possibilities. This chapter will present the many "pathways" these students have pursued, the role higher education institutions—including dominant institutionalized and college masculinities—have played in their journeys, and how their narratives can inform future practice and scholarship. By considering masculinity from a divergent perspective, these students' reflections on their experiences offer us much in the pursuit of meaning.

RELEVANT TERMINOLOGY

The terms most used and relevant in this chapter are trans* and trans*masculine. This chapter uses *trans** to refer to people whose gender identity does not align to one's sex assigned at birth as expected socially. The asterisk at the end of the term is used to "open up *transgender* or *trans* to a greater range of meanings" (Tompkins, 2014, p. 26), specifically inclusion of gender-nonconforming identities, such as genderqueer, agender, and many others. Similarly, the asterisk in *trans*masculine* expands on terms such as trans man or female-to-male to include a broader range of individuals who were assigned female at birth and identify as trans* and with masculinity in some way. Finally, this chapter uses the term *cisgender* or *cis* to describe those who generally experience alignment between their assigned sex at birth and their gender identity. The creation and use of the term is important because it emerged from within trans* communities to challenge positioning cisgender people as normal, traditional, or biological, and thus trans* people as not any of those things (Aultman, 2014).

CONCEPTUAL FRAMEWORK

The literature review and study were informed by a conceptual framework situated in hegemonic masculinity (Connell, 2005) and genderism (Bilodeau, 2009). These contexts are recognized and challenged through the lenses of critical trans politics (Spade, 2011), disidentification (Muñoz, 1999), intersectionality (Crenshaw, 1991), and theory as liberatory practice (hooks, 1994). Finally, these lenses are further supplanted and biased by my own gender journey and identities. I am a trans*man of color, employing both in- and outgroup lenses to the topic and the study's participants. I share commonality as a trans*masculine person of color with all the students in this chapter. As a Middle Eastern person who did not grow up in the United States, my gendered journey is racialized in particular ways. Additionally, as someone who adopts the moniker of "man" and presents as masculine pretty consistently (through attire and secondary sex characteristics that are socially designated as masculine), my gendered journey is also gendered in particular ways. These intersectional aspects of my identities provide me with an outgroup lens for many of the study participants but not all. To continue to check for biases and false analyses based on these concurrent in- and outgroup statuses, I consistently kept a journal throughout the study to acknowledge and then set aside my lens. This process allowed me to be fully present and able to hear participants as they wished to be heard.

Hegemonic masculinity and genderism are part of the social and institutional contexts in which trans*masculine students understand themselves and the world around them, including within higher education institutions. Hegemonic masculinity is "the pattern of practice... that allowed men's dominance over women to continue" (Connell & Messerschimdt, 2005, p. 832), as well as over subordinated masculinities that do not meet patriarchal standards (Connell, 2005). Hegemonic masculinity is invisible, ubiquitous, and maintained and reconstructed by all genders simply by continuing to perform gender-scripted behaviors and practices. Genderism—also referred to as cissexism or cisgenderism—is a cultural and systemic ideology that regulates gender as an essentialized binary based on sex assignment at birth (Bilodeau, 2009). It pathologizes and denigrates nonconforming gender identities through binary sorting and privileging of conforming identities, punishing nonconformity, and isolating gender-nonconforming people and identities.

Intersectionality (Crenshaw, 1991) seeks to name and deconstruct the interlocked nature of systems of oppression. Building off intersectionality, queer people of color's realities offer disidentification (Muñoz, 1999), a political act of resistance that creates new truths rather than either adopting the dominant reality or opposing it entirely. Critical trans politics

(Spade, 2011) further challenges mainstream assumptions that institutional structures are neutral, but rather that administrative systems such as higher education institutions constantly reproduce dominant meanings and boundaries of gender. These lenses taken singularly and together examine and critique intersecting systems of power and pursue transformative theory, which aims to enact practices for liberation (hooks, 1994). Finally, as a trans*masculine person of color, I am invested in the narratives and conceptions of gender like my own, and I believe that the exclusion of our multifaceted realities impacts the matriculation, persistence, success, and well-being of trans* people of color in higher education.

LITERATURE REVIEW

The study of men and masculinities began in the 1970s and 1980s, a pro-feminist endeavor to respond to the men's rights movement. The latter was a conservative backlash to gains made by feminist women and movements up to that point (Brod, 1987; Clatterbaugh, 1990). Thus, studying "men *as men*" (Shapiro, 1981, p. 122) is still fairly emerging, with the focus on college men barely a couple of decades old (Capraro, 2004). Despite the fact that much of the foundational research used in higher education is based on men's development (Evans, Forney, Guido, Patton, & Renn, 2010), men's gender as a construct or process was not examined, thus necessitating the need to study college men's experiences from a gendered perspective (Davis & Laker, 2004; Edwards & Jones, 2009; Harris & Barone, 2011). The literature in higher education thus far overwhelmingly demonstrates that masculinity is associated with violence, harm, and mismanagement of health, both for men and others in their lives (Connell, 2005; Courtenay, 2000, 2011; O'Neil, 2008; O'Neil & Crapser, 2011; Kimmel, 2008, 2010; Kimmel & Davis, 2011).

Despite the growing attention to masculinities on college campuses and the importance of discussing masculinities in their plurality (e.g., Harper & Harris, 2010; Laker & Davis, 2011), these studies are overwhelmingly driven by and about cisgender men. This falsely assumes that masculinity is the exclusive domain of cisgender men (Person, 1999), particularly when terms such as *man*, *male*, and *masculinity* are used interchangeably (Marine, 2013). In addition to masculine-identified or masculine-expressing women (Person, 1999), these studies leave out the experiences and understandings of trans* students who have crucial perspectives to offer. By essentializing masculinity as something that only cisgender men embody, these studies reify the gender binary and inadvertently maintain the supremacy of hegemonic masculinity (Bilodeau, 2009; Connell, 2005; Lev, 2004).

In addition to expanding scholarship on men and masculinities in higher education, the increasing visibility of trans* students at U.S. higher education institutions has enlightened the need for more research exploring their experiences and perspectives (Beemyn, 2003; Beemyn, Curtis, Davis, & Tubbs, 2005). However, this research is limited partly due to the assumption that trans* students are included in LGBTQ research, which is often not the case (Renn, 2010). Even when they are included as participants, most of the scholarship does not differentiate between sexuality and gender, further inappropriately assuming that trans* students' experiences and needs parallel those of their cisgender lesbian, gay, bisexual, and queer peers (Marine, 2011; Pusch, 2003; Renn & Reason, 2013). Most of the existing research points to and emphasizes the oppression and hostility that trans* students face on college campuses (e.g., Bilodeau, 2009; Beemyn, 2003; Beemyn et al., 2005; Rankin, Blumenfeld, Weber, & Frazer, 2010). In addition to being limited as a whole, research on trans* students aggregates the population, leaving the diversity of gender, racial, and all other intersecting identities among them unacknowledged. This practice of mass aggregation of trans* students presents them as a monolithic group, one that is assumed to be White, heterosexual, able-bodied, and so forth. Specifically as it relates to race, the intersection of racism and genderism invisibilizes trans* students of color and their identities even more so (Bilodeau, 2009), which is then made worse by the dearth of narratives and perspectives coming from this population. Additionally, this practice of ignoring race and racism as it informs the experiences of trans* people situates Whiteness as the norm in trans* literature (Bonilla-Silva, 2009). Thus, the intentional recruitment of trans* students of color as well as an explicitly intersectional and raced lens in the study was important to resist the ongoing "whitewashing" of trans* realities.

METHODOLOGY

The study utilized qualitative postintentional phenomenology (Vagle, 2014) and queer phenomenology (Ahmed, 2006) to open up traditional phenomenology to multiplicity and difference. This allowed the study to resist forming a singular essence of trans* masculinity and allowed for divergent voices of trans*masculine students to come through. Through maximum variation and selective sampling, a diverse pool of interested participants was interviewed in person or via Skype or phone anywhere between 40 minutes and 2 hours. From the group of 19 study participants, 11 identified as people of color, and this chapter focuses on their narratives. A table describing each individual participant across the identities provided by them is provided (see Appendix A). The names listed are pseudonyms provided and/or approved by the participants. The participants were also given the opportunity to write in their own descriptors for their various identities, rather than selecting from prechosen options, which is reflected in the table except where the information provided was too long to include in its entirety. The 11 students were diverse racially, regionally, and in terms of their gender identities and ability/disability statuses. Most identified as queer, and socioeconomically all participants identified as middle class or with less means. Only two attended private institutions, with one—Seth—attending a historically women's college. Four were graduate students and seven were undergraduates. The institutions they attended were spread out across four U.S. regions: South (4), Northeast (2), West (3), and Midwest (2).

Data were analyzed using postintentional phenomenology's whole-part-whole method (Vagle, 2014). This began with an initial holistic reading of the data to get a sense of the whole picture, followed by line-by-line readings of each transcript at a time. In addition to my own identification of excerpts and quotes, recruited transcript readers contributed to the final analysis. The final analysis allowed for the emergence of findings that were not thematic but rather in the form of a threshold and pathways, as described in the next section.

FINDINGS

The emergence of the study's findings as a threshold and pathways disputes notions of a singular trans*masculinity or trans*masculine experience, including for trans*masculine students of color. The pathways describe the limitless paths or possibilities of (trans*)masculinities that students take on and that exist within the contexts of hegemony and dominance (Jourian, 2017), as depicted in Figure 8.1. The pathways are not independent of these contexts but rather offer alternatives within them. These pathways are reached through the threshold of dominant masculinities, which function as a sort of passageway or entry point, and are shown as the area encircling the pathways (Figure 8.1). When reflecting on what masculinity means, dominant masculinities were often the first things that came up, demonstrating how ubiquitous and institutionalized they are as trans*masculine students of color seek to define and construct their identities. These dominant and hegemonic examples presented themselves at both individualized and institutionalized levels.

The pathways represent the disidentified (trans*)masculinities that the students in the study took on to (re)define their gendered identities as informed by their intersecting identities. The pathways are not sequentially explored and do not represent a developmental model of sorts. Meaning, trans*masculine students do not start with racialized (trans*)masculinities and arrive at authenticity. Rather the pathways emerge and reemerge at different times in students' lives, can occur concurrently and are not mutually exclusive, are rarely if ever completely resolved, and become more integrated and complex over time. The way that these pathways inform each other is somewhat like taking multiple classes at a time, allowing learning from one to inform another and future ones, and with each semester/quarter, students' approaches to assignments and content become increasingly fused and multidimensional. The study as a whole unearthed the following pathways and subpathways, which are illustrated in Figure 8.1 as darker arrows.

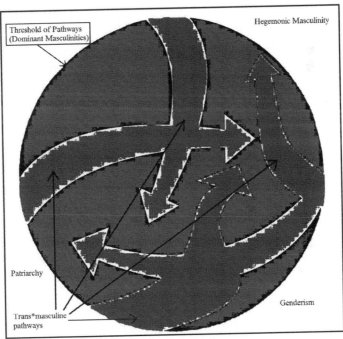

Figure 8.1.   Trans*masculine threshold and pathways.

- Racialized (trans*)masculinities—a significant focus of this chapter, this pathway demonstrates how students' masculinities interact with their racialized identities and experiences, including the systems of oppression that shape those identities and experiences.

  o (Trans*)masculinities of color
  o White (trans*)masculinities

- Reoriented (trans*)masculine embodiments—this pathway explores the ways that participants deconstructed and reconstructed their masculinities, with their identities being in constant formation and negotiation mode as they became exposed to scripts they learned or unlearned. Fashion, sexuality and relationships, disability, and nonbinary identities often informed how this pathway was embodied.

    o Fashioned (trans*)masculinities
    o Sexua-romanticized (trans*)masculinities
    o (Dis)abled (trans*)masculinities
    o Nonbinary (trans*)masculinities

- Authentic (trans*)masculinities—participants expressed strong desires to embody and redefine masculinities in authentic-to-them ways, which did not rely on prescriptive and restrictive performances of harmful scripts, just to be recognized as masculine and/ or men. These authentic (trans*)masculinities required a balancing of gentleness (toward self and others) and intentional approaches to space, voice, and presence.

    o Intentional (trans*)masculinities
    o Gentle (trans*)masculinities

Although race and racism showed up across all the pathways, as well as within the threshold of dominance, this chapter focuses on how trans*masculine college students of color traversed their racialized pathways, with specific attention to (trans*)masculinities of color and Black (trans*)masculinities, and the implications of their reflections. Additionally, some relevant attention is paid to their articulation of institutionalized masculinities and authentic (trans*)masculinities.

Institutionalized Masculinities

When thinking about how their institutions conveyed what masculinity meant, many trans*masculine students of color presented grim and toxic images of institutionalized masculinity embroiled in misogyny and racism, among other systems of oppression. The enactment of dominant masculinities by their peers and individuals on campus was often named as reflective of the institutions. Speaking to institutional masculine culture, RJ said, "Currently, like, this is horrible to say but the culture of [my institution], masculinity equals rape. It's bad shit; it's fucked up to say.... There is a culture of, 'Who gives a shit,' or 'She was asking for it.'" This institutionalized framing and cissexist assumptions that all men are cisgender left Kyle conflicted about his role as a man of transgender experience.

> It's difficult because it's like I want to be able to engage in these conversations, but not knowing how to engage in these conversations. Not knowing how to balance the amount of space I take up. Especially since I am like a hardcore feminist. I believe in the equality of genders. Knowing what that feels like to be seen and treated as a woman, but also transitioning to a more masculine manhood or whatever. I find it hard to find space for me to be able to have these conversations and not feel invalidated by them.... I don't really know because I want to be loud, but I don't want to be demonized. I also don't want to be invisible and not say anything. I just have to pick and choose my battles. But most of the times, I feel like whichever battle I choose I lose.

In addition to seeing dominant masculinity as institutionalized and manifested in rape culture on campus, trans*masculine students of color also talked about the inevitable Whiteness of institutional masculinity. Charles remarked, "We are in the rural Northwest so for me when I think of masculinity specifically here I see straight, White male-bodied, male-identified men." He also talked about how the institution's affinity spaces, such as the multicultural or queer resource center "make [the campus] seem like something that it's not" and function "sometimes [as] a veil." Thus, affinity spaces did not shift the institution's identity, nor did they structurally change the student population, but rather masked its Whiteness and cisheteropatriarchy. Similarly, when thinking about his institution, Earl described it as "White. It's really, really White and as far as specifically about masculinity there are not a lot of men on campus that look like me." That meant that Earl did not consider anyone at the institution as someone who could fulfill an influential role in his life when it came to masculinity because he did not see himself in those around him.

> It really sucks. It's seriously ... I can't tell you.... For me when I think about masculinity I'm thinking about people that I can somehow identify with and it's really difficult for me to identify with a lot of the guys that I see on campus. Seriously, on a daily basis I might see one person that looks like me, if that.

Similarly, Kyle did not feel connected to "any of the authority" on his campus, minimally engaging with any of them, and did not see his institution as playing an influential role on his masculinity. When thinking about employees on campus, he shared, "There is a lot of respectability politics in being a teacher and staff member and stuff like that. And I don't respect that. I don't respect respectability politics." Respectability politics is a strategy that blames the behaviors and attitudes of Black people, particularly poor Black people, for structural inequality rather than racism, White supremacy, classism, and anti-Blackness. Jay also disconnected himself from his institution, commenting on that reality's impact when he said, "It's like people [in higher education] don't have expectations of you as a Black man." When he talked about his on-campus engagement or lack thereof, he said,

> I don't live on campus, I don't fuck with campus, I don't have anything to do with campus. I just go in, get my classes and go back to the south side with the other Black people and I'm good, you know what I'm saying? That's what I do. So I don't really ... I'm immune to the bullshit, you know?

Jay and Kyle both also talked about experiencing anti-Blackness in campus queer spaces when they began presenting as Black men. They experienced being perceived and treated as dangerous, suspicious, and threatening. Jay's relationships with White queer individuals he had previously been in community with began to strain when he physically transitioned. He said, "It was really interesting as I transitioned, as the changes started happening physically you know, going into spaces with White queer people and them being like, 'Who the fuck are you and why are you here Black man?'" Jay felt his masculinity get stripped of its queerness and trans*ness by others' interpretations of Black masculinity as inherently heterosexual and cisgender. Kyle felt "ostracized" and experienced an erasure of his Blackness when he found himself in queer spaces. "I would talk about my queer experience and my trans* experience ... and other people would talk about their queer experience and their trans* experience, but then feeling like, 'Mine doesn't look the same as yours, cause I'm also Black.'"

Experiences of anti-Blackness, like these across institutional spaces, influenced how Earl performed his Black masculinity on campus, including in the classroom. He found himself attempting to "not be the angry Black guy" when in predominantly White environments "with no backup or support." Earl lets "a lot of things go unsaid" and found this performance "exhausting." As an example,

> In [the health equity] class I just didn't say a lot and a lot of times it was really hard to show up to class. It got to the point to where I did my work, I turned in my assignments, but going to that class was a chore. Just kind of like hearing people talk about these different situations or experiences they have had that were like "eye opening" and I was like if I hear one more person say eye opening I'm going to jump out the fucking window.

At Coffee Bean's institution, institutionalized White masculinity, along with classism, all coalesced into "dude-bro" masculinity. They described a dude-bro as "a White fraternity dude, upper class of course."

> I think of someone who is in "Fiji" [Phi Gamma Delta] and "Sammy" [Sigma Alpha Mu]. I think of someone who is obnoxious, someone who is entitled. And that's White masculinity, right, because for me, especially coming to [my institution], it was hard for me to disentangle Whiteness from upper class-ness.... And when we get to masculinity of color, because there's a very clear difference, a very clear divide between the two, I think of some of the Black dudes I know on campus, that most of them, unfortunately, I know because they're football players and how fucked up it is that most of the Black students that you recruit and that you give scholarships to are the ones that are going to make you money as football stars or as basketball players.

The association of Whiteness and masculinity with each other meant Jones held up his Asian male peers to White masculine standards. He described one of his classmates as "very Americanized and he's attractive, very conventionally attractive for an Asian guy. He's buff and he's very social and very cool," and he felt "inferiority compared to him." Another classmate he described as "more approachable to me" and as "nerdier, definitely scrawnier. I think he's more Asian-y than the other guy." Thus, Jones equated being attractive, strong, and cool as a man to being "Americanized," meaning White and being skinny and nerdy as Asian qualities, ones he was not intimidated by and saw himself being like. Thus, "dude-bro masculinity" is something that Jones, as an Asian trans*masculine person, could not and did not want to attain.

(Trans*)masculinities of Color

Trans*masculine students of color explicitly and implicitly named some of the ways they experienced Whiteness, White supremacy, and racism as roadblocks in their desire to witness or embody positive and culturally affirming representations of masculinities. They brought up colonialism, respectability politics, anti-Blackness, and being seen as threats as racialized beings as mediating forces in their experience of masculinities within society as a whole, as well as their own racial and cultural communities. Coffee Bean struggled with their own self-identification as trans* because "even thinking about trans*ness for me has to be disentanglement from Whiteness." Students talked about how this *entanglement* resulted in decisions about cutting their hair in culturally nonaffirming ways (Charles), in linguistic barriers when communicating with family about trans*ness in

Spanish (Seth), a polluting of Lakota masculinity with misogynistic practices (Bastian), and a desire to decolonize machismo (RJ).

As social institutions that are not immune to and which often propagate White supremacy, racism, and colonialism—always in collusion with other forces such as cissexism—trans*masculine students of color experienced hostile environments on campus. Mohammad talked about the intersectional impact of racism, Islamophobia, and masculinity that he experienced as a Palestinian masculine student involved in pro-Palestinian activism on campus.

> My Palestinian [identity] and masculinity intertwined is very interesting in terms of like opposition. The Zionist group on campus, they're very much into LGBTQ rights. But then also they're like quick to label me more as a terrorist. This happened during a divestment [hearing], where I was like accused of carving a swastika into a dorm room, which they never provided evidence of, any pictures or anything. Also I was called a terrorist during the actual hearing. I think that because of my masculinity it's more, it's easier to call me that, a terrorist, than it is for the female Palestinians. Where they're just like, they say that [female Palestinians are] oppressed or they support terrorism, rather than being terrorists.

However, his involvement and leadership in culturally specific activism and spaces allowed Mohammad to find acceptance among his cis peers. Describing himself as "one of the most active Arabs" in his community, he positioned himself among his peers to be "the first person they call . . . when something about Arabs or Muslims comes up in [town]." He believed,

> that has a lot to do with why they respect me too.... I think that I'm also changing stereotypes for them. Because I am so deeply passionate in change and human rights, and Palestine that they're like, "'Oh well not all LGBTQ people are on floats throwing glitter. They actually care about stuff. They're humans too.'"

Despite experiencing resistance to their trans*ness in their sorority, Coffee Bean brought up the organization's history and values, specifically its race-centered activist roots, as a reason they joined in the first place. This was connected to their own personal history and values, the significance of their socialization as a woman of color and anti-misogynistic ideals.

> There's also a part of me that's not interested in denying the fact that I was socialized as a woman of color or that I at some point said yeah I'm a girl, you know what I mean? I don't identify that as like now necessarily, but I feel like it's almost misogynistic in its own way ... to deny the fact that at some point in my life, I was a girl.... That's real and that shapes me and that's who

I was and that will always be a little part of who I am and I think that also informed some of my reason for joining [my sorority].

Trans*masculine students of color often found solace, wholeness, identification, and affirmation when engaging with people of color who lived out diverse presentations and expressions of gender, as well as when they reflected on the messages they received about masculinity from their own communities. This rarely, if ever, occurred at or through their own institutions. A few participants, for example, were alums of the Oakland-based Brown Boi Project (BBP) and had participated in BBP's Leadership Retreat. None of the alums had participated in the retreat in the same cohort as others in the study. BBP is an organization for masculine of center people of color across gender identities who seek and embody nonoppressive masculinities. Charles, who at the time of his participation had not yet begun identifying as trans*, talked about the impact of that space.

We all identified as masculine of center. We were all people of color. I think seeing the spectrum in which you can be within that which is so vast, it was really like, oh my god I think this person that I'm seeing in front of me is like a physical manifestation of all of the feelings that I have and I just didn't know it was possible. So it was such a powerful thing.

Kyle's participation in BBP gave him a vehicle through which to reconnect to his own Cherokee roots. The retreat shifted his perspective on gender by triggering a connection to

the different tribes that existed that actually understood that masculinity and femininity are fluid, [that] they flow into each other rather than just being binary or either side of the spectrum.... I think that if it wasn't for Brown Bois I would probably still have that anxiety, that pressure, to be rigid, to be cold, to try to be hard and all that other stuff. I guess getting connected back to the ancestry that says this never existed before colonialization (sic). This wasn't a part of our culture. We don't even understand what that means ... is what kind of transformed my view of what masculinity means to me and what it can mean in another context.

In addition, one of Kyle's mentors, a community-based activist who "was the first Black trans*man that I ever met," introduced him to the idea of the Black intellectual. Where society, his classes, and student organizations sent him confining and limiting messages about the ability of his identities to coexist in his Black trans* body, this Black-centered mentorship allowed Kyle to reinterpret Black masculinity and embody a counternarrative. It helped him internalize being "a Black man, and that doesn't mean that I will not succeed, or that I am not anything, but I have potential, and I can be an intellectual and I can make change happen."

Finding someone like him also played a big role for James in crafting his masculinity. Incidentally, James was the only trans*masculine student of color to both find this person within a campus context and name a cisgender person as being "like him." When pledging his poetry fraternity, the president of the organization was his inductions master and quickly became someone whom James looked up to and sought to emulate. As others in the fraternity began calling James a "mini Sam"[1] and the two of them became close, he began to feel at ease about his gender around Sam, allowing Sam the opportunity to affirm James' gender.

> When I told him [that I'm trans*] he was like, I've been calling you brother since I met you, which is true. He was immediately like "you're like a little brother to me, for some reason you don't feel like a little sister." So when I told him that I wanted male pronouns he was like, at this point that's only natural and he never slips up or anything.

James' trust in Sam, a cishet Black man, to open up to about being trans male added more pull for James toward Black masculinity. It is where he found affirmation as personified by Sam and likely heightened through their membership and sense of brotherhood within a fraternity. Beyond individual connection, others talked about connections to community and culture as affirming and building their sense of selves. For Bastian this occurred in witnessing change in Lakota masculinity, a going back to historical and precolonial understandings of gender in North America, ones that honored nonbinary genders. Some of this he believed to be in tandem with shifts in the broader trans* community. Having deep historical roots to begin with, he experienced Two Spirit communities as more embracing of gender fluidity than other communities.

> I also think that as the trans* community is beginning to accept more of a fluidity of gender and the general community is starting to accept that, that the Two Spirit community is going through a similar change. But I feel like [the Two Spirit community] might have gotten there just a little bit before the other communities did. That gender is a little more understood as being fluid I guess a little earlier. I like how seamlessly a lot of the members are able to switch from gender to gender.

RJ talked about being in touch with their own ancestors and cultural identity, "like Taíno and Arawak folk and Puerto Rican-ness" and "loving and affirming Black trans*women" as a "beautiful process of decolonizing" and as "survival." They acknowledged this process was hard, a feeling that Jones resonated with when it came to existing at the intersection of multiple marginalized identities, alongside the feeling of being enriched by that existence. He talked about how his gender (transmasculine) and race (Korean-American) "have been the two biggest factors" in shaping him.

> Growing up in [Southern home state] as one of two Asian kids at school you had nobody to mirror you. I had nobody else to look at and oh yeah I'm part of that group. So it's definitely enriched my life culturally in terms of my world view. I'm more understanding of minority status due to my intersecting minority identities. Yet it has also made my life very difficult. I think I had more heartbreak than a normal kid would if they grew up White and straight and stuff in [Southern home state]. I had more stuff to deal with growing up.

Both Jones and Mohammad talked about the ways their particular upbringings imbued them with certain cultural understandings of masculinity that allowed them to resist "American" (which they often used interchangeably with White) masculine ideals. Mohammad brought up the cultural imagery of the *amo*, Arabic for uncle, as the source of his sense of responsibility toward his community as tied to his privileged identities. Pointing to a painting of an amo carrying Jerusalem on his wall, Mohammad described his masculinity as

> carrying the weight of everything. Being able to help out and carry the weight off people. I would describe my masculinity as giving to others. It's what makes me the happiest in life, is when I'm able to give to others. Not necessarily synonymous with masculinity, but for me it is. It's having the ability, having the privilege to help others. Using my privilege and accessibility to do so.

Jones also held that there were contradicting messages he got about masculinity between "Asian culture" and "American people."

> I feel like inherent in Asian culture is kind of this humility and respect thing. So it's hard to be the aggressive masculine that I see a lot in American people. So no matter how much I try to be, not that I would try to be, but like I don't think I have it in me to be American masculine.

Authentic (Trans*)masculinities

Trans*masculine students of color thus contended with notions of masculinity tied with Whiteness and racism as they attempted to embody and redefine masculinities in ways that felt authentic to them, ones that did not involve performing restrictive, prescriptive, and harmful scripts just to be recognized as masculine and/or men. As previously shared, connections to culture and history, as well as individuals and communities of color, allowed them to reground themselves in their genders. Mohammad, another BBP alum, talked about the significance of meeting a gender-diverse group of masculine of center people of color that affirmed to him that "bois cry too." For him, this "was the first time that I actually was told that it's okay to be my authentic self and be okay with it ... to be a masculine person who's sensitive ... in touch with their feminine side, whatever that is."

These authentic ways of being involved being intentional in crafting their masculinities. This often meant being conscious of space and voice and, as Coffee Bean described, embodying a masculinity that was "accountable ... ethical ... without misogyny ... just fun and carefree like my polka dot bowtie." This bowtie symbolized their masculinity because "the way I've placed it and everything, it's masculine, but it's got polka dots on it so it's kind of fruity." They talked about their disidentification with masculinity as wanting "to have the bowties and suspenders and have the flat chest and have all this other stuff ... but I want to do all of that without the cloying paternalism." Coffee Bean embraced their masculinity while rejecting aspects of hegemonic masculinity they were expected to take on.

Authenticity for Seth meant being "more honest" with those around him, and this they believed allowed him to "have stronger bonds with people, because they appreciate when you are honest with them." Ze believed that revealing his trans*identity to others made people "almost ... more invested in you than they would otherwise be." For others, authenticity was about being gentle and centering vulnerability in masculinity (RJ and Charles), talking about hurt and pain with other masculine people (Kyle), embracing their femininity (Jones, Mohammad, and Charles), and self-care (RJ, Kyle, Charles, and Coffee Bean). As Kyle internalized deserving "healthy living [and] care," he learned how to be "a lot more supportive in healthier ways ... not forget[ting] about myself in these larger movements, while also supporting [and advocating for] other people as well."

DISCUSSION

The reflections of trans*masculine students of color divulge incredible insight into how the collusion of multiple systems of oppression come to shape their experiences and identities at the intersections of their marginalized and privileged identities. These reflections have implications for campus educators throughout the institution, from those working in LGBTQ resource centers, to classroom instructors, from those who implement programming for men of color, to those who seek to address the campus epidemic of sexual assaults. Often these environments design curricular and co-curricular interventions in isolation from each other, focusing on a single dimension of students' lives.

LGBTQ campus spaces have much work to do to eradicate racism, particularly anti-Blackness, if they are to be a resource on campus for trans*masculine students of color. Classroom instructors of all disciplines should learn to employ anti-oppressive pedagogy (Kumashiro, 2002). Without such pedagogical practices, students such as Earl, who disengages because of the racism and cissexism he experiences in the classroom, are cheated out of transformational classrooms and misevaluated as being disinterested in academic endeavors. Trans*masculine students of color have also shared about the power of being in community with other masculine people of color, something they overwhelmingly do not experience on their campuses, even though many campuses provide "men of color" programming. Often these programs aim to increase the retention of men of color, as well as create dialogue about positive masculinities. In addition to not considering trans*masculine students as potentially benefiting from and desiring such spaces, the counternarratives shared and crafted by many of these students stand in opposition to racist attributions of danger, threat, and violence that plague masculine people of color, particularly Black men on campus. These counternarratives and the students' unique understandings of how masculine/male privilege and hegemonic masculinity show up, is denied to cisgender men of color who may learn about resisting these intersecting forces from trans*masculine students of color. Cisgender men of color are thus denied the counternarratives of trans*masculine students of color, as well as their unique understanding of how masculine/male privilege and hegemonic masculinity show up. Exposure to these students' articulations of resisting the aforementioned forces could embolden men of color to take even more responsibility in their efforts to eradicate rape culture on campus.

Implications of the articulated realities of trans*masculine students of color go beyond programmatic and practice-related efforts that can benefit all students on college campuses. This study challenges how trans*students as a whole, and trans*masculine students of color specifically, are viewed on college campuses as a population that has to be accommodated. This deficit-oriented viewpoint names trans* students as anomalies or problems to otherwise seemingly well-functioning institutions. Instead, this study radically positions trans*masculine students of color, and their insights and contributions, as assets to institutions that are truly invested in enacting social change.

NOTE

1. Pseudonym for James' inductions master.

REFERENCES

Ahmed, S. (2006). *Queer phenomenology: Orientations, objects, others.* Durham, NC: Duke University Press.

Aultman, B. (2014). Cisgender. *Transgender Studies Quarterly, 1*(1–2), 61–63.

Beemyn, B. (2003). Serving the needs of transgender college students. *Journal of Gay & Lesbian Issues in Education, 1*(1), 33–49.

Beemyn, B., Curtis, B., Davis, M., & Tubbs, N. J. (2005). Transgender issues on college campuses. In R. L. Sanlo (Ed.), *New directions for student services: Gender identity and sexual orientation: Research, policy, and personal perspectives. No. 111* (pp. 49–60). San Francisco, CA: Jossey-Bass.

Bonilla-Silva, E. (2009). *Racism without racists: Color-blind racism and the persistence of racial inequality in America* (3rd ed.). New York, NY: Rowman & Littlefield.

Bilodeau, B. (2009). *Genderism: Transgender students, binary systems and higher education.* Saarbrücken, Germany: Verlag Dr. Müller.

Brod, H. (1987). The new men's studies: From feminist theory to gender scholarship. *Hypatia, 2*(1), 179–196.

Capraro, R. L. (2004). Men's studies as a foundation for student development work with college men. In G. E. Kellom (Ed.), *New directions for student services 107: Developing effective programs and services for college men* (pp. 23–34). San Francisco, CA: Jossey-Bass.

Clatterbaugh, K. (1990). *Contemporary perspectives on masculinity: Men, women, and politics in modern society.* Boulder, CO: Westview Press.

Connell, R. W. (2005). *Masculinities* (2nd ed.). Berkeley, CA: University of California Press.

Connell, R.W., & Messerschmidt, J. W. (2005). Hegemonic masculinity: Rethinking the concept. *Gender and Society, 19*(6), 829–859.

Courtenay, W. H. (2000). Constructions of masculinity and their influence on men's well-being: A theory of gender and health. *Social Science and Medicine, 50*(10), 1385–1401.

Courtenay, W. (2011). Best practices for improving college men's health. In J. A. Laker & T. Davis (Eds.), *Masculinities in higher education: Theoretical and practical considerations* (pp. 177–192). New York, NY: Routledge.

Crenshaw, K. (1991). Mapping the margins: Intersectionality, identity politics, and violence against women of color. *Stanford Law Review, 43*, 1241–1299.

Davis, T., & Laker, J. (2004). Connecting men to academic and student affairs programs and services. In G. E. Kellom (Ed.), *New directions for student services 107: Developing effective programs and services for college men* (pp. 47–57). San Francisco, CA: Jossey-Bass.

Edwards, K. E., & Jones, S. R. (2009). "Putting my man face on": A grounded theory of college men's gender identity development. *Journal of College Student Development, 50*(2), 210–228.

Evans, N. J., Forney, D. S., Guido, F. M., Patton, L. D., & Renn, K. A. (2010). *Student development in college: Theory, research, and practice* (2nd ed.). San Francisco, CA: Jossey-Bass.

Harper, S. R., & Harris III, F. (Eds.). (2010). *College men and masculinities: Theory, research, and implications for practice.* Indianapolis, IN: John Wiley & Sons.

Harris, F., III, & Barone, R. P. (2011). The situation of men, and situating men in higher education: A conversation about crisis, myth, and reality about college students who are men. In J. A. Laker & T. Davis (Eds.), *Masculinities in higher education: Theoretical and practical considerations* (pp. 50–62). New York, NY: Routledge.

hooks, b. (1994). *Teaching to transgress: Education as the practice of freedom.* New York, NY: Routledge.

Jourian, T. J. (2017). Trans*forming college masculinities: Carving out trans*masculine pathways through the threshold of dominance. *International Journal of Qualitative Studies in Education, 30*(3), 245–265. doi:10.1080/0951 8398.2016.1257752

Kimmel, M. S. (2008). *Guyland: The perilous world where boys become men.* New York, NY: HarperCollins.

Kimmel, M. S. (2010). Masculinity as homophobia: Fear, shame, and silence in the construction of gender identity. In S. R. Harper & F. Harris III (Eds.), *College men and masculinities: Theory, research, and implications for practice* (pp. 23–31). San Francisco, CA: Jossey-Bass.

Kimmel, M. S., & Davis, T. (2011). Mapping guyland in college. In J. A. Laker & T. Davis (Eds.), *Masculinities in higher education: Theoretical and practical considerations* (pp. 3–15). New York, NY: Routledge.

Kumashiro, K. K. (2000). Towards a theory of anti-oppressive education. *Review of Educational Research, 70*(1), 25–53.

Laker, J. A., & Davis, T. L. (Eds.). (2011). *Masculinities in higher education: Theoretical and practical considerations.* New York, NY: Routledge.

Lev, A. I. (2004). *Transgender emergence: Therapeutic guidelines for working with gender-variant people and their families.* New York, NY: Routledge.

Marine, S. B. (2011). Stonewall's legacy: Bisexual, gay, lesbian, and transgender students in higher education. *ASHE Higher Education Report, 37*(4).

Marine, S. B. (2013). Book review [Review of the book *Masculinities in higher education: Theoretical and practical considerations*, by J. A. Laker & T. Davis (Eds.)]. *NASPA Journal about Women in Higher Education, 6*(1), 131–134.

Muñoz, J. E. (1999). *Disidentifications: Queers of color and the performance of politics.* Minneapolis, MN: University of Minnesota Press.

O'Neil, J. M. (2008). Summarizing 25 years of research on men's gender role conflict using the gender role conflict scale: New research paradigms and clinical implications. *The Counseling Psychologist, 36*(3), 358–445.

O'Neil, J. M., & Crapser, B. (2011). Using the psychology of men and gender role conflict theory to promote comprehensive service delivery for college men: A call to action. In J. A. Laker & T. Davis (Eds.), *Masculinities in higher education: Theoretical and practical considerations* (pp. 16–49). New York, NY: Routledge.

Person, E. S. (1999). Some mysteries of gender: Rethinking masculine identification in heterosexual women. In *Sexual century: Selected papers on sex and gender.* New Haven, CT: Yale University Press.

Pusch, R. S. (2003). The bathroom and beyond: Transgendered college students' perspectives of transition. *Dissertation Abstracts International, 64*(2), 456. UMI 3081653.

Rankin, S., Blumenfeld, W. J., Weber, G. N., & Frazer, S. (2010). *State of higher education for LGBT people*. Charlotte, NC: Campus Pride.

Renn, K. A. (2010). LGBT and queer research in higher education: The state and status of the field. *Educational Researcher, 39*(2), 132–141.

Renn, K. A., & Reason, R. D. (2013). *College students in the United States: Characteristics, experiences, and outcomes*. San Francisco, CA: Jossey-Bass.

Shapiro, J. (1981). Anthropology and the study of gender. In E. Langland & W. Gove (Eds.), *A feminist perspective in the academy: The difference it makes* (pp. 110–129). Chicago, IL: University of Chicago Press.

Spade, D. (2011). *Normal life: Administrative violence, critical trans politics, and the limits of law*. Brooklyn, NY: South End Press.

Tompkins, A. (2014). Asterisk. *TSQ: Transgender Studies Quarterly, 1*(1–2), 26–27.

Vagle, M. D. (2014). *Crafting phenomenological research*. Walnut Creek, CA: Left Coast Press.

Appendix A

Name	Gendeer	Race/Ethnicity	Sexuality	(Dis)ability	SES	G/UG	Inst. Type & Region
RJ	Transgender, masculine-of-center, genderqueer	Boricua, Latinx	Pansexual	Disabled	Working class	G	South, Private
Kyle	Man of transgender experience	Black Cherokee	Queer	None	Working poor	UG	South, Public
Seth	Transmasculine	Latino	Pansexual	Occasional anxiety	Lower middle class	UG	West, Private
Earl	Queer	African American	Queer	None	Poor	G	West, Public
James	Transmale	White, Black, Native American, and Asian	Queer	None	Middle class	UG	Northeast, Public
Bastian	Two Spirit transman	Lakota Jew (multi-ethnically White)	Heteroflexible, sapioromantic, demisexual	Multiple disabilities	Living in poverty	G	Midwest, Public
Jones	Transmasculine	Korean American	Queer	None	Low middle class	G	South, Public
Mohammad	Transgender man/boi	Palestinian Middle Eastern	Loves femmes	None	Lower middle class	UG	South, Public
Charles	Trans*man, transgender man, FTM	Japanese, Hawaiian, Chinese, Irish, Portuguese, and possibly English	Attracted to femininity in all its forms	None	Middle(ish) working class	UG	West, Public
Jay	Transman	Black	Queer	Yes	Working class	UG	Midwest, Public
Coffee Bean	Tran*masculine non-binary	Lain@, NicaMexiGreek	Queer	PTSD	Working class	UG	Northeast, Public

143

CHAPTER 9

CONFRONTING HATE

Addressing Crimes and Incidents Targeting QPOC Communities

Ashley L. Smith and Joshua Moon Johnson

Queer people of color (QPOC) face numerous challenges related to their racial, ethnic, sexual, and gender identities, such as microaggressions, cultural appropriation, exclusion, and misrepresentation. However, this chapter aims to bring attention to the basic need of physical and emotional safety that many QPOC face on a regular basis. In the last decade, more attention has been placed on addressing LGBTQ bullying in middle schools and even on college campuses. In the last 2 years, there has been a major focus on racism on college campuses. Black Lives Matter movements have made a national impact, including on college campuses. As institutions of higher education focus on campus climate for LGBTQ people and racial minorities, they must also spend time thinking about how those two issues affect a population of people who exist within both communities. QPOC are disproportionately affected by hate crimes and bias incidents, which can greatly affect their ability to succeed in higher education.

The purpose of this chapter is to: (a) understand trends and the impact of hate crimes and bias incidents targeting QPOC faculty, staff, and stu-

---

Queer People of Color in Higher Education, pp. 145–161

dents; and (b) identify resources and recommendations to support QPOC people on college campuses. Little research has examined how hate crimes and bias incidents impact QPOC communities within institutions of higher education. Although this chapter does not provide in-depth lived experiences of QPOC in higher education, it does summarize past literature and bring to the forefront an issue that needs much more attention. Both of us, as authors, work at large predominantly White institutions at least part time in positions that address hate crimes and bias incidents on campus. The summary of literature that we provide comes from a place of sadness, mourning, and hope. Personal experiences have framed perspectives, and our regular interactions with survivors of hate crimes and bias incidents motivated us to research this topic. Even as we were in the middle of writing this chapter, a national tragedy occurred in Orlando, Florida, where a Latinx LGBTQ space was targeted and 49 people were violently killed (Fantz, Karimi, & McLaughlin, 2016). Most of those killed were assumedly QPOC. The impact of this incident served as a persistent reminder that these acts of hate against QPOC are not limited to college campuses; in addressing this issue, it is equally important to bring awareness to the harm that QPOC face daily in the dominant society.

HATE AND BIAS TOWARD LGBTQ PEOPLE AND PEOPLE OF COLOR

The study of campus climate has reemerged in the last few years as higher education struggles to address campus-level racism, sexism, homophobia, and transphobia. Much recent attention has focused on topics such as inclusive language, microaggressions, and cultural appropriation, which all significantly affect campus climate. We aimed to further understand how macroaggressions or hate crimes impacted QPOC on college campuses. There is still little research directly discussing any hate crimes on college campuses, but some national data can provide a broad picture of how hate crimes in the broader society affects campus environments. According to Dunbar (2006), race was the highest motivator of hate crimes—51% of crimes were motivated by race. Sexual orientation was the third-highest motivator of hate crimes in the United States, which was 17% of total attacks. Religious based attacks were at 18%. Many people assume that transgender people are the most targeted, but it is difficult to prove because bias-motivated attacks on the basis of gender identity are not tracked on the federal level (Dunbar, 2006). Moreover, a study of more than 1,000 hate crime reports to the Los Angeles County Human Rights Commission from 1994 to 1995 found that, on average, sexual orientation- and gender identity-motivated hate crimes yielded higher levels of violence than other hate crimes (Dunbar, 2006).

Many college campuses struggle to accurately present the types of hate crimes and bias incidents occurring on campuses; as a result, data on campus hate crimes and bias incidents are limited. Institutions that receive federal aid are expected to collect and report hate crime statistics to the Office of Postsecondary Education of the U.S. Department of Education (Anti-Defamation League, 2012). Additionally, institutions of higher education are required to report information on hate crimes linked to race, gender, religion, sexual orientation, ethnicity, or disability (Anti-Defamation League, 2012). Yet no one specific mandate focuses on how to handle incidents of hate and bias or focus on institutional accountability. Additionally, these crimes have been significantly underreported, and the lack of consistency in definitions of hate crimes across the Departments of Education and Justice has resulted in further gaps of missing data (Anti-Defamation League, 2012). Some campuses have chosen to implement campus climate studies, which have aided their campuses in providing a better understanding of what incidents and crimes were occurring.

Some research on college campus climate has been produced through a few national surveys mostly by Sue Rankin in 2003 and then again in 2010. A report by the National Gay and Lesbian Task Force (Rankin, 2003) concluded that LGBTQ people still encounter hostile climates on college and university campuses, even at campuses with strong support systems and campus LGBTQ support centers. More campuses have been adding LGBTQ-specific centers and services in the last decade. Rankin (2003) also found that one in five respondents feared for their personal campus safety because of their sexual and/or gender identities, and half concealed their sexual and/or gender identities to avoid intimidation. Throughout the rest of the chapter, we will further discuss basic concepts of hate and bias, current trends, the impact of these crimes and incidents, and strategies that institutions can utilize to address hate and bias affecting QPOC students.

HATE AND BIAS IN HIGHER EDUCATION

Implications and Definitions

Issues of hate and bias continue to plague college campuses and administration. Yet today we are seeing resistance taking place: Students are demanding administration to respond and comply with these issues, instead of continuing to "sweep them under the rug." As institutions of higher education that receive federal funding, the Office of Civil Rights requires campuses not to contribute to a hostile environment. As mandated in Title IX, factors that contribute to hostile environments are understood as alleged conduct that is "sufficiently serious to limit or deny a student's ability to participate in or benefit from the school's educational program" (U.S. Department of Education, 2014). Title VI of the Office of Civil Rights mandates that institutions receiving federal funding cannot exclude any person in the United States on the grounds of race, color, or national origin from participating in, be denied the benefits of, or be subjected to discrimination under any program or activity (Office for Civil Rights, 2016). Additionally, the anti-discrimination mandate focuses in particular on race, color, and national origin. Based on both of these government mandates, it would seem as if incidents of hate and bias occurring on college campuses would be deemed inappropriate and could potentially put institutions at risk of being incompliant.

It also becomes increasingly difficult to handle these incidents because states have varying definitions and protected classes under which these kinds of incidents can be categorized. This also makes implementing processes increasingly difficult for administrators because there are different expectations and protocols depending on the types of incidents reported. As a result, when institutions begin to hold themselves accountable and implement processes to handle issues of hate and bias, it becomes increasingly important to clarify what hate and bias are and who the necessary actors are who need to be present in specific incidents. Typical incidents are categorized as hate crimes, hate and bias incidents, and microaggressions; moreover, within each of these categorizations, key distinctions are found.

Types of Incidents

A hate crime is "a criminal offense intentionally directed at an individual or property in whole or in part because of the victim's actual or perceived race, religion, national origin, gender, gender identity, sexual orientation, or disability" (Anti-Defamation League, 2012, p. 2). These crimes' impact often expand beyond just the victim; they have the potential to intimidate other members of the victim's community, which leaves many of them feeling isolated, vulnerable, and unprotected (Anti-Defamation League, 2012). Common examples of hate crimes are graffiti or vandalism with speech targeting a specific population, such as a race or an ethnic group, that insinuate some form of harm against an individual, group, or community. According to the Anti-Defamation League (2012), some inconsistency exists with the category hate crime, as "each state defines criminal activity that constitutes a hate crime differently—and the breadth of coverage of these laws varies from state to state, as well" (p. 4). More specifically, protected identities vary under the definition of a hate crime across states, which in turn impacts the ways in which incidents of hate are handled. Under the legal definitions, only specific identities are listed, and others, such as gender identity, gender expression, socioeconomic status, and citizenship, are not typically listed. As a result, if a hate incident specifically addressed one of these unprotected identities, it cannot be considered a hate crime.

When an incident is not considered a hate crime, a campus might classify it as a hate or bias incident. Hate and bias incident definitions vary by campus, but most are similar to the University of Wisconsin-Madison's, which states,

> Single or multiple acts toward an individual, group, or their property that have a negative impact and that one could reasonably conclude are based upon actual or perceived age, race, color, creed, religion, gender identity or expression, ethnicity, national origin, disability, veteran status, sexual orientation, political affiliation, marital status, spirituality, cultural, socioeconomic status, or any combination of these or other related factors. Bias or hate incidents include, but are not limited to: slurs, degrading language, epithets, graffiti, vandalism, intimidation, symbols, and harassment that are directed toward or affect the targeted individual or team. Incidents of bias or hate contribute to a hostile campus environment and can occur even if the act itself is unintentional or delivered as a joke, prank, or having humorous intent. (University of Wisconsin-Madison, 2016)

Hate and bias incidents do not meet the level of criminal standards; however, their potential to create a hostile environment is what makes these incidents a top priority in ensuring that the campus environment is safe and secure for all students, especially QPOC students as they face these incidents at alarming rates. Some may suggest that implicit bias is a major factor in why these incidents are occurring and that the lack of cultural competencies and awareness across groups and identities allows for these incidents to continue happening. It is fair to argue that some implicit bias may be present because often college campuses are the first places where students are required to live and engage with individuals who are different from their majority cultures. Yet institutions must begin addressing these issues and providing a platform for biases to be discussed on a deeper level. For this reason, we also find it equally important to address and provide a space for students to report microaggressions that they face both inside and outside the classroom environment.

Hate and bias can often show up on campuses as microaggressions, which are subtle putdowns, indignities, and/or invalidation directed toward a marginalized group (Sue et al., 2007). Microaggressions can include slurs, epithets, and degrading language, and many microaggressions are directed toward marginalized people based on race, gender, and sexual orientation (Shelton & Delgado-Romero, 2011). People on the receiving end of microaggressions often goes through a guessing game in their mind trying to figure out exactly what the person meant by his or her comment, if he or she intended to harm them, or if they are just overreacting. Additionally, these short comments can cause victims to think about the incident many times over for an hour, 4 weeks, 5 months and even years later. In our experience as members of a Hate and Bias Response Team, we have received reports of microaggressions from as far back as 3 or 4 years. Microaggressions don't leave victims' minds as quickly as they leave the perpetrator's mouth. However, it is additionally important to understand that we all carry biases and microaggress others on a daily basis. Although often little can be done with microaggressions through criminal or conduct processes, it is important to hear and address them in an educational and a supportive manner.

When addressing microaggressions from a hate and bias point of view, we encourage reporting of these incidents. Yet in the collection of the data reporting, we look to see whether patterns in these incidents occur (i.e., the same faculty member committing microaggressions or multiple incidents reported against the same student organization). Persistent microaggressions contribute to the same hostile environment as hate crimes and hate and bias incidents. It is not possible to accurately and effectively engage in this work against acts of hate and bias on college campuses without also including microaggressions at the core.

Intersectionality and QPOC

Violence faced by QPOC is a direct attack on the intersections of their race, gender, and sexuality. Intersectionality is a critical starting point to critique, theorize, and understand how QPOC face oppression and inequality as a result of identity-based politics. Yet it is equally important to acknowledge and note, as intersectional scholars have argued, that Black women were at the core of intersectionality's foundation (Alexander-Floyd, 2012; Luft, 2010). Intersectionality, coined by Kimberlé Crenshaw, is defined as the connection of race, gender, class, and sexuality and focuses on the ways these interconnecting identities maintain injustices among Black women (Collins, 2000; Crenshaw, 1991; Lugones, 2007). However, intersectionality theory has been used to address other identities beyond individuals who are both Black and female, and methods have also been developed to explore intersectional privilege, creating awareness of how an individual can be "simultaneously an oppressor and oppressed" (Collins, 2000; McIntosh, 1989; Sacks, 1998; Kimmel,1994). Hancock (2007) suggests that intersectionality needs to "start moving conversations at a broader level of analysis, beyond just exploring the experiences of women of color"

(p. 249). In her approach, she promotes using intersectionality as a research paradigm that focuses on "causal complexity," which "requires recognition of categories that are multiple but not mutually independent" (Hancock, 2007, pp. 251–252).

One of the conflicts for intersectional scholars is the method in which we examine individuals and their identities. The greatest conflict is whether to explore from an additive approach, in which we evaluate an individual's oppression based on their additional marginalized identities (i.e., she is Black plus female plus lesbian plus low income) or to view her as a queer woman of color at a predominately White institution. In using additive approaches, we run the risk of developing a measurement scale that suggests one person is more oppressed than another just because of who he or she is. Hancock (2007) suggests that we move beyond a content specialization based on individual identities and eliminate the "oppression Olympics" that takes place when exploring and categorizing specific experiences. When we approach this work with QPOC, we must also realize that they do not face violence or oppression as a result of one identity more than another; the connection of all their identities and expression (race, gender, gender expression, and sexuality) at once results in their negative experiences. To understand individual identities as being interlocked with one another resists viewing them separately or through an additive model, which is "firmly rooted in the either/or dichotomous thinking of Eurocentric, masculinist thought" and results in a ranking, "quantification and categorization of identities" (Collins, 2000, p. 2). Intersectional analysis must be completed at "multiple levels … by means of an integrative analysis of interaction between the individual and the institution" (Hancock, 2007, p. 251). This would then require a multistep approach when addressing violence faced by QPOC because it is critical to understand how and why QPOC face violence as a result of their intersecting identities, how these identities operate within predominate and hegemonic White heteropatriarchal institutions, and how QPOC's experiences with violence are intersectionally addressed (or excluded) in anti-discrimination laws and policies.

Anti-Discrimination Law for Whom?

In its current structure, the laws and statutes around hate crimes are presented as a form of anti-discrimination law. According to the Anti-Defamation League (2012), "in language, structure, and application, the majority of the nation's hate crime law are directly analogous to anti-discrimination civil rights laws" (p. 2). Yet we question who exactly receives full protection under the current laws. The way in which the protected categories are listed is not representative of all marginalized groups and furthermore lacks the inclusion and protection across varying and multiple, intersecting identity categories, especially for queer people of color. Crenshaw (1989) suggests, "antidiscrimination law is so limited, sex and race discrimination have come to be defined in terms of the experiences of those who are privileged but for their racial or sexual characteristics" (p. 218). In Crenshaw's (1989) article, she argues further that sex discrimination is linked to White women's experiences, and race is linked to those of Black men, which as a result excludes discrimination against Black women. In a similar way, we see this same thing occurring with QPOC because their protection against violence is not guaranteed in the current framing of hate crime definitions. For example, the legal definition of a hate crime in the state of Wisconsin lacks class and gender identity and expression, therefore limiting the ways in which queer and trans people of color (QTPOC) may be protected, under the law, as it relates to the hate violence they experience as a result of one of their central identities. It is also equally important to remember that class, gender, and sexuality are also racialized, so even in the instance that an incident is directly attacking a queer person's gender or sexuality, if he or she is also experiencing this incident as a person of color, there are additional implications to the crime they faced, which differs from a White queer individual because their (marginalized) racial identity is interlocked with their gender and sexuality. Yet with the way in which the law is set up, one could potentially not receive the justice one deserves because of the lack of intersectional and cultural consistency and the exclusion of one's various identities. For QPOC, their experiences with violence and hate are not based on an either/or framework but instead as multiple and interlocked oppression happening at the same time for every one of their identities (Collins, 2000; Mattias de Vries, 2014).

Additionally, as mentioned earlier, each state has differences within its legal definition of a hate crime, and "the breadth of coverage of these laws varies from state to state as well" (Anti-Defamation League, 2012, p. 4). The majority of states include race, religion, and national origin/ethnicity in their list of protected classes for hate crime incidents. Yet only 31 states and the District of Columbia include sexual orientation-based crimes; 26 states and the District of Columbia include coverage of gender-based crimes; 9 states and the District of Columbia include gender identity-based crimes; and 30 states and the District of Columbia include coverage for disability-based crimes (Anti-Defamation League, 2012).

TRENDS AND IMPACTS

When hate crimes and bias incidents occur on campuses, they create hostile environments in the same exact spaces that we expect students to learn, develop, grow, and, most important, live. As we think about hate crimes and bias incidents, it is important to be aware of how they show up in current society and how they might show up on college campuses. According to the Anti-Defamation League (2012), most hate crimes are still motivated by race: 52% of all reported hate crimes in the United States. As one looks deeper into race-motivated hate crimes, 66% of those were anti-Black. The next highest category is motivated by religion: 19% of hate crimes reported are directed toward Jewish and Muslim people (Anti-Defamation League, 2012).

LGBTQ+ people are sadly also highly targeted on college campuses. LGBT people in higher education reported fearing for physical safety, regularly hearing derogatory remarks or jokes regarding sexual identity, observing anti-gay graffiti, and noticing a lack of institutional policies that address anti-LGBT camps climates (Rankin, Weber, Blumenfeld, & Frazer, 2010). An earlier study by Rankin (2003) also showed that 41% of LGBT people believed their institutions were not adequately addressing issues related to sexual and gender identity, and 43% felt their college or university curricula did not represent LGBT people's contributions. Transgender individuals, or those perceived as transgender, face hostile climates that include behaviors such as verbal harassment, threats of violence, acts of discrimination, destruction of their property, and even physical assaults (Rankin, 2003). These incidents of discrimination will lead to fear. Fear not only affects the individual who was the victim but many others who share similar identities. In one study, the researcher found that 54% of LGBT people say they are concerned about being the victim of a hate crime (Harris Interactive, 2006). This fear contrasts strongly with the feelings of most Americans. Fewer than 1 in 10 people in the general population (6% in 2007 and 7% in 2006) frequently worries about hate violence, and just more than half (55% in 2007 and 52% in 2006) never worry about becoming the victim of a hate crime (Carroll, 2006).

In Rankin's (2003) study, which studies 30 campuses and more than 17,000 participants, she found that 42% of lesbian, gay, and bisexual respondents indicated they were the target of harassment based on their sexual orientation; additionally, 30% of people of color reported harassment based on race. Rankin had numerous studies where her primary focus was the experiences of LGBT people on campuses, but she included race as a factor. Although Rankin shared great new knowledge on LGBTQ people of color, White LGBTQ people have set the norms for the LGBTQ community (Nadal, 2013).

Little information is available about how race and LGBTQ+ identity intersect in the research on hate crimes. However, Rankin et al. (2010) found that lesbian, gay, and bisexual people of color were more likely than White lesbian, gay, and bisexual people to experience negative campus climates. In a study examining LGBTQ American Indians, researchers found that 100% of participants reported verbal insults, 79% had experienced threats of attacks, 57% had been chased or followed, 36% had had objects thrown at them, 36% were spat on, 36% were physically assaulted with a weapon, and 29% had been sexually assaulted. All of these percentages were substantially higher than non-American Indian participants. The physical assaults were primarily perpetrated by non-American Indians (Walters, Simoni, & Horwath, 2001).

As a result of negative campus climates, students who have experience with anti-LGBT incidents will have responses that impact not only their academics but their overall health and wellness (Rankin et al., 2010). Rankin et al. (2010) found that "LGBT students who are members of a negative campus climate are at an increased risk for psychological, vocational, and physical health concerns" (p. 34). Meyer (2012) found that hate crimes have long-term effects on students' emotional well-being; moreover, hate crimes often have longer term mental health effects than other crimes (Meyer, 2012).

Bard and Sangrey (1979) found that long-term emotional effects could also lead to ongoing physical effects. The long-term emotional impacts included lower self-esteem, depression and helplessness, fear, internalized hate, and devaluation of self (Bard & Sangrey, 1979). Survivors of hate crimes reported having high levels of psychological distress, which led to sleep disturbances and nightmares, headaches, uncontrollable crying, agitation and restlessness, and increased use of drugs and alcohol (Bard & Sangrey, 1979). According to Mallon (2001), ongoing verbal harassment eroded people's self-worth, self-esteem, and internal sense of feeling accepted. Meyer (2012) found that for gay men who had faced anti-queer violence, the verbal insults they experienced had as much impact as physical assaults.

Many people from marginalized groups have been told their whole lives that they are less valuable, immoral, or living in sin. After a hate crime, QPOC may feel internalized hate and devaluation of self. Walter, Simoni, and Horwath (2001) found that victims of hate and bias struggled with internalized homophobia and felt like their mistreatment was punishment for the way they were living. Most hate crimes toward QPOC are interracial, but Meyers (2012) found that QPOC felt like they were being punished for their queerness when the perpetrator was of the same race as them (Meyer, 2012). Meyer (2012) found that after experiencing anti-queer violence, QPOC felt they have disappointed their entire race. They felt like they have negatively portrayed their racial group, whereas White people did not feel this way.

LGBTQ people do not all have the same experiences, and we should look particularly at how racism and sexism overlaps with homophobia and heteronormativity. Much anti-queer violence is rooted in sexism and misogyny; women and feminine people are often higher targets (Meyer, 2012). Significant intersectional differences exist, and LGBTQ people evaluate anti-queer violence in different ways (Meyer, 2012). The vast differences between the LGBTQ and people of color communities lead us to know that there is no one single way in which QPOC experience anti-queer violence (Meyer, 2012). As much as we might want to generalize how QPOC experience hate crimes and bias incidents, differences are found based on gender, race, and gender expression.

Many factors influence how and why QPOC face hate and bias. Meyer's (2012) research shows that queer women of color often faced violence from heterosexual men when they refused advances from them. Masculine lesbians of color who dated more feminine women often reported they were verbally and physically attacked by heterosexual men (Meyer, 2012). Meyer suggests that these men were punishing the masculine lesbians for converting the feminine women into lesbians. As hate crimes are discussed, the conversation usually turns to who the perpetrators are. For QPOC, it still varies, and little is known about perpetrators. A report from the Human Rights Commission shared that when race was known in hate crimes toward QPOC, White people were the main perpetrators, which was 46% of all attacks (Marzullo & Libman, 2009). Regardless of perpetrators, the impact of hate crimes and bias incidents can significantly affect the academic success of QPOC students. Feeling racism and heterosexim on a daily basis negatively influences students' mental health (Nadal, 2013).

As students deal with the physical and emotional responses to a hate crime, their academics can greatly suffer. The long-term emotional effects can lead to physical responses, such as not being able to sleep or using drugs and/or alcohol as coping mechanisms. Campuses have seen increases in reports of hate and bias incidents, but the mechanisms to support them are often still not in place. Students of color and LGBTQ+ people are the highest targets of hate and bias; therefore, we know that QPOC students have multiple identities that lead them to feeling unsafe and unwelcomed on their campuses. The conversations addressing hate and bias are finally reemerging, and higher education must look at these incidents and students from a complex lens. Institutions of higher education should consider the following recommendations.

RECOMMENDATIONS

The Basics

As we jumped into conversation about supporting QPOC during hate and bias incidents, we are aware that some campuses are still working on creating reporting systems and protocols. A first step is to create a robust reporting system that allows people to report crimes, even if anonymously. Reporting should be easy to access and navigate and be widely publicized. Offer personal outreach to vulnerable populations, such as QPOC, LGBTQ, and religious minorities. Create a campus-wide response plan that considers the many different types of incidents and which campus and community members should be connected to it. Campuses have demanded action, open communication, and transparency. Campuses should be ready to address campus climate issues but also be prepared to have actions that move the campus forward.

Police Training

It is also important to understand that the hate and violence that QPOC face is not isolated to just student-to-student incidents. QPOC also experience bias- and hate-motivated violence at the hands of the state and state actors. Mattias de Vries' (2014) study on transgender people of color found that "fourteen of the Latino, Black, and mixed-race trans men interviewed reported experiencing greater stigmatization by police officers after transitioning, regardless of social class" (p. 16). For this reason, we must also begin to get both campus and local police involved before their first interaction or incident with a QPOC. Law enforcement should participate in cultural trainings and be provided with resources to gain an awareness of the experiences, issues, and needs of QPOC students. Additionally, police and state officials should be proactively integrated into the campus culture and not just reactively as incidents happen. It is critical to establish a liaison through both the campus and local city forces who can be present at large events for student organizations or support groups as a means to build rapport with the student body (e.g., an officer who serves as a campus liaison to fraternity and sorority organizations who is present when they have large house events and also attends their meetings and retreats). The students will build trust with the officer and be able to ask for clarification or help dealing with an issue. This would be equally beneficial for QPOC because they often lack trust in and relationships with police and campus security, possibly causing their issues to go underreported, mishandled, and unnoticed. Additionally, an officer or a staff member from the force is a beneficial asset to any committees or response teams that work to address cases and incidents of hate and bias directly because they can provide guidance, clarification, and effective protocols around hate crimes and bias incidents, categorizations of individual experiences, as well as ensure that each incident is properly handled and investigated.

Counseling Resources

Rankin et al. (2010) found that participants in their study who experienced "both ambient and heterosexist harassment had the lowest overall well-being" (p. 173). Additionally, because more students on college campuses are identifying as transgender, a greater need exists to provide adequate counseling and support for and cater to the direct needs of these students (Rankin et al., 2010). Some of their recommendations for adequate support services include offering support groups for individuals wanting to connect with, share, or disclose related to their sexual identity and gender identity; training for counseling and healthcare staff for LGBTQ needs physically, mentally and emotionally; and offering health insurance support for counseling services for transgender students and staff as well as for surgeries and procedures for gender and hormone reconstruction (Rankin et al., 2010). Finally, we suggest incorporating culturally competent counseling services and staff who are aware of and can address the needs of queer students of color, as well as be fully aware of the struggles they face as students of color on the campus and as queer students.

Intersectional Approaches

Moving forward, intersectional scholars should attempt to further define the ways in which intersectionality can be used to address multiple subjects who experience oppression. As practitioners, we have to give credit to the additive approaches, in which we understand a person to be American Indian + queer + female to understand the complexities of the identities that QPOC students contain. Yet we have to simultaneously push beyond this approach to understand and analyze how these identities are interlocking and the ways in which these students face the impacts of hate and bias based on their race, gender identity and expression, and sexual orientation all at once, and not as one prioritizing the other on any given day or incident. Additionally, we must begin to further explore and analyze how gender and sexual orientations are also racialized, further contributing to the interlockedness of students' experiences based on their identity. Intersectional oppression is also tied to oppressive racialized and gendered experiences related to sexuality. Wadsworth (2011) suggests, "gendered norms, as social control mechanisms, were also simultaneously racialized, with expectations and restrictions—such as concerned labor or sexual availability—allocated differentially across racial groups according to access to white and/or male dominance" (p. 205). This articulation forces us to begin exploring the ways in which QPOC face violence and hate incidents that are not explained or explored through heteronormative, binary, cisgendered privileges and dominant White, LGBT lenses (Mattias de Vries, 2014).

In addition, the expansion of intersectional approaches must continue further the exploration of how to do this work in a way that also addresses structural and institutional factors. Institutions should use what Crenshaw (1991) describes as structural and political intersectional approaches when working to eliminate hostile environments on campuses for QPOC students. In Crenshaw's (1991) articulation, through the structural approach, we further understand how "one burden interacting with preexisting vulnerabilities create yet another dimension of disempowerment" (p. 281). The political approach "highlights the fact that women of color are situated within at least two subordinated groups that frequently pursue conflicting political agendas" (Crenshaw, 1991, p. 282). In using the structural and political approaches to address issues faced by QPOC students, we can begin to explore and critique hate crime laws and institutional policies that include protected classes that maintain a binary understanding of identity that reinforces dominant identities (Mattias de Vries, 2014). This is particularly important when we begin to question how much of the categorizations and protected classes listed in the laws are still based on dominant or heteronormative, binary understandings (i.e., man and woman for gender identities and feminine and masculine expressions; Mattias de Vries, 2014). We recommend exploring other policies at your institutions that may also be categorizing and defining students based on these normative standards, and begin addressing them both intersectionally and inclusively for all students who make up the campus community.

Additionally, the structural and political approaches are helpful when critiquing how we are putting intersectionality into practice and when we ask what true intersectional support looks like. Another recommendation is to begin exploring the support services on campus and the ways in which they intersectionally provide a space for QPOC students. Often we fall short in ensuring there are Black student unions or Latino cultural centers on campus, and we assume this is enough for students of marginalized racial backgrounds to find and create community. Yet we know that students of color who also represent queer and transgender populations are often hypermarginalized in these communal spaces due to lack of acceptance around their sexual orientation, gender identity, or expression. These issues are not isolated to predominately White institutions. Even at minority-serving institutions, such as historically Black colleges and universities, LGBT students still face bias and microaggressions based on their gender and sexual orientation, especially Black lesbian women (Patton & Simmons, 2008). Patton and Simmons (2008) argue, "receiving acceptance of their sexual identities within their racial group may be difficult, particularly if they are expected to deny or hide their sexual orientation" (p. 198). Similarly, the issues they face as a result of their racial identity may also be neglected in spaces where "sexual orientation holds greater value" (Patton & Simmons, 2008, p. 198). In what ways can your cultural and LGBT centers collaborate to ensure support services are implemented for QPOC students on your campuses and not in isolation? Another important recommendation centers on visibility. As much as space is important for QPOC students, it is equally as important to see people represented on campus who are just like them. As practitioners, we find it important to have speakers and guests on campus who are activists, organizers, and celebrities of color, but we must also invite QPOC to increase this visible representation for our students and increase awareness of their experiences and issues to the campus at large.

CONCLUSIONS

Addressing hate crimes and bias incidents on campuses is a daunting task and can leave multicultural, LGBTQ, and social justice workers exhausted and hopeless. Thus, the goal of addressing hate and bias cannot be the responsibility of one team, staff member, or department. Prevention and education efforts must be in place. Regular campus climate assessments must be in place to gain an accurate picture of your campus. Many campuses assume that because they are not getting reports, their students are not being victimized. We seriously question this assumption. Most campuses are afraid to ask the questions because they do not know how they will respond to the answer. As overwhelming as hate and intolerance is in society, as leaders in higher education we must address our campuses and make them safer and more inclusive places than our outside societies.

QPOC are highly targeted with violence, exclusion, and marginality. Although some may assume these are small campus populations, they are populations deeply targeted and neglected once they experience hatred and violence. Our hope is that our campuses can begin to structure systems to take incidents seriously and swiftly. Until we meet vulnerable populations' basic needs, their academic pursuits will suffer and campuses will suffer as well. This chapter is sadly one of few pieces that address violence directed toward QPOC. We encourage researchers and administrators to use this information but take the next step in furthering the research on QPOC. This is the beginning of a conversation long overdue. We wish you hope, peace, and resilience as we take on a long-long effort to end racism, sexism, homophobia, and transphobia.

REFERENCES

Alexander-Floyd, N. G. (2012). Disappearing acts: Reclaiming intersectionality in the social sciences in a post-Black feminist era. *Feminist Formations, 24*(1), 1–25.

Anti-Defamation League. (2012). Hate crime laws: The ADL approach. Retrieved from http://www.adl.org/assets/pdf/combating-hate/Hate-Crimes-Law-The-ADL-Approach.pdf

Bard, M., & Sangrey, D. (1979). *The crime victim's book*. New York, NY: Basic Books.

Collins, P. H. (2000). *Black feminist thought: Knowledge, consciousness, and the politics of empowerment*. New York, NY: Routledge.

Carroll, J. (2006). Americans' crime worries. Gallup Organization. Retrieved July 12, 2016, from www.gallup.com/poll/25081/ Americans-Crime-Worries.aspx

Crenshaw, K. (1989). Demarginalizing the intersection of race and sex: A black feminist critique of antidiscrimination doctrine, feminist theory and antiracist politics. *The University of Chicago Legal Forum*, pp. 139–167.

Crenshaw, K. (1991). Mapping the margins: Intersectionality, identity politics, and violence against women of color. *Stanford Law Review, 43*(1241), 1241–1299.

Dunbar, E. (2006). Race, gender, and sexual orientation in hate crime victimization: Identity politics or identity risk? *Violence and Victims, 21*(3), 323–337.

Fantz, A., Karimi, F., & McLaughlin, E. C. (2016). Orlando shooting 49 killed, shooter pledged ISIS allegiance. Retrieved July 5, 2016, from http://www.cnn.com/2016/06/12/us/orlando-nightclub-shooting/

Hancock, A. (2007). Intersectionality as a normative and empirical paradigm. *Politics and Gender, 3*(2), 248–254.

Harris Interactive. (2006, September 7–14,). Retrieved from www.harrisinteractive.com/news/allnewsbydate.asp?NewsID=1099

Kimmel, M. S. (1994). Masculinity as homophobia. *Sexuality and Intimate Relationships*, pp. 147–151.

Lugones, M. (2007). Heterosexualism and the colonial/modern gender system. *Hypatia, 22*(1), 186–219.

Luft, R. E. (2010). Intersectionality and the risk of flattening difference: Gender and race logics, and the strategic use of antiracist singularity. *The Intersectional Approach: Transforming the Academy Through Race, Class, & Gender*, pp. 100–115.

Mallon, G. P. (2001). Sticks and stones can break your bones: Verbal harassment and physical violence in the lives of gay and lesbian youths in child welfare settings. In M. E. Swigonski, R. S. Mama, & K. S. (Eds.), *From hate crimes to human rights: A tribute to Matthew Shepard* (pp. 63–81) Binghamton, NY: Harrington Park Press.

Marzullo, A. M., & Libman, A. J. (2009). *Research overview: Hate crimes and violence against lesbian, gay, bisexual, and transgender people*. Washington, DC: Human Rights Campaign. Retrieved from http://hrc-assets.s3-website-us-east-1.amazonaws.com//files/assets/resources/Hatecrimesandviolenceagainstlgbtpeople_2009.pdf

Mattias de Vries, K. (2014). Transgender people of color at the center: Conceptualizing a new intersectional model. *SAGE Ethnicities, 0*(0), 1–25.

McIntosh, P. (1989,). White privilege: Unpacking the invisible knapsack. *Peace and Freedom Magazine*.

Meyer, D. (2012). An intersectional analysis of lesbian, gay, bisexual, and transgender (LGBT) people's evaluations of anti-queer violence. *Gender & Society*, *26*(6), 849–873.

Nadal, K. L. (2013). *That's so gay: Microaggression and the lesbian, gay, bisexual, and transgender community*. Washington DC: American Psychological Association.

Office for Civil Rights. (2016). *Education and Title VI*. Retrieved from http://www2.ed.gov/about/offices/list/ocr/docs/hq43e4.html

Patton, L. D., & Simmons, S. L. (2008). Exploring complexities of multiple identities of lesbian in a Black college environment. *Complexities of Multiple Identities*, *59*(3–4), 197–215.

Rankin, S. (2003). *Campus climate for gay, lesbian, bisexual, and transgender people: A national perspective*. The policy institute of the national gay and lesbian task force. Retrieved from http://www.thetaskforce.org/static_html/downloads/reports/reports/CampusClimate.pdf

Rankin, S., Weber, G., Blumenfeld, W., & Frazer, S. (2010). *2010 state of higher education: For lesbian, gay, bisexual & transgender people*. Charlotte, NC: Campus Pride.

Sacks, K. B. (1998). *How Jews became white*. New Brunswick, NJ: Rutgers University Press.

Shelton, K., & Delgado-Romero, E. A. (2011). Sexual orientation microaggressions: The experience of lesbian, gay, bisexual, and queer clients in psychotherapy. *Journal of Counseling Psychology*, *58*(2), 210–221.

Sue, D. W., Capodilupo, C. M., Torino, G. C., Bucceri, J. M., Holder, A. M., Nadal, K. L., & Esquilin, M. E. (2007). Racial microaggressions in everyday life: Implications for counseling. *The American Psychologist*, *62*(4), 271–286.

U.S. Department of Education. (2014). *Questions and answers on Title IX and sexual violence*. Retrieved from http://www2.ed.gov/about/offices/list/ocr/docs/qa-201404-title-ix.pdf

University of Wisconsin-Madison. (2016). *Hate and bias on campus*. Retrieved from https://www.students.wisc.edu/doso/reporting-and-response-to-incidents-of-biashate/

Wadsworth, N. D. (2011). Intersectionality in California's same-sex marriage battles: Acomplex proposition. *Political Research Quarterly*, *64*(1), 200–216.

Walters, K. L., Simoni, J. M., & Horwath, P. F. (2001). Sexual orientation bias experiences and service needs of gay, lesbian, bisexual, transgendered, and two-spirited American Indians. In M. E. Swigonski, R. S. Mama, & K. S. (Eds.), *From hate crimes to human rights: A tribute to Matthew Shepard* (pp. 133–149). Binghamton, NY: Harrington Park Press.

CHAPTER 10

FINDING AND MAKING SPACE

What QPOC Students Face in Rural Places

Vivie Nguyen

This chapter will delve into the ways in which administrators and staff who oversee college LGBT centers/services on rural campuses mindfully understand and provide support for Queer People of Color (QPOC) while considering minimal or nonexisting campus and community resources, bias and discrimination in rural communities, QPOC relationships with communities of color and LGBTQ communities, and rural dating opportunities.

Although some literature exists on QPOC and LGBT people in rural communities, respectively, a dearth of research exists regarding the intersection of these identities and places: QPOC in rural areas. This chapter is based on a study implemented to both confirm and give further visibility to challenges noted in the literature for QPOC and rural LGBT persons, particularly centered on how these unique challenges apply when QPOC identities interface with a rural college setting.

Queer People of Color in Higher Education, pp. 163–178
Copyright © 2017 by Information Age Publishing
All rights of reproduction in any form reserved.

LITERATURE REVIEW

Rural Campus and Community Resources

Rural campuses and communities may lack the visibility and resources for LGBT persons to create and find substantial community. Mitchell (2008) describes a 2-year rural college campus in which few students and faculty openly identified as LGBT. She recounts a faculty member advising a student to conceal his or her sexual orientation while living in a rural community, whereas another student was denied the opportunity to be a leader of a minority student organization based on his gay identity. D'Augelli (2006) reported that the rural university he was a faculty member of, as well as the rural area of his residence, provided no "gay community": the student organization was a handful of students, there were many closeted LGBT people, and one night a week a local dance club was "gay."

Drumheller and McQuay (2010) detail the difficulty of rural LGBT community members to admit their sexual orientation as well as seek out services (if provided) at rural centers in places where religious dogma takes priority over social justice. LGBT persons are quick to conclude that mentalities in highly religious areas are also related to uneducated, conservative, and racist viewpoints, and thereby compartmentalize areas and social spaces where they feel safe and supported apart from the broader community.

Ethnic-Racial and LGBT Community

Emerging adulthood is a significant time for identity development and learning how to be in community and relationships with others (Munsey, 2006). Students of color may opt to join racial-ethnic affinity groups as a conduit to exploring significant aspects of identity. Phinney (1992) conceptualizes ethnic identity as comprised of ethnic identity affirmation, belonging, and commitment. Ethnic identity is also related to self-concept and self-esteem.

In line with ethnic identity research, maintenance of networks and relationships in racial and ethnic communities could be necessary for maintaining self-esteem for gay men of color (Han, 2007) as well. Unfortunately, many communities of color still grapple with understanding and accepting LGBT identities. African American communities may be influenced by heterosexist attitudes (Mays, Cochran, & Rue, 1993; Malebranche, Fields, Bryant, & Harper, 2009), whereas the belief that lesbianism is strictly Western, as well as restrictions on gender roles and sexual restrictions for Asian Americans, contribute to concealment of sexual orientation for people of color (Bridges, Selvidge, & Matthews, 2003).

One can imagine the need for a sense of belonging in one's ethnic affinity group(s) could be especially important within a campus where students of color are few. However, QPOC may be met with traditional values in communities of color that are unaccepting of LGBT identities. Furthermore, QPOC students who seek out LGBT student organizations or campus communities may find that these groups consist of primarily White men. Parallel to national movements and perceptions, LGBT student organizations may mirror the use of White, middle-class male clout to gain support from the broader community (Teunis, 2005), rendering the voice and issues of QPOC silent.

Rural Climate: Bias and Harassment

The often conservative and homogenous nature of rural communities, as well as lower levels of education and socioeconomic status of inhabitants, can contribute to the creation of an unaccepting environment for those who are perceived as different. In a study on LGBT youth (ages 13–21), youth in communities of higher poverty were more victimized based on their gender expression and sexual orientation compared with individuals in affluent areas. Communities with a higher proportion of college graduates had fewer LGBT youth reporting hostility in their school climate. Regional differences may also exist because LGBT youth in the Midwest and South are more likely to report victimization in a school setting than youth in the Northeast (Kosciw, Greytak, & Diaz, 2009). Overall, LGBT youth and adults are the most unsafe in rural communities, which tend to harbor negative attitudes toward LGBT people, lack diversity, and have a higher concentration of people with conservative values and intolerant religious beliefs. As a consequence, these rural perspectives create a more densely concentrated "homophobia" in rural communities compared with non-rural areas (Herek, 2002; Preston et al., 2004; Snively, 2004).

With regard to considering multiple minority identities, LGBT people of color are subject to not only microaggressions and discrimination based on heterosexism but race as well (Balsam, Molina, Beadnell, Simoni, & Walters, 2011). The subjection to microaggressions based on multiple marginalized identities may further emphasize the benefits of communities and organizations to validate the experience of and process discrimination for QPOC, especially within rural areas where conservative and homogenous ideologies are prevalent.

QPOC and Rural Dating

Discrimination, racism, and erasure of non-White identities within the LGBT community can greatly hinder QPOC's experiences in interracial dating. Although Black lesbians may be more likely to have interracial relationships than their White counterparts, to some extent due to their small numbers, challenges arise when White partners are inexperienced and/or insensitive to racial barriers and insults (Jackson & Greene, 2000). Black lesbians may be more inclined to seek non-White partners in relationships if they perceived that discrimination occurred with a White partner in previous relationships (Mays et al., 1993). In instances where White men are interested in African American men, it has been reported by African American gay males that they are often automatically expected to be put in a dominant position during intercourse; if taking on the more submissive role, a power dynamic at times leads to derogatory language and racist expression from White partners. These dynamics strongly play into the trope of African Americans as hypersexual and powerful (Mercer, 1994) or to be of service to White male privilege if taking a submissive role (Teunis, 2005). In contrast, gay Asian men are given the narrative of being exotic and submissive, with gay Latino men also reporting feeling fetishized by White men (Han, 2007). One could imagine how interracial dynamics are potentially exacerbated when dating in a rural community or campus, where the majority of potential partners for people of color are White and may also have limited interactions with diverse populations.

Rural places have unique obstacles with regard to finding romantic or intimate encounters with potential LGBT partners. Utilizing online networks is now the main avenue in which same-sex couples find each other (Ansari, 2015). Although online dating has opened opportunities for LGBT relationships, it also has limitations that are directly related to the locations in which users live. In rural or more isolated communities, virtual dating allows for the opportunity to meet LGBT partners or those interested in same-sex encounters when no physical gay venues or places are available to find each other. However, because a rural campus or community may be particularly limited in LGBT-identified persons, the consistently same group of users is available; variety in partner options only occurs when users search in further cities (Blackwell, Birnholtz, & Abbot, 2014). Furthermore, the stronger stigma of same-sex behavior in rural areas compared with urban communities contributes to many individuals in rural environments being closeted (Preston et al., 2004), which as a consequence may lead to an even sparser virtual or visible community presence of LGBT-identified persons in rural communities.

If we are able to expand all the aforementioned factors related to rural communities as impactful to a college campuses located in rural areas, then the glaring deficit for QPOC to feel fully accepted and supported by a rural campus and local community, other persons of color, predominantly White LGBT communities, and potential dating partners is undeniable.

CURRENT STUDY

The aforementioned literature provides a foundational perspective into the lives of LGBTQ persons in rural areas and the challenges faced by QPOC with regard to discrimination, dating, and navigating belonging to the LGBTQ community and communities of color. However, a significant dearth exists in the literature on how LGBTQ identities in rural areas intersect and interface with being a QPOC.

College can be perceived as an ideal time for some QPOC to come out, as has been noted with gay Korean college men (Strayhorn, 2014). Surely, a rural location and limited racial demographics of an institution can impact the QPOC experience of coming out and finding community. Young adults in the queer community may choose to build on identity experiences both within academia (student organizations) and outside campus, where a sense of anonymity or social life beyond their peers may occur: bars, online dating, and LGBT community resources or events in the surrounding area. However, living and learning in a predominantly White and rural campus poses additional obstacles, including but not limited to: lack of visibility of QPOC in student organizations, fewer dating opportunities in rural versus metropolitan areas, racism within the LGBT community, and discrimination against race and sexual orientation in a rural community.

The current study surveyed rural college campus administrators to assess how various factors—such as campus and community resources, bias and climate concerns; QPOC relationships with student organizations, law enforcement, and dating—impact the experience of QPOC populations at their respective rural colleges.

METHOD

The survey titled *LGBTQ Students of Color on Rural College Campuses* utilized a mixed-methods approach and was comprised of 25 questions (24 open ended and 1 closed), which were topically sectioned into separate survey pages: Campus Demographics; Campus and Community Resources; Bias, Climate, and Relationships; and Overall Assessment of Campus Community in Rural Locations. The survey was inherently programmed to be anonymous/deidentified to ensure participants' confidentiality.

A link to the survey was e-mailed to administrators who work within LGBTQ- or diversity-related services representative of 30 rural college institutions, as well as an electronic list-serv for Student Affairs administrators who work and/or have interest in social justice issues. The survey return rate was 23 participants, reflective of 20 rural institutions (three responses fit the demographic of one institution and will thereby be utilized as an aggregate; one response did not fit the requirements of a rural institution and was omitted from analysis).

For the purpose of the survey, the following definitions were utilized:

> **Rural:** "Rural" encompasses all population, housing, and territory not included within an urban area. Whatever is not urban is considered rural according to the U.S. Census definition. The Office of Rural Health Policy accepts all nonmetro counties as rural (metro defined as a core urban area of 50,000 people or more by the White House Office of Management and Budget).
>
> **Person (student) of color:** "Person of color refers to racial and ethnic minority groups. People of color is an all-inclusive term that incorporates African Americans, Latinas/os, Asians and Pacific Islanders, and Native Americans (for this survey, we are also including individuals who identify as Middle Eastern and multiracial as persons of color).... Among the terms linked to or derived from people of color is queer people of color."—Salvador Vidal Ortiz

Campus Demographics

- The majority of campus institutions that responded to the survey were from the Midwest (74%, 14 institutions), followed by 3 from the Northeast, 1 from the Great Plains, and 1 from the Southwest.
- Sizes of the institution were categorized as small (<5,000 students), midsized (5,000–15,000), or large (>15,000). Seventeen schools (89%) indicated that they were small in size, with one being midsized and one large.
- Institutions ranged from 35 to 75 miles away from a major metropolitan area, with a collective average of 52 miles.
- The range in percentage of the student of color population reported for all campuses was 8% to 35%.

Due to the small survey population, demographic data are not compared between groups; rather, the following study findings are presented in aggregate form and within corresponding/numbered thematic categories that parallel the literature review presented at the beginning of the chapter.

RESULTS

Rural Campus and Community Resources

Recruitment and Retention

The vast majority of responses indicated that the location of their campus impacted recruitment and retention efforts for minority and marginalized communities. Obstacles that influenced recruitment and retention included proximity to metropolitan areas, isolated campus area and size, fear and hesitation of prejudice and conservative values of surrounding campus area, and lack of diversity on campus and surrounding community.

> I would say that the location makes a huge difference because many students of color come from urban environments that tend to have more "excitement" or appeal than (campus). Because (campus) is in (Midwest), many people have this idea that it is somehow disconnected from culture or diversity, which tends to be true in some respects, and lacks healthy or safe places for people of color to grow and thrive in this area.

> Who the hell wants to be in (Midwest) when you're black and queer? Certainly not me, and I'm both. The lack of social options, recreational landscape, a small population, etc., make the campus incredibly unappealing. POC from more racially diverse areas find the small Midwestern town and landscape incredibly jarring, boring, and uncomfortable.

> The area outside of (campus) is fairly conservative which might dissuade minority/ marginalized populations.

Campus (Student and Administrative/Staff)-Based Resources

Survey participants were asked about student- and administrative/ staff-based resources on their respective campuses. An example of a student-based resource would be a student organization or group, whereas an administrative/staff-based resource would be a center or office overseen/ supervised by professional staff.

LGBTQ (Q for Queer and/or Questioning). All survey respondents who answered questions on LGBTQ student- and administrative/staff-based resources reported that their institution has a student-based organization for LGBTQ-identified persons. The majority of participants stated that their campus also offered student groups specific to various identities within the LGBTQ community, such as a trans advocacy, women's, and men's groups. Of these campuses, two stated that they have an LGBTQ-themed housing option.

With regard to administrative/staff-based resources, the majority of participants mentioned an inclusion or a multicultural office and/or a gender, sexuality, LGBTQ-based center. A few respondents noted cultural-awareness weeks, academic courses, and faculty and staff support for LGBTQ students. Two participants stated that they were not sure whether any administrative/staff-based resources for LGBTQ students existed. Two respondents noted that there was an LGBTQ office but that the office was only staffed by one person.

Students of Color. All but one response reported having student-based organizations and/or leadership opportunities for students of color. These student groups included but were not limited to groups centered on racial affinity, international, and religious identities. With the exception of one participant, all respondents reported that administrative/staff-based resources were present and consisted of offices dedicated to diversity, inclusion, multicultural, and international efforts and populations.

Queer People of Color. When asked about student- and administrative/staff-based resources for QPOC, the majority of respondents reported that a QPOC student group did not exist or they had no answer/knowledge of one; two responses noted that a QPOC student group existed on their campus.

> There is nothing that is specific to LGTBQ students of color, rather our students, faculty/staff move throughout all of these groups. We are small enough that there is a lot of overlap within many of our affinity groups and resources provided.

> There is no formal QPOC group on campus, though there have been some attempts. It seems as though QPOC are dispersed in other student organizations and affinity groups. The LGBTQ student organization on campus has been primarily white and male-centered in the past 2–3 years, which has caused some hesitation for QPOC to join.

With regard to administrative/staff-based resources specific to QPOC, two participants responded with none or no answer. The rest of the participants alluded to aforementioned departments such as diversity, inclusion, and multicultural-type offices and/or gender and sexuality centers. No response specifically spoke to structural or institutional offices, centers, and/or staff whose role was primarily to serve QPOC.

Queer Faculty/Staff of Color. Participants were asked whether they were aware of any queer faculty or staff of color on campus. This was the only survey question posed as a closed yes/no. Although the majority of responses were "yes," more than a third of participants reported that they were not aware of any queer-identified faculty or staff of color on their campus.

Of those who responded "yes" to having an awareness of queer faculty/staff of color on campus, the next question inquired whether the queer faculty/staff of color population was numerous and visible. The vast majority of participants spoke to the visibility of queer faculty/staff of color; however, half of respondents reported that the queer faculty/staff of color population was not numerous on their campus. "Some professors are open about their sexuality while others are not as much … some professors "come out" to their students while some may not think it important. That being said, I know that my school's LGBTQ Center is organizing a monthly talk with queer faculty and staff. Staff members are typically out to students, however they are not numerous. I would say they are neither numerous nor visible; I can count them on one hand. Half that number for those that are out. Of those that are not out, it has less to do with personal confidence in identity and more to do with perceived/real politics as well as how much of their personal lives they wish to keep, theirs.

Community-Based Resources

In line with the literature review, all survey respondents conveyed a complete lack of weekend and night-life social options in the surrounding rural community for LGBT-identified young adults. Any LGBT social spaces that participants alluded to or were aware of consisted of events put on by their campus, not the local community.

On availability of LGBT weekend and night-life social options in the local, rural community:

Not outside the heteronormative context of socialization. On campus, yes … in the local community, definitely not.

Findings related to the *Rural Campus and Community Resources* component of the survey aligned with challenges noted in the literature for individuals who reside within campuses and/or communities in rural areas. The location of a rural campus impacts recruitment and retention of minority and marginalized persons because students who are coming from more diverse environments have hesitations of places that are demographically homogenous and may hold more conservative values than nonrural environments. Although the rural LGBTQ campus resources found in this study are quite robust in contrast to the lack of LGBT campus resources noted in the articles by Mitchell (2008) and D'Augelli (2006), as well as unanimous participant reports of resources available for people of color, there is a lack of specific student spaces, staff, and resources dedicated to QPOC. Thereby, queer students of color on rural campuses must straddle between what resources are available for the LGBT community and for people of color, respectively. Furthermore, although most of our participants reported that queer staff and faculty of color were "out" in most settings, the population is notably few in number (as validated by more than a third of respondents not being aware of a queer faculty/staff of color presence on their campus).

QPOC and Their Relationships With Racial/Ethnic and LGBTQ Student Organizations

Although some survey respondents noted that QPOC students generally have a good relationship with racial-ethnic affinity communities and/or organizations, many participants answered that QPOC feel alienated in ethnic-racial spaces where QPOC identities are not made visible.

They (LGBTQ people of color) are members (of ethnic/racial-affinity orgs.) generally, but few of the orgs highlight or make visible queer identities.

I believe students are pretty involved with the ethnic-racially based groups.

From what I've seen and heard, this varies student to student. Some love the queer people of color organization because it fulfills a need whereas some do not like it for reasons like: they don't like who is in it, they do not have time to go, or do not feel they have to go to this group to validate them. Overall, though, I think the relationship isn't entirely positive.

I'm not sure that there is that much interaction between them. It feels like the ethnic- racially based groups work together, but that there isn't that much cross over between the two.

Communities of color can very much be conservative when it comes to queer identity due to strong religious ties or traditional ideology passed on through generations.

When asked about QPOC relationships with LGBTQ-based student organizations, participants reported that, although some QPOC are part of these organizations, a lack of racial visibility and addressing of racial dynamics is present.

Most of the LGBTQ club membership is White.

They (LGBTQ people of color) are members generally but few of the orgs highlight or make "visible racial dynamics."

About half of queer students of color participate in queer groups on campus.

QPOC may not see themselves reflected in the LGBT student organization's leadership or programming. Thereby, it may be difficult for them to assess whether they would belong in such a space or feel validated.

Survey responses related to QPOC and their relationship to communities of color and LGBTQ communities directly reflect obstacles previously mentioned in the literature: QPOC have difficulty feeling validated and visible in their queer identities within communities of color and, in reverse, for their racial/ethnic identities in primarily White LGBT communities

Overall, participants responded that resources for QPOC are few, and the lack of availability of community both on and off campus is difficult for QPOC to both find and navigate.

Many (QPOC) are secretive about their identities and do not share widely so there is no support to speak of—it's generally avoided. Many feel that there are few resources on campus for queer students of color, and there are none in our town. The main difficulty is that there is little to no support for students unless they turn to other students.

Rural Climate: Bias and Harassment

Two-thirds of institutions conveyed that they have a hate or bias reporting system on campus. When asked about bias/harassment that QPOC may face on campus, participants alluded to more subtle forms of discrimination, such as microaggressions. Only one response conveyed overt use of hate language for LGBTQ/QPOC identities. The participants' responses convey various views: LGBTQ and racial identities may be seen as separate issues to one individual, whereas another perspective can convey that these marginalized identities are intertwined.

> My perception is that we are a very open campus. We are known to incoming students as being a LGBTQ friendly campus. We are struggling with our populations of color in the same way the other campuses are ... working with campus safety to ensure they are stopping students with cause, that microaggressions in the classroom are being addressed, etc. But I am unaware that students belonging to both identities feel that they are harassed or treated with bias because they hold both identities. Rather it is more likely that something happens more likely due to race.

> Although students claim to be accepting and politically correct in every way, they are unknowingly microaggressive. I, for example, have experienced students (and on one occasion a college employee) mocking my mannerism such as using gesturing with my hands. Students are also uncomfortable when queer students, two queer men especially, engage in public displays of affection like holding hands and kissing. While these are not directed at a student's race/ethnicity and sexuality, I believe they are inextricably linked.

> There have been a few situations that have occurred at fraternity parties or houses where LGBTQ students and QPOC students have been called derogatory names related to sexual orientation and have been shouted at to leave the premise. Students of color have also been called racial slurs as they walk past certain Greek houses.

Compared with bias-related situations on rural campuses, all responses conveyed that more overt forms of discrimination occur in the surrounding local community.

> While the college is relatively progressive, the town it is in is not as accepting. Students have had racist slurs and epithets yelled at them by townspeople driving by and many students of color (especially women of color) fear walking around alone especially at night. Queer students also feel the need to hide their sexuality and act/pass as straight in order to avoid harassment. On a few occasions, pick-up trucks have driven through campus with confederate flags on them.

> More likely to be overt homophobia or racism (in local community).

> If you're brown you're probably going to get stared at and if you're gay you're going to get stared and grumbled at.

Reports on student relationships with campus and local law enforcement were mixed; half of the responses noted that the relationship between students, particularly those of communities of color, and law enforcement needed improvement or was poor in nature. Other responses conveyed that they have not heard of any negative relationship existing between law enforcement and the QPOC community.

> Low faith in campus police and safety. Communities of color report being profiled. The relationship between queer students of color and campus security/law enforcement is fine. I've never heard of negative experiences between students and them. I'm Black and I don't call local police. I only call the college security. Students in general do not have a good relationship with the security or police system at our school and in our town, respectively.

Findings related to bias, harassment, and climate from this survey paralleled the literature that rural communities are perceived to be and are experienced as more overtly homophobic in nature when it comes to bias and discrimination against the LGBTQ community than nonrural areas. The survey responses related to campus climate conveyed that individuals on a college campus were more likely to convey bias and discrimination through more subtle means (e.g., microaggressions), but racial and homophobic undercurrents are still present. In validation of the literature, responses conveyed that QPOC have to deal with discrimination for racial as well as LGBTQ identities.

QPOC and Rural Dating

With regard to rural dating, responses conveyed the lack of options on campus and in the surrounding and nearby rural community, with even fewer opportunities when it comes to a desire to date another QPOC. Mention was also made of lack of anonymity in a small community as well as hesitations for White LGBTQ individuals to date people of color.

> Because this population is growing within both of these identities one would believe that they feel the prospects are increasing. However, I still see a lot of students dating people from other schools or the local community. This could be because we are a small school and it is difficult for anyone to date and break up and/or hookup when so many people know each other.

> There are very few queer students of color and students often joke that the pickings are slim but there is some truth to this. Students have a difficult time finding partners of color because there are so few.

> There are few options. White queers remain exclusive. Brown queers remain alone.

> I think LGBTQ students of color are definitely having a very different experience than LGBTQ students that do not identify as kids of color. I think that there is more of a stigma being an LGBTQ student of color so I don't think people are as willing to engage in a relationship with them.

> I've had queer men of color tell me that their "taste" for an ideal mate has changed after moving from an urban area to this campus. That now, they prefer White men over men of color. I am not sure if this has to do with a true change in attraction or adapting to a situation. However, they are also internalizing or are disappointed in how gay White men are disinterested.

As noted in the literature, interracial dynamics are at play for dating within the LGBTQ community. Specifically, participants mentioned stigma as well as disinterest for QPOC partners from White LGBTQ persons. Furthermore, our respondents' answers also show the limited dating options in the LGBTQ community in rural areas, such as already knowing or having experienced most if not all LGBTQ partners available in the area and the need to expand beyond proximity to find dating opportunities.

SUMMARY AND FUTURE IMPLICATIONS

In summary, the findings in this survey align with the literature on QPOC and LGBT persons in rural communities, respectively. When these identities intersect, QPOC in rural communities face the same as well as the combined challenges noted in the literature for QPOC and LGBT persons in rural communities. QPOC on rural college campuses and communities are hesitant of conservative ideologies in rural areas as are the recipients of discrimination (based on race and sexual orientation) related to those values; have difficulty feeling validated and visible in both communities of color and in the primarily White LGBTQ community on campus; lack numerous and visible adult role models who are also QPOC; and struggle with the lack of rural LGBTQ dating opportunities, especially when attempting to find a relationship with another QPOC.

Additional findings in the study note the QPOC community's mistrust of campus and local law enforcement. This skepticism could be influenced by perceived discrimination; interactions with law enforcement; and national attention of law enforcement, which has shown numerous cases where people of color, individuals of the LGBTQ community, and QPOC are mistreated. Throughout the survey, participants noted how their campuses have more resources and spaces for QPOC compared with the local rural community, but that campus resources, too, are limited.

Recommendations for campus administrators and professionals include:

- Mentor and guide racial/ethnic affinity groups as well as LGBTQ student organizations to consider an intersectional and inclusive lens toward membership in considering the need for community from QPOC, and encourage students to either consider forming a QPOC organization and/or provide events and dialogues that directly address and include QPOC issues within existing racial-ethnic and LGBTQ organizations on campus.
- Capitalize on the ability of "out" faculty/staff of color to mentor, guide, and provide role modeling for QPOC students.
- Offer campus-wide, departmental, and student organizational discussions on issues of mistrust and mistreatment of QPOC by national law enforcement and how this applies to or is perpetuated by campus law enforcement; and implement inclusive training modalities to campus and local law enforcement within the context of national news and mistrust of law enforcement by marginalized persons.
- Ensure that a bias and hate crime report system is in place on your campus through advocacy and the use of student information, surveys, focus groups, and other forms of information gathering to compel the administration that a hate/bias-response team and/or report system is necessary in supporting the safety of all student identities on campus.
- If a bias response system is already in place on your campus, talk with members of the team or initial responders to be sensitive to and competent with QPOC issues; provide outreach and visibility that the bias and hate crime reporting system is open to and supportive of situations experienced by QPOC; and ensure that a team member who is well versed in QPOC issues is available for QPOC students to speak to if they so choose.

REFERENCES

Ansari, A. (2015) *Modern Romance*, 85. New York, NY: Penguin Press.

Balsam, K. F., Molina, Y., Beadnell, B., Simoni, J., & Walters, K. (2011). Measuring multiple minority stress: The LGBT People of Color Microaggressions Scale. *Cultural Diversity & Ethnic Minority Psychology, 17*(20), 163–174.

Blackwell, C., Birnholtz, J., & Abbot, C. (2014). Seeing and being seen: Co-situation and impression formation using Grindr, a location-aware gay dating app. *New Media & Society*, 1–20.

Bridges, S. K, Selvidge, M. M. D., & Matthews, C. R. (2003). Lesbian women of color: Therapeutic issues and challenges. *Journal of Multicultural Counseling and Development, 31*, 113–120.

D'Augelli, A. R. (2006). Coming out, visibility, and creating change: Empowering lesbian, gay, and bisexual people in a rural university community. *American Journal of Community Psychology, 37,* 203–210.

Drumheller, K., & McQuay, B. (2010). Living in the buckle: Promoting LGBT outreach services in conservative urban/rural centers. *Communication Studies, 61*(1), 70–86.

Han, C. S. (2007). They don't want to cruise your type: Gay men of color and the racial politics of exclusion. *Social Identities, 13*(1), 51–67.

Herek, G. M. (2002). Heterosexuals' attitudes toward bisexual men and women in the United States. *Journal of Sex Research, 39*(4), 264–274.

Jackson, L. C., & Greene, B. (2000). African-American lesbian and bisexual women in feminist- psychodynamic psychotherapies: Surviving and thriving between a rock and a hard place. In L. C. Jackson & B. Green (Eds.), *Psychotherapy with African-American women: Innovative psychodynamic perspectives and practice* (pp. 82–125). New York, NY: Guilford Press.

Kosciw, J. G., Greytak, E. A., & Diaz, E. M. (2009). Who, what, where, why, and when: Demographic and ecological factors contributing to hostile school climate for lesbian, gay, bisexual, and transgender youth. *Journal of Youth and Adolescence, 38,* 976–988.

Mays, V. M., Cochran, S. D., & Rue, S. (1993). The impact of perceived discrimination on the intimate relationships of Black lesbians. *Journal of Homosexuality, 25,* 1–15.

Mercer, K. (1994). *Welcome to the jungle: New positions in black cultural studies.* New York, NY: Routledge.

Mitchell, D. (2008). I thought composition was about commas and quotes, not queers: Diversity and campus change at a rural two-year college. *Composition Studies, 32*(2), 23–50.

Munsey, C. (2006). Emerging adults: The in-between age. *American Psychological Association, 37*(6), 68.

Phinney, J. (1992). The Multigroup Ethnic Identity Measure: *A new scale for use with adolescents and young adults from diverse groups. Journal of Adolescent Research, 7,* 156–176.

Preston, D. B., D'Augelli, A. R., Kassab, C. D., & Starks, M. T. (2007). The relationship of stigma to the sexual risk behavior of rural men who have sex with men. *AIDS Education and Prevention, 19*(3), 218–230.

Snively, C. A. (2004). Building community-based alliances between GLBTQQA youth and adults in rural settings. *Journal of Gay & Lesbian Social Services, 16*(3/4), 99–112.

Strayhorn, T. L. (2014). Beyond the model minority myth: Interrogating the experiences of Korean American gay men in college. *Journal of College Student Development, 55*(6), 586–594.

Teunis, N. (2005). Sexual objectification and the construction of whiteness in the gay male community. *Culture, Health, & Sexuality, 9*(3), 263–275.

CHAPTER 11

MEETING AT THE INTERSECTIONS

Using Queer Race Pedagogy to Advance Queer Men of Color in Higher Education

Jonathan P. Higgins

In recent studies, issues relating to equity, access, and retention for men of color in higher education have become topics of high priority. Because men of color often struggle with issues pertaining to identity development in higher education (Stevens, 2004), it is important to discuss the needs that queer men of color have when seeking higher education. In these discussions, the intersecting identities that these young men of color have play a pivotal role in examining what higher education institutions must do to retain them. However, queer (gay, bisexual, same gender-loving) men of color (QMOC) are often marginalized in higher education (Woodson, 2013); this leaves room to discuss the issues that QMOC have academia and what needs to be done to help them find academic success during such an important time of their lives.

The experiences that QMOC have in higher education can only be defined as complicated. Many QMOC are the first in their family to go to a

Queer People of Color in Higher Education, pp. 179–194
Copyright © 2017 by Information Age Publishing
All rights of reproduction in any form reserved.

4-year institution and are often the first to leave home to aspire to any form of higher education (Strayhorn, Blakewood, & DeVita, 2008). Granted, many QMOC are offered access to multiple resources when seeking higher education, but the "one-size-fits-all" mentality of advising and mentoring does not address the sociocultural needs of QMOC within the university community.

Research finds that QMOC often struggle when negotiating the intersections of both race and sexuality (Higgins, 2015). For these young men, assistance is needed when navigating campus climate as well as when trying to acclimate to the demands of the first-year experience (Sanlo, Rankin, & Schoenberg, 2002).

In 2005, the majority of research conducted about queer student experience has focused primarily on students who self-identify as white or not of color (Goode-Cross & Tager, 2011). The primary focus maintains conversation on leadership but never addresses the need for conversations on intersectionality (Misawa, 2010a). Since 2009, the California Postsecondary Education Commission has reviewed research and data and worked with local higher education officials on issues relating to queer students of color, particularly QMOC. The commission found that queer students from different institutions face multiple challenges when seeking to obtain higher education, with retention being the greater issue for QMOC (Angeli, 2009).

Most of the information pertaining to the needs of the queer population has come from institutions that are recognized as predominately white institutions (Patton & Simmons, 2008). Current research indicates that as issues evolve for queer students, so does the need for research regarding the intersectional identities of QMOC. The research must be centered on the intersectional experiences that QMOC have related to both sexuality and race because for many, problems are not just connected to their racial experiences but also how their sexual orientation shapes their sense of belonging within society and higher education.

QMOC AND HIGHER EDUCATION

The experiences that QMOC have when seeking higher education can be both exclusive and uninclusive. QMOC often deal with ideals that promote and reinforce the whiteness of gay life (Han, 2007). Many of these ideals deal with concepts of privilege and experiences that do not take into consideration experiences related to the intersections of their identity. Each of these concepts promotes institutionalized racism and oppression, never taking into consideration the need for queer voices to be included in the narrative of higher education experience. For many QMOC, issues related to the intersections of race and sexuality are often overshadowed as the reality remains for many that "to be gay in America means to be gay and white" (Han, 2007, p. 54). According to Han (2007), the reality for many QMOC is:

> Despite the civil rights dialogue used by the gay community, many "gay" organizations and members of the "gay" community continue to exclude men of color from leadership positions and "gay" establishments, thus continuing to add to the notion that "gay" equals "White." Likewise, gay men of color experience homophobia within their racial and ethnic communities. (p. 51)

Han's (2007) narrative explained how QMOC often suffer from lower levels of self-esteem and issues connecting to higher identity development and high levels of internalized homophobia (Goode-Cross & Tager, 2011). P. B. Harper (2000) expressed that often anything related to queer studies is tied to topics involving "whiteness." This negates the experiences of QMOC, further marginalizing them within the higher educational spectrum. That significance extends far beyond the objection—as valid and urgent as it is—that what is currently recognized as queer studies, for instance, is unacceptably Euro-American in orientation, its purview effectively determined by the practically invisible—because putatively nonexistent—bounds of racial whiteness (Grzanka, 2014, p. 57). Grzanka (2014) further explained that QMOC sit in silence about their experiences because the conversations do not allow for them to include issues related to intersections of their identities.

Although many QMOC feel invisible in the gay community, the greater issue focuses on providing space for QMOC to share their experiences (Fine, 2012). As shared by Chang and Culp (2002), higher education professionals must move toward a way of thinking post-intersectionality while allowing QMOC the opportunity to tell their stories beyond marginalization. This postintersectionality movement must include conversations that dissect the issues that both men of color and QMOC have within higher education and how higher education professionals are going to support the needs of both intersecting identities (Fotopoulou, 2012). Because intersections are just more than race and sexuality, recognizing each element of the discourse will allow for these stories to be better understood. Further, it will allow for "individuals in power relations" to give greater attention to the needs of QMOC (Robinson, 1999) due to the issues these men face when navigating the intersections of their racial and sexual identities in a higher education setting.

FROM THEORY TO PRACTICE: PEDAGOGY FOR UNDERSTANDING EXPERIENCES

Queer race pedagogy and intersectionality help to substantiate the experiences that QMOC have when negotiating both race and sexuality. Utilizing concepts of queer race pedagogy and intersectionality when talking about a QMOC's experience in higher education not only validates each individual experience but also provides voice and context to how each student negotiates his experience.

Queer race pedagogy evolves from the theories of critical race theory (CRT) and queer theory. CRT allows us to describe the hierarchical categories that influence power relations in different racial groups (Misawa, 2010b). As for queer theory, the concept notes that identities are not who we are but a part of which we are (Sullivan, 2003).

Misawa's (2005) queer race pedagogy (QRP) concept focuses on the needs of queer students of color to be recognized on a systematic level. Misawa (2010a) explained that QRP is designed to assist QMOC in discussing issues related to their racial and sexual experiences. He also believed that the experiences of QMOC are typically overlooked and ignored in mainstream discourse of queer rights in higher education and therefore need further attention. Misawa (2010a) went on to explain that conventional pedagogy is not enough to serve the needs of QMOC because these students often deal with more complicated issues when seeking a higher education. QRP embodies conceptual frameworks taken from ideas of intersectionality and allows further discussion of how identities converge (Crenshaw, 1989).

QRP serves more than one purpose. It demands that educators address as many issues as possible when dealing with QMOC in relation to sociocultural issues, power dynamics, and equity of education (Misawa, 2010a). This pedagogy pushes educators out of their comfort zones in the classroom while taking into account the various identities that intersect in the classroom. QRP helps educators to see the sociocultural issues in relation to power and challenges those in positions of power to use critical thinking in creating systems to help queer students of color succeed.

QRP can be applied in helping to empower QMOC in higher education by implementing space for counterstorytelling. Misawa (2010) states that allowing counterstorytelling in spaces such as pride centers or classrooms helps to create a learning community and environment where QMOC can feel safe about sharing elements of their lived experiences. The author also states that implementing QRP into elements of class assignments and events allows for the exploration of said positionalities such as race and sexual orientation.

Queer Race Pedagogy and Positionality

Misawa's (2005, 2010a) concept of QRP is heavily informed by the concept of positionality. Positionality in QRP shows that queer students of color should not be defined by their fixed identities. For QMOC to succeed, institutions must acknowledge that the campus population is made up of all races, classes, genders, and sexual orientations.

Positionality sets the foundation for QRP, helping to contextualize current issues in higher education in relation to the needs of queer students of color. Misawa (2010b) explained that before QRP can be used to help prescribe a solution to issues related to queer students, one must get the "position" of issues in higher education. Misawa (2010a) made it clear that the most prevalent issues for QMOC are related to access of power, racism, and homophobia. Knowing this, institutions must acknowledge that all of the identities held by QMOC are relational and complex to effectively fix issues related to power and social control. Positionality allows us to acknowledge the fluidity of the identities associated with QMOC. QMOC must not be categorized or labeled, and those in positions of power should not categorize the needs of QMOC as universal. Examining concepts of intersectionality allows for more discussion of how race and sexuality play a role in the first-year experience of QMOC on a systematic level.

QRP and Intersectionality

The concept of intersectionality is often viewed as an important paradigm to queer research (McCall, 2014). Intersectionality introduces the important problems in relation to the practice of queer research, and it also brings to the forefront the political struggles that queer people of color have when discussing their lived experiences (Phoenix & Pattynama, 2006).

The concept of intersectionality defines the systematic study of differences that are interlinked with perceptions of race, gender, sexuality, class, and ethnicity (Fotopoulou, 2012). Intersectionality gives attention to how all these issues connect while giving attention to the interrelation of one's identities. When using intersectionality as a point of focus, difference is seen as the central concept in relation to subordination. Intersectionality provides better insight into the experiences and offers an explanation as to why they are important.

The term and topic is now being used to discuss the needs of QMOC (Brown, 2012), though the concept was introduced over 20 years ago. This concept discussed how intersectionality focuses on gaining better insight into the "limitations of one-dimensional, identity-based structures of inequality and oppression" (Brown, 2012, p. 542). Because educators often only focus on one side of oppression when discussing issues related to access and equity for QMOC, professionals risk negating the experiences that these students have by ignoring the intersections of their identity. Brown (2012) explained that the goal of Crenshaw's (1989) theory was to specify the experiences of those who are oppressed while preventing the "occlusion of center oppressions when analyzed by political forces" (p. 542). Intersectionality looks at all forms of oppression while providing a solid solution to the issues QMOC have at the institutional level, specifically relating to their racial and sexual identities.

QRP positionality and intersectionality allow for discussion related to the need for higher education to recognize the experiences that QMOC have when seeking a higher education. Although these concepts provide a framework for discussing issues pertaining to identity, more conversation must be had regarding the need for identity development, and for identity development to focus not just on acknowledging the intersecting identities but providing QMOC with a better knowledge of how to negotiate said identities.

QUEER IDENTITY DEVELOPMENT

> *Living our identities is much like breathing. We don't have to ask ourselves each morning who we are. We simply are.... Identity is never fixed; it continually evolves. But something in it stays constant; even when we change, we are recognizably who we have always been. Identity links the past, the present and the social world into a narrative that makes sense. It embodies both change and continuity.*

(Josselson, 1996, p. 29)

Recent studies showed that a larger part of understanding one's race and sexuality is linked to identity development. Bilodeau and Renn (2005) wrote that there continues to be a wealth of growing research regarding the new perspectives of experiences and how they relate to the intersections of identities. These new perspectives related to queer-identity development expound on the notion of how QMOC negotiate their multiple intersecting identities and how the identity development process is much different than that represented by white, Westernized men.

Although the Cass (1979) Identity Development Model is referenced when discussing the coming-out experiences of queer men, Stevens (2004) believed that this development model is not inclusive of QMOC. This model does not give light to diversity within the community and fails to provide greater insight as to how QMOC negotiate their multiple identities when going through each stage. Although the Cass (1979) model provides insight into the process of learning about one's identity, it fails to give attention to the racial and cultural dimensions as they relate to queer identity (Stevens, 2004).

The identity of QMOC is often shaped by how each of them views his life experiences within the classroom and at home (Torres, Jones, & Renn, 2009). Torres et al. (2009) wrote this is where many of them begin to formulate belief systems that relate to their multiple intersecting identities. For many QMOC, the identity development process begins to center on "fitting in" and how they can be like the majority (their white counterparts who are often heterosexual) versus coming up with their own definition as to what it means to have multiple identities. Torres et al. (2009) continued in stating that in order for QMOC to know who they are, we must give attention to the multiple identities that these young men carry.

Identity development for QMOC must go beyond viewing elements of their identity as mutually exclusive. For QMOC to fully know who they are, "attention must be given to racial identity and sexual identity" (Torres et al., 2009, p. 586). Further, one must realize that for QMOC to fully be developed, social identity must not overshadow the need to better comprehend each intersecting identity. One must be willing to reflect more on the lived experiences of QMOC and how each of their identities goes beyond the limiters of a single identity within the campus community.

For many QMOC who enter higher education, many of their experiences relate to how they negotiate the intersections of their identity. The first step to making sense of their experiences begins with learning how race plays a role in their first-year experience. For many QMOC, race is often the hardest identity to negotiate when discussing elements of queer identity due to the pressures that come with being a man of color within a college institution (Goode-Cross & Tager, 2011).

For many QMOC seeking a higher education, accepting the intersectionality of their queer and racial identities is often a difficult process. Because of previous life experiences, many QMOC often struggle when recognizing how both identities can exist in the same accord. Rosado (2011) wrote that for many QMOC, personal experiences and upbringing often shape the way they learn and interact with other students in college in relation to their sexual identity. Because many QMOC face issues pertaining to the intersections of their racial and sexual identities, some QMOC struggle with coming to terms with their identity and what it means for their overall experience.

The issues that QMOC face are not just about race or sexuality. Woodson (2013) wrote that the issue for many QMOC is tied to concepts of positionality, where many of them feel as if they are not being given the attention they need to excel as a person who identifies as both queer and of color.

The battle of QMOC is not only connected to how they are treated by nonmembers of the queer community who do not identify as a person of color, but also how they are often treated by other white men in the community. For these young men, the issue is connected to the validation of their struggles and how they feel they do not belong in a community that promotes being white.

The common problem that many QMOC face when dealing with the complexities of their sexual orientation and race falls in line with the expectations of having to hide or deny their sexual orientation as a person of color (Wall & Washington, 1991). It is often found that the issue of dismissing race and sexual orientation is common when attending a 4-year institution. Although queer sexual preference remains synonymous with being a woman (Harper & Harris, 2010), programs and discussion of sexuality and gender within higher education are often noninclusive of male experiences. It can also be stated that when talking about gender expression, race, and sexuality within higher education, studies often only focus on "the binaries of sexuality and gender roles" (Harper & Harris, 2010, p. 6). It is a common notion that most QMOC often struggle with concepts of masculinity because masculinity is often seen as a word that promotes heterosexism. Harper and Harris (2010) helped us to see that for many QMOC, the concept of being queer is usually separated from the idea of masculinity, leaving a hole in the discussion of what it means to be a young QMOC in higher education. The issues are not just centered on the identity of sexuality of QMOC but why QMOC fear coming out to their peers within their college campuses.

In the last decade, issues related to the fear of coming out in college have been given some attention. These discussions failed to address the issue of what it means to be a QMOC who embraces both his race and sexuality and why there is so much shame around the topic of sexuality in the colored community (Stockton, 2006). Woodson (2013) claimed that the dilemma of racial acceptance and sexual acceptance is one that is common for QMOC. He wrote that as a person of both the queer and black communities, a constant identity struggle overshadows the educational experience that many QMOC have while seeking a higher education.

Woodson (2013) continued to express that as a student in college, he often felt rejected by the queer community because of his darker skin. In different social settings, he dealt with issues of self-hatred not just because of his sexuality but also because of his racial identity. Woodson's story is one that expressed issues related to the exclusion from college peers but also self-hatred learned early on in his college experience. From dating to academic occurrences, Woodson's (2013) experiences provided a dominant narrative of what QMOC face when navigating elements of their identities while seeking a higher education.

INSTITUTIONAL EXPERIENCE FOR QMOC

Examining campus climate in relation to the retention of QMOC is important because it provides insight into experiences that QMOC have at their respective institutions. Focusing on campus climate in relation to retention provides background as to how 4-year colleges can make experiences more inclusive and affirming for QMOC.

The campus climate at 4-year institutions for QMOC can often be defined as hostile and uninviting. In recent studies, Rankin (2006) stated that for most students who identify as queer, campus climates are often seen as being highly discriminatory environments that have negative effects on both the academic experiences and intellectual development. This finding is important to explore because for QMOC, environmental contexts play a vital role in identity development (Stevens, 2004). As QMOC become more visible within the campus community, the issue becomes how colleges will assist them in becoming comfortable within the intersections of their identities (Evans & Herriott, 2004).

The National Information Center for Higher Education (2010) stated that 23% of first-time freshman will leave their current institution due to the campus climate. Mancini's (2011) data were alarming because more than 50% of the students surveyed in her study who identified as queer stated they voluntarily left their first college or university within the first few months because of the experiences they had. Mancini (2011) continued to explain that 46% of QMOC will never earn a degree due to believing that they are not vital to the institution while feeling marginalized and oppressed.

Since 2010, the State of Higher Education for queer people noted that more than 38% of students who identify as queer and of color have seriously considered leaving their institution (Rankin, Blumenfeld, Weber, & Frazer, 2010). When asked why these students were looking to leave their institution, many of them expressed that they did not feel supported by professional staff due to the lack of programs and services provided to queer students of color, specifically QMOC.

The issues that QMOC face within higher education are not simply related to issues of acceptance but to issues related to interactions (Rankin & Reason, 2005). For students of color who openly identify as queer, there needs to be a link of quality interactions happening among staff, faculty, and other queer students, specifically those who share the same experiences. Further, these interactions should not be limited to the classroom but should involve campus clubs, groups, and organizations. Rankin and Reason (2005) expressed that providing QMOC the opportunity to be involved can "maximize cross-racial [& sexual] interactions [that] encourage ongoing discussion that are essential to the personal and academic development" (p. 45).

In one study of 14 campuses nationwide, it was found that three-fourths of the participants label their campuses homophobic (Dugan & Yuman, 2011). Subsequently, more than half of the study participants stated that they have experienced being called derogatory names such as "queer" or "fag," whereas others stated that they experienced some form of physical assault in their first year. One study done at Yale University explained that 26% of students who identified as queer reported threats of physical violence, and more than 50% of queer students shared that they had experienced some form of verbal assault (Longerbeam, Inkelas, Johnson & Lee, 2007, p. 219). This experiences often shapes the retention of QMOC and how they connect with their campus community.

Davis (2008) explained that issues related to low retention rates in higher education are often connected to the lack of reform and programs in place for QMOC. Davis also expressed that most African American men in the queer community are often an oppressed subgroup in campus culture and are left to deal with issues related to their sexuality in the "backdrop" of campus matters. Although retention is a general issue for higher education in relation to all students of color, the needs of African American men who identify as queer have not been surveyed or been met yet.

Renn (2010) writes that, to retain QMOC in higher education, an institution must have pedagogy that is inclusive and constantly evolving to fit the needs of an ever-changing queer movement. Because the movement is in a constant state of change, higher education leaders must be willing to do the research to find out what QMOC need to feel valued and supported through the first year of their academic journey. For QMOC to find true academic success, additional resources must be provided, along with services that help develop the foundation of their intersecting identities (Angeli, 2009; Walpole, 2003).

Smith and Jaffer (2012) continued to stress the important role that higher education has on the lives of QMOC. For QMOC to find success in their academic endeavors, they must believe that all those who work for the institution are committed to being a resource. QMOC must know that those who serve in higher positions are invested for both their academic and personal successes both in- and outside of the classroom while feeling as "if said professionals," whether positive or negative, validate their experiences. By having this support, QMOC will not just find academic success but will have the needed support to remain invested in their academic aspirations.

Recognizing Privilege in Higher Education

It was said that privilege is often seen as a phenomenon within both society and educational systems (Blanchett, 2006). Be it belief systems, the structure of an organization, or the access that a student has within the organization, elements of privilege continue to afford opportunities to students of European decent in relation to educational equity.

This notion of privilege, which was often defined as an inherited right, keeps queer students of color from sharing the full truths of their intersecting identities. For many queer men who identify as white and cisgender, an unwillingness to acknowledge that they are overprivileged in academia seems prevalent (McIntosh, 2003). Further, this privilege is followed by ideas tied to the overrepresentation of white cisgender queer men in the media and the notion that many white cisgender queer men have the option to stay "color blind" when focusing on issues related to other marginalized groups in the LGBTQ community, specifically QMOC (Yosso, Parker, Solorzano, & Lynn, 2004). The context of privilege, specifically privilege held by white cisgender males in the queer community, only extends the idea that the voices of QMOC are more frequently disproportioned in higher education because of the lack of discussions held in- and outside the classroom in relation to their intersectional experiences. Understanding this, one must examine why the topics related to privilege are so salient when discussing the needs of QMOC in academia.

Authors such as Han (2007) and Woodson (2013) state that many of the stories that QMOC share about their higher education experiences relate to their campus climate, and many of the experiences that queer men of color are often overshadowed with moments of white privilege. This privilege, which often "others" the voice of QMOC, is not something that just happens within higher education. Both authors share in their work that many young men experience moments of invisibility in places such as bars, pride centers, or LGBT-related events, leaving them feeling doubly marginalized as both men of color and queer. Both Han (2007) and Woodson (2013) express that, to move QMOC from feeling as if they are the "other" in the campus community, deconstruction of privilege, specifically privilege that benefits white cisgender queer men, must be deconstructed.

It is important to understand that, to denaturalize privileges, we have to give attention to the way it has been imbedded into the culture of LGBT rhetoric (Logue, 2005). The full deconstruction comes when educators, specifically educators who are of color, begin to challenge the invisibility and normativity of whiteness in LGBTQ culture. The culture of whiteness in the LGBTQ community has remained relatively free from interrogation (Logue, 2005) because the ownership of said privilege has not been challenged in a way that lifts up the voices of QMOC to speak from a place of authentic truth.

When asking how we can deconstruct privilege to gain a better understanding of how being a QMOC affects the overall higher educational experience, it is important to analyze how we engage queer white cisgender men about topics related to privilege in the LGBT community (Banks,

Pliner, & Hopkins, 2013). Rocco and West (1998) wrote that, for privilege to be deconstructed in a matter that will serve QMOC, one must allow marginalized voices to be uplifted. Each experience must be normalized in a way that not only creates space for QMOC to share intimate details of their intersectional experiences but provides spaces both inside and outside of the classroom that openly challenge topics related to power, privilege, and the full visibility of QMOC in higher education.

CONCLUSIONS

The quality interactions that queer students of color have with higher education professionals allow for the feeling of being better connected to their universities while helping to reinforce learning outcomes that benefit the overall higher education experience for QMOC (Rankin & Reason, 2005). Rankin and Reason (2005) go on to express that the connections between underrepresented groups such as QMOC and higher educational professionals are imperative not just because they provide a better likelihood for a positive educational outcome but because they will lead QMOC to have other positive interactions with students who may share the same identity. Higher education professionals must serve as mentors and allies who assist in helping QMOC navigate the first-year experience.

To better serve QMOC, it is recommended that higher education professionals move toward a more inclusive and capital building ideology (Wall &Washington, 1991). It is important for QMOC to feel as if they have those who advocate for both their racial and sexual identities because they often feel invisible. Opportunities for them to directly identify those who advocate for their intersecting identities gives QMOC validation and much needed support within the campus community (Brockenbrough, 2013).

By implementing Misawa's (2005, 2010a) concept of QRP, components of theory and practicality not only help to better understand the experiences that QMOC have when seeking a higher education but how gender identity, race, and sexuality shape every element of their lived experience. Misawa's (2010b) work also points to a larger issue in place when talking about both race and sexuality and its position within both society and higher education. By using the Cass (1979) identity model to guide the development of QMOC both before and during their academic experience, we are only focusing on sexual identity. The Cass (1979) identity model does not take into consideration how race, power, and privilege affect the experiences of QMOC and how many of the experiences they have with higher education are related to race first and sexuality second. Further, it does not take into consideration the struggles that QMOC have with integrating their racial experiences into their lived experiences as QMOC with campus culture.

Overall, for many QMOC, racial experiences shape and mold how they view their identities and how each of them "shows up" within the campus community. By using this model to develop QMOC, it not only ignores their racial identity and the affect it has on their sexual identities, but it furthers the issues that many of them have with coming to terms with their lived experiences as QMOC. For QMOC, life is more than just their sexuality.

Life is related to struggle and strife because of racial marginalization and gender roles/expectations. For many QMOC, a greater sense of self is never developed out of fear of being ridiculed or worse, being rejected because of racial and gender norms. If the Cass (1979) model is going to continue to be used to support the identity development of QMOC, consideration must be given to how one's full identity (gender, race, and sexuality) is going to be fully developed while taking into consideration one's full lived experience. Because identity is multidimensional for QMOC and a greater understanding of self is not usually found until the first year of higher education, all aspects of their identity should be considered when discussing the needs that QMOC have when seeking a 4-year degree.

It is important to remember that we must utilize experience, theory, and research to grasp the vast complexities that QMOC face when seeking a higher education. Although the complexities alluded to in this chapter are all interrelated in connection with issues of race and sexuality, greater attention needs to be given to how educators create space to analyze the voice and experiences of QMOC who are seeking higher education. By utilizing concepts of queer race pedagogy and intersectionality, higher education becomes a place that supports the full development of QMOC and is a place of fair and equal representation.

REFERENCES

Angeli, M. (2009). Access and equity for all students: Meeting the needs of LGBT students. *California Postsecondary Education Commission*, *9*(14), 1–4.

Banks, C. A., Pliner, S. M., & Hopkins, M. B. (2013). Intersectionality and paradigms of privilege. In K. A Case (2013). *Deconstructing privilege: Teaching and learning as allies in the classroom* (pp. 102–114). New York, NY: Routledge. Retreived from https://www.safaribooksonline.com/library/view/deconstructing-privilege/9780415641456/017_9780203081877_chapter7.html

Bilodeau, B. L., & Renn, K. A.(2005). Analysis of LGBT identity development models and implications for practice. *New Directions for Student Services*, *111*, 25–39

Blanchett, W. J. (2006). Disproportionate representation of African American students in special education: Acknowledging the role of White privilege and racism. *Educational Researcher, 35*(6), 24–28.

Brockenbrough, E. (2013). Introduction to special issues: Queers of color and anti-oppressive knowledge production. *Ontario Institute for Studies in Education of the University of Toronto, 43*(3), 426–239.

Brown, M. (2012). Gender and sexuality: Intersectional anxieties. *Progress in Human Geography, 36*(4), 541–550.

Chang, R. S., & Culp, J. M., Jr. (2002). After intersectionality. *University of Missouri-Kansas City Law Review, 71*(2), 485–492.

Crenshaw, K. (1989). Demarginalizing the intersection of race and sex: A Black feminist critique of antidiscrimination doctrine, feminist theory and antiracist politics. *The University of Chicago Legal Forum, 140,* 138–167.

Davis, R. J. (2008). African American men in college. *The Journal of Higher Education, 79*(3), 360–363.

Dugan, J. P., & Yurman, L. (2011). Commonalities and differences among lesbian, gay, and bisexual college students: Considerations for research and practice. *Journal of College Student Development, 52*(2), 201–216.

Evans, N. J., & Herriott, T. K. (2004). Freshman impressions: How investigating the campus climate for LGBT students affected four freshmen students. *Journal of College Student Development, 45*(3), 316–332.

Fine, L. E. (2012). The context of creating space: Assessing the likelihood of college LGBT center presence. *Journal of College Student Development, 53*(2), 285–299.

Fotopoulou, A. (2012). Intersectionality queer studies and hybridity: Methodological frameworks for social research. *Journal of International Women's Studies, 13*(2), 19–32.

Goode-Cross, D. T., & Tager, D. (2011). Negotiating multiple identities: How African-American gay and bisexual men persist at a predominantly White institution. *Journal of Homosexuality, 58*(9), 1235–1254.

Grzanka, P. (2014). *Intersectionality: A foundations and frontiers reader.* Boulder, CO: Westview Press.

Han, C. (2007). They don't want to cruise your type: Gay men of color and racial politics of exclusion. *Social Identities, 13*(1), 51–67.

Harper, P. B. (2000). The evidence of felt intuition: Minority experience, everyday life, and critical speculative knowledge. *A Journal of Lesbian and Gay Studies, 6*(4). 641–657.

Harper, S. R., & Harris, F., III. (2010). *College men and masculinities.* San Francisco, CA: John Wiley & Sons.

Higgins, J. (2015). *Working at the intersections: Examining the first-year experiences of queer men of color in higher education* (Doctoral dissertation, University of Redlands).

Josselson, R. (1996). The ethical attitude in narrative research: Principles and practicalities. In D. J. Clandinin (Ed.), *Handbook of narrative inquiry* (p. 29). Thousand Oaks, CA: Sage.

Logue, J. (2005). Deconstructing privilege: A contrapuntal approach. *Philosophy of Education Archive,* 371–379.

Longerbeam, S. D., Inkelas, K. K., Johnson, D. R., & Lee, Z. S. (2007). Lesbian, gay, bisexual college student experiences: An exploratory study. *Journal of College Student Development, 48*, 215–230.

Mancini, O. (2011). Attrition risk and resilience among sexual minority college students. *Columbia Social Work Review, 2*, 8–22.

McCall, L. (2014). The complexity of intersectionality. *Signs, 40*(1).

McIntosh, P. (2003). "White privilege and male privilege." *Privilege: A Reader*, 147–160.

Misawa, M. (2005, June). *The intersection of race and sexual orientation in adult and higher education.* Paper presented at Proceedings of the 46th annual Adult Education Research Conference, Athens, Georgia.

Misawa, M. (2010a). Queer race pedagogy for educators in higher education: Dealing with power dynamics and positionality of QUEER students of color. *The International Journal of Critical Pedagogy, 3*(1), 26–35.

Misawa, M. (2010b). Racist and homophobic bullying in adulthood: Narratives from gay men of color in higher education. *New Horizons in Adult Education and Human Resources Development, 24*(1), 7–23.

National Information Center for Higher Education Policymaking and Analysis. (2010). *Retention rates: First-time college freshmen returning their second year—four-year total.* Retrieved from http://www.higheredinfo.org/dbrowser/index.php?measure=92

Patton, L. D., & Simmons, S. L. (2008). Exploring complexities of multiple identities of lesbians in a Black college environment. *The Negro Educational Review, 59*(3), 197–215.

Phoenix, A., & Pattynama, P. (2006). Intersectionality. *European Journal of Women's Studies, 13*(3), 187–192.

Rankin, S., Blumenfeld, W. J., Weber, G. N., & Frazer, S. (2010). *State of higher education for LGBT people: Campus pride 2010 national college climate survey.* Retrieved from http://campuspride.org/research/

Rankin, S. R. (2006). LGBTQA students on campus: Is higher education making the grade? *Journal of Gay & Lesbian Issues in Education, 3*(2/3), 111–117.

Rankin, S. R., & Reason, R. D. (2005). Differing perceptions: How students of color and White students perceive campus climate for underrepresented groups. *Journal of College Student Development, 46*(1), 43–61.

Renn, K. A. (2010). LGBT and queer research in higher education: The state and status of the field. *Educational Researcher, 39*(2), 132–141.

Robinson, T. L. (1999). The intersections of dominant discourses across race, gender, and other identities. *Journal of Counseling & Development, 77*(1), 73–79.

Rocco, T. S., & West, G. W. (1998). Deconstructing privilege: An examination of privilege in adult education. *Adult Education Quarterly, 48*(3), 171–184.

Rosado, S. (2011). *Browning the rainbow: The academic persistence and multiple identities of lesbian, gay, bisexual Latino/a students* (Doctoral dissertation). University of California San Diego. Retrieved from https://escholarship.org/uc/item/8j8666v5

Sanlo, R., Rankin, S., & Schoenberg, R. (Eds.). (2002). *Our place on campus: Lesbian, gay, bisexual, transgender services and programs in higher education.* Westport, CT: Greenwood Press.

Smith, M. S., & Jaffer, F. (2012). *Beyond the queer alphabet: Conversations on gender, sexuality, and intersectionality* [E-reader version]. Retrieved from https://the-menace.s3.amazonaws.com/uploads/Beyond_the_Queer_Alphabet_20March2012-F.pdf

Stevens, R. A. (2004). Understanding gay identity development within the college environment. *Journal of College Student Development, 45*(2), 185–206.

Stockton, K. B. (2006). *Beautiful bottom, beautiful shame: Where "Black" meets "queer."* Durham, NC: Duke University Press.

Strayhorn, T. L., Blakewood, A. M., & DeVita, J. M. (2008). Factors affecting the college choice of African American gay male undergraduates: Implications for retention. *National Association of Student Affairs Professionals Journal, 11*(1), 88–108.

Sullivan, N. (2003). *A critical introduction to queer theory.* New York, NY: New York University Press.

Torres, V., Jones, S. R., & Renn, K. A. (2009). Identity development theories in student affairs: Origins, current status, and new approaches. *Journal of College Student Development, 50*(6), 577–596.

Wall, V. A., & Washington, J. (1991). Understanding gay and lesbian students of color. In N. J. Evans & V. A. Wall (Eds.), *Beyond tolerance: Gays, lesbians and bisexuals on campus* (pp. 67–78). Alexandria, VA: American College Personnel.

Walpole, M. (2003). Socioeconomic status and college: How SES affects college experiences and outcomes. *The Review of Higher Education, 27*(1), 45–73.

Woodson, C. F. (2013). *The experience of gay and lesbian students of color in counterspaces.* Retrieved from http://www.slideshare.net/cwoodso1/cornells-comps-final-draft-2

Yosso, T. J., Parker, L., Solorzano, D. G., & Lynn, M. (2004). From Jim Crow to affirmative action and back again: A critical race discussion of racialized rationales and access to higher education. *Review of Research in Education,* 1–25.

CHAPTER 12

EXPERIENCES OF QUEER STUDENT LEADERS OF COLOR

Expanding Leadership Paradigms in Higher Education

Annemarie Vaccaro and Ryan A. Miller

What do we know about the leadership experiences and perspectives of queer students of color? Unfortunately, very little. With a dearth of empirical research about student leadership development for queer students of color, institutions are forced to draw on limited and often exclusionary research to develop leadership programs and services. In this chapter, we share selected results from a phenomenological study of six queer leaders of color. By using an asset-based lens and centering student narratives, this chapter begins to fill the gap in the literature about what it means to be a queer student leader of color at a predominately White institution. Our participants led through their multiple, intersecting social identities, exuded passion for fighting oppression through social justice leadership, crafted "family-like" counterspaces for students from marginalized identities, and committed themselves to ongoing growth as student leaders.

Queer People of Color in Higher Education, pp. 195–210

Insights from queer student leaders of color offer educators paradigm-shifting perspectives—perspectives that extend our understanding of leadership beyond White-normed leadership literature and problem-based perspectives on students from minority backgrounds. Our goal for sharing rich student narratives is to offer tangible ideas for crafting campus programs and services to meet the unique needs of queer students of color. This chapter concludes with practical recommendations for leadership development programs, leadership advising, and the creation of welcoming campus counterspaces.

WHAT WE [DON'T] KNOW ABOUT QUEER STUDENT LEADERS OF COLOR

As the study of student leadership has expanded in higher education, researchers have begun to document differences in leadership perceptions based on social identities. Studies utilizing quantitative survey methods to examine leadership have drawn comparisons between groups, such as students of color and White students or women and men (Dugan & Komives, 2007; Dugan, Komives, & Segar, 2008; Kezar & Moriarty, 2000). Although making important contributions to the literature on leadership and diversity, these studies are not designed to deeply investigate how marginalized groups conceive of leadership in relation to their identities. This approach has also ignored intersectional and within-group differences in leadership perceptions.

In the following sections, we summarize the small but growing body of literature examining student social identities and leadership. Although most of these studies are written from a single identity lens (i.e., race or sexual orientation), they begin to move the field toward empirical understandings about connections between leadership and social identity. First, we focus on student leaders of color and LGBTQ student leaders. Then we conclude this section with the limited literature emphasizing intersectionality and the leadership experiences of queer students of color.

Student Leaders of Color

Students of color may view leadership to be group-oriented, departing from hierarchical notions of leadership (Arminio et al., 2000; Dugan et al., 2008; Liang, Lee, & Ting, 2002). Arminio and colleagues (2000) interviewed 106 African American, Asian American, and Latina/o student leaders. Student leaders of color in that study often enacted loyalty to the group and expended significant personal energy and resources in a leadership role (Arminio et al., 2000). Others have noted that students of color may not participate in campus-wide student activities and governance to the same extent as their White peers, which may weaken a sense of belonging on campus and negatively impact retention (Lavant & Terrell, 1994). This finding suggests the importance of promoting leadership development in both culture/ethnicity-specific organizations as well as campus-wide groups. Sometimes ethnic student organizations offer leadership development opportunities for students of color goals. In predominantly White institutions, culture/ethnicity-specific organizations can offer students "venues of cultural familiarity, vehicles for cultural expression and advocacy, and sources of cultural validation" (Museus, 2008, p. 580). Such group settings can also be valuable opportunities for students of color to learn and practice leadership skills.

LGBTQ Student Leaders

Although the literature about LGBTQ students has increased on topics such as campus climate, mental health, and identity development, studies examining LGBTQ student leadership are rare. One national study found that lesbian and gay students were more involved in activism than their heterosexual peers (Longerbeam, Inkelas, Johnson, & Lee, 2007). Other studies have explored LGBT student organizations, tangentially referencing student activism and involvement. Renn and Bilodeau (2005) explored the relationship between LGBT identity development and leadership of an LGBT student organization. They asserted that LGBT leadership experiences support identity development of LGBT students. In another study, Renn (2007) classified student leaders of LGBT organizations into the following categories: LGBT leaders, LGBT activists, and queer activists. These categories were based on interviews and indicated whether students primarily worked within existing systems (positional leadership) or challenged systems of power (postpositional or transformational leadership).

Leadership and Intersectionality: LGBTQ Students of Color

Although an emerging body of research has advanced our general understandings of LGBTQ students of color (Misawa, 2010; Patton, 2011; Wall & Washington, 1991), this scholarship has not focused primarily on leadership. Only three studies have begun to address this void in research.

Renn and Ozaki's (2010) study of psychosocial and leadership identities among 18 student leaders of identity-based organizations at a large public institution concluded that students followed either a parallel but separate path of experiencing leadership and psychosocial identities or a merged path in which the identities intersected. In one of the few studies on leadership and activism exhibited by queer students of color, Vaccaro and Mena (2011) described the challenges experienced by self-identified queer student activists of color. Students in the study discussed juggling multiple responsibilities on and off campus while desiring spaces to safely explore their multiple, intersecting identities—spaces that were few and far between or virtually nonexistent.

Most recently, Miller and Vaccaro (2016) documented the leadership experiences and perceptions of queer students of color who served as leaders within a predominantly White queer student organization. Students in the study sought to lead authentically, collaboratively, and within a culturally competent framework. Students faced disrespect, stereotyping, and tokenization from their peers, illustrating challenges that queer student leaders of color can face in predominantly White campus and student organization contexts.

THE STUDY

Data for this chapter were gleaned from a phenomenological study with six queer student leaders of color. Phenomenology is an effective method for understanding an individual's lived experiences with a particular phenomenon, such as campus leadership (Giorgi & Giorgi, 2003; Husserl, 1913/1962; Wertz, 2005). It is also considered to be one of the most effective methods for studying the complex lived experiences of queer people of color (DeBlaere, Brewster, Sarkees, & Moradi, 2010).

Study participants were undergraduate students between the ages of 18 and 21 who self-identified as queer people of color and student leaders. All held a formal leadership role in a predominantly White queer student group (QSG) as well as other groups on campus (e.g., Black Student Association, Latino Fraternity, HIV Awareness Club). Participant genders were as follows: women ($n = 2$), men ($n = 3$), and ($n = 1$) was considering a genderqueer identity. Students self-identified as Latino ($n = 2$), African American ($n = 2$), Chinese American ($n = 1$), and biracial ($n = 1$). The study was conducted at a private, mid-size, predominantly White research university.

Students were invited to a series of two intensive 60- to 120-minute interviews conducted a year apart. One student left the university and did not complete the second interview. Semistructured interview questions included: "Tell me a little bit about how you self-identify"; "What are your experiences as a queer person of color on campus?"; "Tell me about your experience of being a member of the QSG"; "Tell me about your definition of leadership"; "What leadership activities and roles have you engaged in, on and off campus?"; and "What is it like being a queer student leader of color on a predominantly White campus?" Using phenomenological analytic techniques, we documented student perspectives on the essence—or what it means to be—a queer student leader of color on a predominantly White campus. Although we have written elsewhere about queer student leaders of color and authentic leadership (Miller & Vaccaro, 2016), this chapter highlights a plethora of other important perspectives on leadership from a student point of view.

Addressing credibility and trustworthiness is imperative in any qualitative research project (Jones, Torres, & Arminio, 2014). To do this, we invited participants to review emergent findings. All participants agreed that our conclusions reflected their lived realities. We also clarified researcher bias throughout the study. We wrote analytic memos and engaged in researcher conversations about the ways our perspectives and social identities shaped our analyses. In qualitative work, the researcher *is* the research instrument (Jones et al., 2014). As a White, queer, bisexual woman who serves as a faculty member and a White queer man who is an administrator and researcher, our identities surely shaped this project. We acknowledged that, although we are active members of queer communities and work to support queer communities of color through our professional and personal commitments, we also benefit from privileges as White and cisgender people. It is important to acknowledge our positionality, privileges, and the impact of the two on all of our published works—including this chapter.

LEADERSHIP THROUGH THE EYES OF QUEER STUDENTS OF COLOR

Leadership Is Honoring and Leading Through Intersecting Identities

To be a successful leader, queer students believed they should honor and lead through their intersecting privileged and minoritized social identities. To do this, they needed a solid foundation of self-awareness. All participants described an ongoing process of identity and leadership self-reflection. They believed that effective leaders considered the ways their minoritized and privileged identities intersected to shape their leadership perspectives and actions. Ricardo self-identified as a queer, Chicano, biological male. All of these identities, not just his minoritized identities as a queer person of color, shaped his leadership perspectives and experiences. He explained:

> What makes me? What motivates me? What gets me to push to lead? And I feel like it really should come from that real quality, that core [as a queer person of color].... But acknowledge that I'm given degrees of White privilege, also thinking about the way that I'm speaking, and the way that I'm, how much space I'm taking up as a biological man, and . . . even the way that I speak entitles me to privilege, you know, being very educated ... so having to be very conscious of all those things. (Ricardo)

As Ricardo's quote showed, queer students of color lived at and led from the intersections of minoritized and privileged identities. Those complicated intersections shaped how they felt about and engaged in leadership. By understanding and honoring their complex heritages, histories, and intersecting identity realities, they believed they could lead more authentically. Corey's perspectives on leadership were transformed once he began reflecting on his multiple intersecting identities as a gay African American man. Through self-reflection, Corey began to understand that his complex and layered social identities shaped every decision he made as a queer leader of color:

> If I'm in a leadership position, I want to share as much of myself as I can with my group.... Because I feel like there's a great [responsibility]. You know? I get what it means to be a person of color who's queer.... So it's almost these identities within identities kind of. You know? So now I'm just figuring out that—wow ... here's another layer that just got peeled back from me, so now I have to get to that layer [to lead effectively].... It's completely, I don't know, it's kind of changed the way that I think about things, and how I'm intentional about the things that I do. Like I'm still kind of—now I feel like I'm at this crossroads ... learning about my multiple identities and how they intersect, and leading through them. (Corey)

Jun also discussed how recent explorations of her cultural roots led her to understand herself and, in turn, think differently about manifestations of marginalization. Her increased self-awareness as a woman of color with a rich ethnic heritage helped her grow as an individual and a leader. Jun said:

> My ethnic identity ... is a lot stronger now, especially knowing myself being Asian American.... And ever since I have discovered how powerful my name is, I don't care that everybody ... mispronounce[s] my name, but that's still my name.... That's the name I was given by my parents and my family. And um, my family traces back to the [identifier removed] legacy and has a lot of history. This summer, especially when I was back in China, I learned a lot [about my ethnic heritage].... It's really helped me to grow as an individual [and a leader] ... especially being a queer woman of color. (Jun)

Leadership is inherently relational. Queer students of color realized that their intersecting social identities helped them relate to others. According to the Relational Leadership Model (Komives, Lucas, & McMahon, 2013), this is indeed a strength and hallmark of effective leadership. Luis explained how identity-based relationships allowed him to "know" people better, which in turn made him a more effective relational leader:

> I can get to know people within my various communities, because of my identities ... [as] a gay Latino male ... raised in a lower middle class family with an immigrant mom.... So I use my skills of networking, and knowing who is who, and who does what on campus, to get our name out and to get the resources that we need.... So my thing has been to network not only throughout campus, but also in [the city].... That's been one of my major accomplishments—I feel like I have a lot of name recognition. I can call people whenever I want and ask them for help, my thing is also being a person of support. (Luis)

Students also realized that by honoring their multiple identities and intersectionality, they were being role models for leaders who came after them. Ricardo explained:

> Of course like everything, [leadership is] a process ... because it is just so much like ... the being conscious of your identities.... But then, it's almost like, take it up another level, to become a leader, because in becoming a leader you become a role model, in certain degrees. (Ricardo)

In summary, queer student leaders of color lived at, led from, and role modeled intersectionality and leadership. Their perspectives show how important it is for student leaders to be self-aware, be authentic, and honor intersectionality.

Leadership Is Challenging Oppression and Doing Social Justice Work

Queer students of color engaged in leadership to promote social justice. They were advocates and allies for queer people of color as well as a host of individuals from minoritized backgrounds. Luis explained:

> The reason that a lot of us are successful is because we advocate for ourselves. We don't let people try to push us around. We don't let people try to tell us, "You're not good enough." People haven't even tried to tell me that, because I walk into a room with my head held high, and also shaking my hips. People who are recognized on campus are the people who advocate for themselves, who let people know, I am around, and if you really want to push me around,

you're going to feel it, twice as hard. So these students cannot feel like they are inferior, cannot feel like they don't belong here. (Luis)

Embedded in Luis' quote is the reality that microaggressions, in the form of messages of inferiority (Sue, 2010), are ever-present realities for members of minoritized social identity groups. As a queer student leader of color, Luis felt it was his job to stand up for minoritized groups and challenge oppression. Ricardo also used his leadership skills to challenge microaggressions of assumed inferiority (Sue, 2010). Sometimes this meant proving his legitimacy as a student and a leader by excelling at both roles:

And just being very conscious ... of the way that I may be being judged.... But it almost feels sometimes like ... I have to do more work to prove my legitimacy, to prove that I actually have a stake in what's happening, or I know about what's going on. I'm not just like another affirmative action kid.... I totally deserve to be here regardless of affirmative action.... As a leader ... sometimes I really feel that pressure [to prove my legitimacy]. (Ricardo)

Having to prove one's legitimacy can be an emotionally taxing process for members of minoritized social identity groups (Sue, 2010). Challenging oppression can also be unsafe. Corey juxtaposed his desire to do social justice leadership by standing up for minoritized communities with the reality that it was not always physically or emotionally safe to do so. He also challenged the oppressive assumption that the onus should be on queer people of color to name and challenge marginalization.

And there was this one guy, he told me, "Well, I think people of color, when they're being attacked, or being oppressed, they need to speak out. You know? So we can be informed." And I'm like, "No! That's just you using your privilege to have us, like speak out for you. It's not our job to speak out, and it's not safe for us to always speak out." (Corey)

Students realized that social justice work was a long and difficult task. Challenging oppression was not easy, yet they believed it was a foundation for effective leadership. In addition to reacting to instances of marginalization, queer leaders of color worked to be proactive by educating peers about inclusion. Unfortunately, this leadership task of educating others about social justice was an arduous one—especially when students with privilege resisted or simply "did not get it." Corey shared,

Getting people to see an issue, or you know, raising the most awareness— sometimes it takes time and sometimes you're not going to raise awareness. [You] realize that people are people and they're going to take what you give them or they're not going to take what you give them and that's just something as a person that you have to deal with.... People just worry and stress so much, and I'm just like, "Relax and do what you have to do and realize that if you affect some people, great, if not, oh well, there's next time." You know? (Corey)

As Corey's quote suggests, queer students of color realized that social justice education was a long process. It was unrealistic to expect heightened peer awareness after one interaction, conversation, or educational program.

Because working toward social justice was an ongoing process, students learned to be content with "next time" (Corey) or planting a seed. Jun recognized she was planting a seed and building a legacy of socially just leadership that would hopefully live on after she graduated. She said, "I've set tradition. And it's up to the new leaders to, to flower that. I plant[ed] it, they need to flower it. I can't stay at this college forever." In summary, queer students of color believed that one important role of leadership was to do the difficult work of social justice. They challenged oppression, educated peers, and passed on the tradition of social justice activism to student leaders who followed in their footsteps.

Leadership Is Creating Counterspaces and Building Community

As student quotes and prior research have suggested (Miller & Vaccaro, 2016; Vaccaro & Mena, 2011), students from multiple minoritized social identities encounter oppression not only on campus but also within supposedly safe campus groups such as the QSG. James recounted an incident where he experienced exclusion from fellow White LGBT activists. As a queer leader of color, he was forced to challenge injustice within the queer community—a place where he sought refuge from oppression.

> They were talking about issues that affected the GLBT community. And [queer people of color] were like, "These issues don't affect us. We're people of color [too and] there are different issues that affect us." ... For the first time in a gay-oriented group, I felt like people were really racist ... and I had to fight that racism and be like, "No, I am not going to do this."... It was interesting, but I had to affirm myself as a queer person of color. (James)

Because they knew how challenging it was to navigate marginalization within campus spaces, queer leaders of color felt a responsibility to create safe and affirming spaces for individuals living at the intersections of multiple marginalized identities. Much literature has extolled the benefits of culture-specific organizations. Specifically, they offer students a space to express and explore their cultural heritage and glean support and validation from those with similar social identities (Museus, 2008). Yosso, Smith, Ceja, and Solórzano (2009) used the term counterspaces to describe unique spaces where students from similar social identities can "vent frustrations and cultivate friendships with people who share many of their experiences" (p. 677). Such spaces can be a student organization like a Queer People of Color Club or a campus office like an LGBT Center or Latino/a Student Union. As part of their leadership initiatives, queer students of color in our study attempted to create safe and validating counterspaces. Luis described his vision of such counterspaces:

> These are advocating groups where these students get together and they identify with their community, and they feel like they have somewhere to go. Because [this university] ... isn't always welcoming to everybody, students feel like they're by themselves.... So these students actually get together and they help each other. They see each other and they feel like they're accepted. So for me it's been part of that, being at these student alliances and telling them ... "I *am* you and I will always be around [to support you]." (Luis)

Others like Ricardo, Jun, and Laila sought to transform the sometimes racially oppressive QSG into a counterspace where queer people of color felt welcomed and affirmed. These student leaders hoped these counterspaces would have a welcoming family-like atmosphere. Jun explained,

> I would say that it means to me ... being in a big family, because everybody is ... my friends and family. [So, when oppression gets] really bad, you have that connection with someone, and that great minds think alike. And I'm surrounded by people who think like me who really support everything that I do. And yes, we do have conflicts, but it's like [all family disagreements]— we will be alright. (Jun)

As the president of QSG, Ricardo's vision was "being supportive. And [creating] that safe space is really important, too. I think that's always been my vision for QSG ... like I want to build a family." Laila also used the analogy of family in her description of her ideal campus counterspace. Activism and social justice politics were important to her. But, in her mind, those leadership initiatives had to be built upon a solid foundation of "community" and family-like relationships. Laila explained, "I really want to, really, really, really want to build a family with my group before we can really like do a whole lot of political things. I really want to like build a community." In sum, queer student leaders of color recognized the importance of creating safe counterspaces where they could find reprieve from oppression and have their lived realities validated by people who shared similar intersecting social identities. In these family-like spaces, students could glean support, regenerate, and renew their commitment to dong the hard work of socially just leadership.

Leadership Is an Ongoing Developmental Process

Queer student leaders of color in our study were smart, knowledgeable, and committed. They talked about how they were constantly growing and learning new skills through leadership activities. During the year between his two interviews, Corey developed many new leadership skills. He was proud of this growth, saying: "So I think for me that's pretty nice, and that's a big accomplishment for me is, you know, really being like, looking back and like, 'I really did learn those skills.'" Despite their growth, students never purported to know everything there was to know about leadership. They believed leadership was about constantly growing and learning. For queer student leaders of color, leadership was a complex and often challenging phenomenon that required continuous development. In fact, leaders like Ricardo believed they became more effective by learning from their mistakes.

> The leadership piece is so big. And I feel there are so many mistakes that are made with it. And not to say that I haven't made mistakes myself, by any means. I've made a lot of mistakes in facilitating leadership workshops and being a leader. But it's about learning from those mistakes, right? (Ricardo)

James echoed these sentiments. He even suggested he learned more through trial and error as a student leader than he did in most classes.

> Well, I personally felt like it was a learning experience for me because I had never been in any activist kind of things. We didn't even have a GSA at my [high] school ... I just felt like I learned a lot ... it was more of a giant education. I felt like I should've gotten credits [for my leadership activities] because I learned more in QSG over the year than I did in any of my classes. I just felt like I learned a thousand times more than I learned in any of my classes! (James)

To queer student leaders of color, leadership was not a role that was mastered quickly; it was an ongoing developmental journey where they continuously learned and honed new perspectives and skills.

HOW CAN CAMPUSES SUPPORT QUEER LEADERS OF COLOR?

In order to create inclusive leadership development opportunities for students, higher educators must understand and incorporate the leadership experiences and perspectives of queer students of color. Listening to voices of queer student leaders of color can offer valuable insight for college campuses. Given the themes presented in this chapter, we offer a few practical recommendations for leadership development programs, leadership advising, and the creation of counterspaces on campus.

Leadership Development

Programs designed to develop students' leadership capacities have proliferated at colleges and universities. Yet an examination and reconsideration of the paradigms informing such programs is needed. Without critical engagement, leadership development programs run the risk of reaffirming leadership as an individual, hierarchical, position-based phenomenon. This chapter, as well as our prior work (Miller & Vaccaro, 2016), offers evidence that queer student leaders of color may crave leadership development programs that affirm leadership as collectively oriented and non-hierarchical. Students were also passionate about infusing their social identities into socially just leadership practice whereby they challenged oppression while creating welcoming counterspaces. Educational and programmatic efforts to support student leadership ought to intentionally engage these leadership paradigms. Leadership education related to diversity must approach identity from an intersectional standpoint that validates the experiences of queer students of color.

Queer student leaders of color may feel immense personal responsibility to create change on and off campus, which can lead to burnout and other negative health-related consequences (Vaccaro & Mena, 2011). Given this, leadership programs might also address the role of self-care, mental health, and wellness strategies in particular for students who face multiple forms of oppression and who lead within identity-based groups.

Leadership Advising

To effectively meet the needs of queer students of color on campus, faculty, administrators, and student affairs professionals must educate themselves about social justice, intersecting oppressions, and how marginalization manifests within higher education. Specifically, professionals must develop their cultural competence through sustained engagement with these topics (Pope, Reynolds, & Mueller, 2004). Students may seek out advisors whom they view as role models. Regardless of whether advisors share similar social identities with queer students of color, all professionals must educate themselves on how to ally with students working against interlocking forms of oppression. Increasing cultural competence by understanding their own social identities, as well as the historical and theoretical underpinnings of privilege and oppression, positions advisors to best support queer students of color. Culturally competent professionals who engage in deep, personal reflection and continually educate themselves on intersectional identity issues are poised to more effectively serve queer students of color in their leadership development.

Queer student leaders of color believed challenging oppression was a central aspect of their leadership role. Fighting oppression, however, can be a taxing endeavor (Sue, 2010), especially when students feel like they are engaging in the fight alone. As such, advisors can encourage students to participate in coalition building with other social justice-minded leaders on and off campus. Such collaborations can potentially reduce the burden on queer students of color who often feel they are doing this important work in isolation. Yet, practitioners must also acknowledge that coalition building can be a challenge. Queer people of color do not make up a monolithic group. Moreover, as students in this chapter noted, tensions between, and within, identity groups are bound to surface. Professional faculty and staff advisors need the cultural competency skills to effectively navigate disagreements from coalition members about the nature of oppression and specific plans for campus action.

Campus Counterspaces

Queer students of color, who experience multiple forms of marginalization on campus, may benefit from the cultivation of intentional spaces on campus where intersecting identities are acknowledged and centered. Such counterspaces might include the development of queer people of color organizations, centers, or classes (Solórzano, Ceja, & Yosso, 2000). Although single-identity spaces, such as a queer student group or Black Student Alliance, might offer valuable support, such spaces may still neglect intersecting social identities, suggesting the need for counterspaces (Yosso et al., 2009). These venues may simultaneously function as environments that promote leadership development for queer students of color as well as offer support for those navigating racism, heterosexism, and other intersecting oppressions on and off campus (Vaccaro & Mena, 2011).

Queer student leaders in our study felt it was their duty to create family-like counterspaces on campus. However, this work must not fall squarely on the shoulders of students. Faculty and staff should work to institutionalize counterspaces for queer people of color. University employees can teach courses about queer people of color. They can also lobby to support the creation of campus organizations and centers for queer students of color. Dedicating physical space, fiscal resources, and personnel support are great first steps toward creating validating campus counterspaces for queer students of color. Of course, educators must invite students to code-sign and help implement these spaces. Students might profess varied goals for the counterspace, such as activism, visibility, community building, and/ or service. Certainly, divergent perspectives can cause counterspace tensions. However, as Jun noted, "we do have conflicts, but it's like [all family disagreements]—we will be alright" (Jun). Disagreements are a natural part of community life. Instead of viewing divergent student perspectives as negative, they should be seen as positive building blocks for counterspaces that truly honor the diverse and complicated perspectives of queer students of color on campus.

CONCLUSIONS

In this chapter, narratives from queer student leaders of color offered valuable insight into their leadership experiences and perspectives. The interconnections between their intersecting social identities and leadership perspectives ran deep. Leadership for queer students of color was informed by their intersecting identities, passion for fighting oppression through social justice leadership, desire to build a sense of community through counterspaces, and commitment to ongoing leadership development. These perspectives on leadership can be used in higher educators to develop inclusive leadership programs, affirm advising models, and validate campus counterspaces.

REFERENCES

Arminio, J. L., Carter, S., Jones, S. E., Kruger, K., Lucas, N., Washington, J., Young, N., & Scott, A. (2000). Leadership experiences of students of color. *Journal of Student Affairs Research and Practice*, *37*(3), 184–198.

DeBlaere, C., Brewster, M. E., Sarkees, A., & Moradi, B. (2010). Conducting research with LGB people of color: Methodological challenges and strategies. *The Counseling Psychologist*, *38*(3), 331–362.

Dugan, J. P., & Komives, S. R. (2007). *Developing leadership capacity in college students: Findings from a national study. A report from the Multi-Institutional Study of Leadership*. College Park, MD: National Clearinghouse for Leadership Programs.

Dugan, J. P., Komives, S. R., & Segar, T. C. (2008). College student capacity for socially responsible leadership: Understanding norms and influences of race, gender, and sexual orientation. *Journal of Student Affairs Research and Practice*, *45*(4), 475–500.

Giorgi, A. P., & Giorgi, B. M. (2003). The descriptive phenomenological psychological method. In P. M. Camic, J. E. Rhodes, & L. Yardley (Eds.), *Qualitative research in psychology: Expanding perspectives in methodology and design* (pp. 243–273). Washington, DC: APA.

Husserl, E. (1962). *Ideas: General introduction to pure phenomenology* (W. R. B. Gibson Trans.). New York: Collier Books. (Original work published 1913)

Jones, S. R., Torres, V., & Arminio, J. (2014). *Negotiating the complexities of qualitative research in higher education: Fundamental elements and issues* (2nd ed.). New York: Routledge.

Kezar, A., & Moriarty, D. (2000). Expanding our understanding of student leadership development: A study exploring gender and ethnic identity. *Journal of College Student Development, 41*(1), 55–69.

Komives, S. R., Lucas, N., & McMahon, T. R. (2013). *Exploring leadership: For college students who want to make a difference* (3rd ed.). San Francisco, CA: John Wiley & Sons.

Lavant, B. D., & Terrell, M. C. (1994). Assessing ethnic minority student leadership and involvement in student governance. *New Directions for Student Services, 66*, 59–71.

Liang, C. T., Lee, S., & Ting, M. P. (2002). Developing Asian American leaders. *New Directions for Student Services, 97*, 81–90.

Longerbeam, S. D., Inkelas, K. K., Johnson, D. R., & Lee, Z. S. (2007). Lesbian, gay, bisexual college student experiences: An exploratory study. *Journal of College Student Development, 48*, 215–230.

Miller, R. A., & Vaccaro, A. (2016). Queer student leaders of color: Leadership as authentic, collaborative, culturally competent. *Journal of Student Affairs Research and Practice, 53*(1), 39–50. doi:10.1080/19496591.2016.1087858

Misawa, M. (2010). Racist and homophobic bullying in adulthood: Narratives from gay men of color in higher education. *New Horizons in Adult Education and Human Resource Development, 24*(1), 7–23.

Museus, S. D. (2008). The role of ethnic student organizations in fostering African American and Asian American students' cultural adjustment and membership at predominantly white institutions. *Journal of College Student Development, 49*(6), 568–586.

Patton, L. D. (2011). Perspectives on identity, disclosure, and the campus environment among African American gay and bisexual men at one historically Black college. *Journal of College Student Development, 52*(1), 77–100.

Pope, R. L., Reynolds, A. L., & Mueller, J.A. (2004). *Multicultural competence in student affairs*. San Francisco, CA: Jossey-Bass.

Renn, K. A. (2007). LGBT student leaders and queer activists: Identities of lesbian, gay, bisexual, transgender, and queer identified college student leaders and activists. *Journal of College Student Development, 48*(3), 311–330.

Renn, K. A., & Bilodeau, B. (2005). Queer student leaders: An exploratory case study of identity development and LGBT student involvement at a Midwestern research university. *Journal of Gay & Lesbian Issues in Education, 2*(4), 49–71.

Renn, K. A., & Ozaki, C. C. (2010). Psychosocial and leadership identities among leaders of identity-based campus organizations. *Journal of Diversity in Higher Education, 3*(1), 14.

Solórzano, D., Ceja, M., & Yosso, T. (2000). Critical race theory, racial microaggressions and campus racial climate: The experiences of African-American college students. *Journal of Negro Education, 69*(1/2), 60–73.

Sue, D. W. (2010). *Microaggressions in everyday life: Race, gender, and sexual orientation.* Hoboken, NJ: John Wiley & Sons.

Vaccaro, A., & Mena, J. A. (2011). It's not burnout, it's more: Queer college activists of color and mental health. *Journal of Gay & Lesbian Mental Health, 15*(4), 339–367.

Wall, V. A., & Washington, J. (1991). *Understanding gay and lesbian students of color. Beyond tolerance: Gays, lesbians, and bisexuals on campus.* Alexandria, VA: American College Personnel Association.

Wertz, F. J. (2005). Phenomenological research methods for counseling psychology. *Journal of Counseling Psychology, 52*(2), 167–177.

Yosso, T., Smith, W., Ceja, M., & Solórzano, D. (2009). Critical race theory, racial microaggressions, and campus climate for Latina/o undergraduates. *Harvard Educational Review, 79*(4) 659–669.

ABOUT THE AUTHORS

EDITORS

Joshua Moon Johnson Much of Dr. Joshua Moon Johnson's work stems from his personal identity as a Christian, queer, multiracial Asian-American/Euro-American, man who grew up in Mississippi. He is currently the Special Assistant to the VP of Student Life/Assistant Dean of Students. He previously served as the Assistant Dean/Director of the Multicultural Student Center at the University of Wisconsin- Madison. Joshua's understanding of identity and conflict has led him to a career educating on topics of social justice and has led to becoming a best-selling author with his first book, *Beyond Surviving: From Religious Oppression to Queer Activism*. Joshua received a doctorate in higher education and a certificate in LGBT studies from Northern Illinois University, and a master's degree in social sciences, student affairs, and diversity from Binghamton University, State University of New York. Joshua also has a master's degree in marketing from The University of Alabama as well as a bachelor's in business from the University of South Alabama.

Gabriel (Gabe) Javier serves as Assistant Dean of Students and Interim Director of the Multicultural Student Center. Gabe is also the Director of the LGBT Campus Center. Previously, Gabe served as the Assistant Director of the Spectrum Center and Assistant to the Dean of Students at the University of Michigan-Ann Arbor. Originally from St. Louis, MO, Gabe was raised Roman Catholic and is a member of Pi Kappa Alpha Fraternity.

Gabe is proud of his Filipino identity and how the richness of his intersectional experiences inform his work. Gabe has presented across the nation on topics such as intersectionality, intimate partner violence and sexual assault, digital identity development, and the design, implementation, and assessment of LGBTQ Ally Training programs.

CONTRIBUTORS

Paulina Abustan is a Queer Pinay scholar-activist and Doctoral Student of Washington State University's Cultural Studies and Social Thought in Education program. Her research and activism centers the intersections of race, gender, sexuality, and disability in education and society. She seeks to connect the decolonizing Kapwa Pedagogies of Queer Pilipinx educators with Queer Studies and DisCrit Studies in Education.

Ashish Agrawal is a PhD Candidate in the Department of Engineering Education. He is from a small town called Dalsinghsarai in the state of Bihar in India. He received his Bachelor of Technology in Electrical Engineering from Indian Institute of Technology Roorkee (IIT Roorkee) in 2010, and Master of Science in Electrical Engineering from Virginia Tech in 2015. Passionate about teaching, he tries to implement liberative and culturally-inclusive pedagogies in the first year engineering classes he teaches at Virginia Tech. His research interests include exploring and understanding the experiences of international faculty, teaching assistants, and students in universities in the United States. Ashish is also deeply involved in LGBTQ+ advocacy at college campuses. He along with a fellow graduate student and friend started AcrossBorders@VT, a group of international LGBTQ+ students/faculty/affiliates of Virginia Tech. The aim of the group is to support one another by providing a friendly space for the international LGBTQ+ population at the university to discuss concerns about their sexuality, gender identity, and coming out.

Danielle Aguilar's passion for social equity and justice is rooted in her identity as a queer Chicana. Danielle is currently the Assistant Director in the Office for Multicultural Learning at Santa Clara University. Danielle received her MEd in Higher Education and Student Affairs Administration from the University of Vermont and a BA in Feminist Studies with a minor in Black Studies from the University of California, Santa Barbara.

Mario Alejandro Rodriguez is a first generation, gay, Latino and his parents are from Jalisco, Mexico. Most of Mr. Rodriguez work comes from personal identity as well as working at various years in student affairs at

Hispanic Serving institutions. In addition, to sailing to on Semester at Sea 2009, he has done multicultural work in California, Florida, Illinois, Wisconsin and currently in Maryland. He is the Associate Director for Student Diversity and Development at Towson University where he primary overseas LGBTQ+ and Latinx student populations. Mario previously served as the Assistant Director of the Multicultural Student Center at the University of Wisconsin-Madison. He received a masters degree in higher education administration from Florida International University, and a bachelors degree in nternational Business and Spanish from University of La Verne.

Christian D. Chan is a doctoral candidate in Counseling at The George Washington University and currently serves as a Lecturer in Counseling at The George Washington University. He also received his Master of Arts degree in Clinical Mental Health Counseling with The George Washington University and Bachelor of Arts degree with the majors of Psychology and Computer Applications and a Theology minor. As a Queer Person of Color, intersectionality plays a significantly central force in Christian's life both personally and professionally. His prior professional experiences include working as a case manager with foster care adolescents, higher education administration, intensive outpatient counselor, and an outpatient counselor, providing individual, couples, parent-child, group, and family counseling services.

Brittany Derieg is the current Assistant Director for Reporting in the Office of the Vice Chancellor of Student Affairs and Campus Diversity at UC Davis, and in this role has responsibility over the development and ongoing evaluation of campus programs and projects. She works with campus and community constituencies as part of the research and planning phase of many system-wide and campus-wide initiatives linked to student success and campus climate. Brittany is also a doctoral student at the UC Davis School of Education, with previous research experience in fields as diverse as higher education, primate behavioral development, and neurodevelopment. Brittany has previously held research positions at Lajuma Research Center in South Africa and at the UC Davis Center for Neuroscience. Prior to joining the Office of the Vice Chancellor in 2014, Brittany also worked at the Community College Foundation, where she supported and built relationships with California K–12 school districts, teachers and counselors.

Adrienne N. Erby is a faculty member in the Counselor Education program at Ohio University. Her scholarship and service centers on multicultural issues in counseling, intersectionality, cultural identity, and social justice advocacy. She has a PhD in Counseling with a Multicultural Counseling cognate from The University of North Carolina at Charlotte and a Master's degree in Community Counseling from Oklahoma State University. She has practiced clinical mental health counseling in university counseling centers, and in community mental health settings. Dr. Erby's teaching and scholarship uses an integrated multicultural and developmental lens in understanding mental health and promoting wellness.

David Julius Ford, Jr., holds a BA in Psychology and an MA in Clinical Mental Health Counseling, both from Wake Forest University. In May 2014, he earned his PhD in Education with a Concentration in Counselor Education and Supervision at Old Dominion University. Dr. Ford is a Licensed Professional Counselor in North Carolina and Virginia. He is a National Certified Counselor (NCC) and Approved Clinical Supervisor (ACS). Dr. Ford recently began his third year as an Assistant Professor of Counselor Education in the Department of Graduate Psychology at James Madison University, where he serves as the faculty adviser to the Nu Lambda chapter of Kappa Alpha Psi Fraternity, Inc., and the JMU Gospel Choir.

Erika L. Grafsky, PhD, is an Assistant Professor of Human Development and a faculty affiliate of Women and Gender Studies, as well as Health Sciences at Virginia Tech. She received her master's degree from the University of Kentucky's Marriage and Family Therapy Program, and doctorate in Human Development and Family Science from The Ohio State University. Erika's scholarship is focused on psychosocial health and well-being of sexual and gender minority individuals and their families and affirmative therapy practices.

Jonathan P. Higgins is a speaker, educator and thought leader. With over 10 years of experience in education, social justice and grass roots movements, Dr. Higgins is focused on public speaking and working with the media on issues centered on people of color, LGBTQ storytelling and marginalized communities. Dr. Higgins is committed to using his voice to highlight and bring focus to the issues that affect both the Black and LGBTQ community. In September of 2016, Dr. Higgins launched a YouTube page where he posts weekly videos about social justice issues, and began sharing pieces of his a mini-documentary highlighting stories related to his life as a queer Black man growing up in the inner city of San Bernardino, as well as being the first person in his family to attain a doctoral degree.

T. J. Jourian is a social justice scholar, advocate, and consultant, having spoken, taught, and facilitated trainings at hundreds of college campuses, conferences, and community-based organizations across the U.S. As a queer Middle Eastern Armenian transman, T.J.'s passion lies with supporting, learning from, and participating in justice and liberation work that is critical, intersectional, empowering, and dynamic. Central to T.J.'s evolving agenda is the use of intersectional scholarship to trans*form postsecondary education and experiences, foregrounding trans people in achieving the democratic and emancipatory potentials of higher education. His research interests involve trans* and queer student, staff, and faculty campus experiences and leadership, particularly those of queer and trans* people of color, justice-centered curriculum and pedagogy, and student activism. T.J.'s contributing chapter comes from his dissertation work titled "My masculinity is a little love poem to myself": Trans*masculine college students' conceptualizations of masculinity, which revealed the racialized, embodied, and authentic pathways undertaken by trans*masculine college students. He is affiliated with Oakland University.

Ryan A. Miller, PhD, is assistant professor of educational leadership at the University of North Carolina at Charlotte, where he teaches courses in higher education and research methods. His research agenda focuses on the conditions for creating inclusive campus cultures in higher education. As a first-generation college graduate, Ryan is committed to the pursuit of equity and social justice in education through his research, teaching, and practice. He has presented nationally and published scholarship primarily addressing sexual orientation, gender identity, race/ethnicity, and disability in higher education. His dissertation on intersections of disability and LGBTQ identities received the 2016 Melvene D. Hardee Dissertation of the Year award from NASPA Student Affairs Administrators in Higher Education. Prior to becoming a faculty member, Ryan worked for 8 years in higher education, including roles in student affairs and diversity affairs. He holds graduate degrees in education from The University of Texas at Austin and Harvard University.

Hoa N. Nguyen is a therapist and researcher in the field of family therapy. Her work focuses on empowering LGBTQ+ individuals and families and understanding how experiences of immigration and diaspora may shape their lives. She is working on her doctorate in Human Development at Virginia Tech, and completing her dissertation on the coming in and coming out stories of international LGBQ students in the United States. Hoa currently teaches at Valdosta State University's Marriage and Family Therapy Program, where she received her master's degree

Vivie Nguyen is the daughter of Vietnamese immigrants who instilled in her the importance of education, a strong work ethic, and humility. Vivie received her BA from the University of California, Irvine and obtained her MA in Counseling Psychology at the University of California, Santa Barbara. Her professional and deeply personal livelihood focused on well-being, support, success, and equity for marginalized and/or minoritized persons directly arose from colorful and transformational friendships throughout her emerging and current adulthood. Vivie served as the Director for the Cultural Resource Centers and Coordinator of LGBT Services at DePauw University for a number of years. She is back on the West Coast, amongst her natural habitat of sea & trees, as the Director for the Office of Intercultural Engagement at the University of Puget Sound.

Ashley L. Smith is currently a third year doctoral student in the Department of Educational Policy Studies with a focus on Gender and Women's Studies at the University of Wisconsin-Madison. Her passions and research focus on the experiences of Black Women and girls in education as it relates to the intersections of their race, gender, class, and sexuality. In 2015 the Association of Black Sociologists honored her for her paper "#BlackWomenMatter: The Invisible Victims of the Movement in the Wake of State Violence." Additionally, she serves as the Graduate Assistant for Bias Prevention Initiatives through the Division of Student Life at UW-Madison. Ashley received a master's degree in Higher Education from Syracuse University and a bachelor's in Business Management from DePaul University.

Emily Prieto-Tseregounis currently serves as an Assistant Vice Chancellor and Chief of Staff to the Vice Chancellor of Student Affairs and Campus Diversity at the University of California, Davis. In her role, Dr. Prieto-Tseregounis assists the Vice Chancellor in the management of all units in the Division of Student Affairs and provides campus wide influence on issues impacting student life. Her other responsibilities include oversight of the AB 540 and Undocumented Student Center, the Center for Student Affairs Assessment, Student Affairs Marketing and Communication, College Opportunity Programs, and the Internship and Career Center. Prior to her arrival at UC Davis, Dr. Prieto-Tseregounis was the Director of the Latino Resource Center at Northern Illinois University, and she also served in various faculty roles at teaching courses on "U.S./Mexico Border Relations" and "Multicultural Education." She was awarded Fulbright Specialist Grants to teach and conduct research at the University of Ibadan in Nigeria and Sophia University in Tokyo, Japan. Dr. Prieto-Tseregounis received her Ph.D. in Education with a specialization in Language, Literacy and Culture, and her Master's in Education with a specialization in Sociocultural Studies both from the University of California, Davis.

Annemarie Vaccaro, PhD, is a faculty member and Program Director for the College Student Personnel Program at the University of Rhode Island. She identifies as a queer, white, cisgender woman who is passionate about conducting critical research that will (hopefully) be used to inform socially just practice. Her research explores the intersections of college student experiences and the social identities of gender, race, class and sexual orientation. Her most recent book is *Centering Women of Color in Academic Counterspaces: A Critical Race Analysis of Teaching, Learning, and Classroom Dynamics* (Vaccaro & Camba-Kelsay, 2016: Lexington). Annemarie's LGBTQ research can be found in a variety of journals, including her co-authored book *Safe Spaces: Making Schools and Communities Welcoming to LGBT Youth* (Vaccaro, August Kennedy, 2012; Praeger). She earned her PhD in Higher Education Administration and an MA in Sociology from the University of Denver. She also has an MA in Student Affairs from Indiana University of Pennsylvania.

Chris Woods, influenced by his identities as a queer biracial man of Latinx and Catholic upbringing, has dedicated much of his academic and professional career to the intersections of faith and sexuality on the college campus. He has presented nationally at conferences and colleges/universities on topics centering queer and trans people of color, racial justice and intersectionality, bi/multiracial identities, and the intersections of faith, race, and sexuality. Chris serves as the Associate Director of Multicultural Affairs and LGBTQ Outreach at Columbia University. He previously served as the Program Administrator of the NYU LGBTQ Student Center. In addition to his professional roles, Chris has contributed to the field of LGBTQ student services in higher education by serving on the board of the Consortium of Higher Education LGBT Resource Professionals as the Recorder and previously as the Racial Justice Chair. Chris received his BA in English and Religious Studies from New York University and his MA in Higher Education and Student Affairs from The Ohio State University.

Made in the USA
San Bernardino,
18 August 201